THE HUMAN CONSTITUTION

THE HUMAN CONSTITUTION

St. Thomas Aquinas

Translated and with an Introduction
by Richard J. Regan

Scranton: University of Scranton Press

Library of Congress Cataloging-in-Publication Data

Thomas, Aquinas, Saint, 1225?-1274.
　　[Summa theologica. Pars 1. Quaestio 75–118. English]
　　The human constitution / Thomas Aquinas ; translated and with
an introduction by Richard J. Regan.
　　　　p.　　cm.
　　Includes bibliographical references and index.
　　ISBN 0–940866–62–5 (hard). — ISBN 0–940866–63–3 (pbk.)
　　1. Man (Christian theology) — Early works to 1800.
2. Philosophical theology.　I. Regan, Richard J.　II. Title.
BT740.T4913　　1997
233'.5—dc21　　　　　　　　　　　　　　　　　　96–49915
　　　　　　　　　　　　　　　　　　　　　　　　　　CIP

Marketing and Distribution

University of Scranton Press
Chicago Distribution Center
11030 S. Langley
Chicago　IL　60628

CONTENTS

ST I

PREFACE

The writings of St. Thomas deserve wide circulation for several reasons. First, they have had so much influence on other thinkers. Second, no serious student of Western thought can be considered well-educated without acquaintance with St. Thomas's grand synthesis of faith and reason. Third, St. Thomas's thought, in my opinion, has intrinsic merit and perduring relevance. Even those who do not share St. Thomas's philosophical and theological perspective should find his writings intellectually stimulating.

This volume is an anthology of St. Thomas's thought about the human constitution as expressed in the first part of the *Summa theologiae*: the human soul, its immortality, its union with the body, the senses, the intellect, and free will. As the selections make clear, St. Thomas generally approaches these topics about the human constitution from the perspective of human reason. Reading these selections in isolation from the rest of the *Summa*, however, risks misrepresenting his thought. The *Summa* is professedly a summary of theology, not philosophy, and St. Thomas's perspective is that of a believer seeking to understand his faith. Nonetheless, St. Thomas proposes certain propositions and analyses on the basis of reason, and it is important for believers and nonbelievers to weigh their merit precisely as rational arguments. Within that context, the anthology is selective, and informed readers can judge for themselves whether the texts selected are sufficiently representative and comprehensive.

My first purpose, then, is to make available to scholars and the general public in a single, relatively comprehensive volume the thought of St. Thomas on the human constitution. My second purpose is to provide a translation superior to previous translations.

The English Dominican Fathers' translation dates from the first third of this century. That translation is accurate and literal for the most part, but its English rendition of certain key terms is misleading, and its style is by contemporary standards, stilted. The more recent Blackfriars' translation of a quarter century ago renders key terms more accurately but translates the text very freely and sometimes misleadingly. I believe that only a painstakingly literal translation can capture the nuances of St. Thomas's thought. I aim, therefore, to provide a translation that is more faithful than that of the Blackfriars, and more felicitous than that of the English Dominican Fathers.

To assist the reader, I have provided a glossary of key terms. Hackett Publishing Company has graciously allowed me to incorporate definitions from the glossary Professor William P. Baumgarth and I provided in our anthology of St. Thomas's ethical and political writings, *On Law, Morality, and Politics.*

I wish to thank Professor Baumgarth, my colleague in the Department of Political Science of Fordham University, for his help in selecting the texts in this volume. I also wish to thank the Reverend W. Norris Clarke, S.J., Professor Emeritus of Fordham University, and the Reverend Brian Davies, O.P., Professor at Blackfriars, Oxford University, for their helpful suggestions for the bibliography, and Father Davies for his helpful comments on the introduction.

NOTE ON THE TEXT AND TRANSLATION

This translation is from the 1952 Marietti recension of the Leonine text of the *Summa*. In citing books of the Bible and numbering the Psalms, I have followed the Revised Standard Version. I have translated St. Thomas's biblical quotations as he phrases them, not as they appear in the Vulgate. I have cited Plato according to the Stephanus divisions, and Aristotle according to the Bekker divisions. For patristic citations or quotations, I have referred the reader to the Migne edition. Unless otherwise indicated, note references to the *Summa* are to the first part.

Translators should be faithful to the text and express the meaning of the text in felicitous English. The two objectives are often difficult to reconcile. Fidelity to the text has been my highest priority, although I am confident that the reader will find the translation clear and idiomatic. The translation of certain key words inevitably involves interpretation. I have, for example, generally translated participial use of the Latin infinitive *esse* as "existing" or "existence." Since I interpret that St. Thomas takes "being" in the absolute participial sense to mean "existing," I have chosen to make that interpretation explicit. The translation of other key words varies with the context. I have, for example, translated *ratio*, the generic Latin word for reason, as "argument," "aspect," "consideration," "nature," "reason," "reasoning," or "respect" as appropriate for different contexts.

Richard J. Regan

INTRODUCTION

From its earliest days, Christianity found itself at odds with many facets of the dominant pagan culture of the Greco-Roman world, and Christians essentially regarded themselves as pilgrims and aliens in that world. The conversion of the Roman Empire and its barbarian invaders relieved some of the tension between Christian belief and secular culture, but the introduction of the corpus of Aristotle's philosophy into the Latin West during the years 1130 to 1280 precipitated a new, expressly intellectual challenge to the now dominant Christian religion. From the religious perspective, the nub of the problem was that Aristotle assumed or affirmed certain things that were incompatible with important tenets of Christian belief; Aristotle and Greeks generally, for example, believed in the eternity of matter. Moreover, in order to distinguish the acceptable wheat from the unacceptable chaff in Aristotelian and Hellenic thought, Christian thinkers needed to learn how to philosophize systematically.

Christian thinkers, of course, had from the beginnings of Christianity reflected deeply on the mystery of God's creative and redemptive love for the human race. John the Evangelist, St. Paul, the Apostolic Fathers, and the Fathers of the Church had expressed theological reflections in their writings. And early medieval Christian writers focused on the interior life, of which they were masters; they generally saw no need to study the physical world except for the purpose of spiritual or moral instruction. The introduction of the corpus of classical Greek, especially Aristotelian, philosophy and the treatises of Arab commentators, however, challenged Christian thinkers to find ways to understand the very constitution of the world and the human person into which they believed God had so lovingly inserted himself. The contrast between the concerns of St. Bernard of Clairvaux (1090–1153) and St. Thomas Aquinas (1225–1274) illustrates the shift of intellectual focus. Where St. Bernard concerned himself with the supernatural gift of Christian wisdom, St. Thomas concerned himself with the natural gift of human reason as the foundation of Christian wisdom; where St. Bernard sought to discover in the mysteries of faith the ways of God toward man, St. Thomas in addition sought by the use of reason to trace the ways of man to God.

The massive infusion of Hellenic thought into the culture of Western Europe in the twelfth and thirteen centuries transpired in the context of two important institutional changes. Universities were emerging in the thirteenth century as centers of learning, and the University of Paris was the foremost in the area of theology. With this transition from the cathedral schools to the universities, the focus of formal learning shifted from logic and rhetoric to philosophy and theology. Second, the Dominican and Franciscan religious orders were founded in the thirteenth century, and they, unlike monks, were active in apostolic ministeries. And so, among the leading masters (i.e., professors) of the University of Paris School of Theology in the thirteenth century were the Dominican St. Thomas and the Franciscan St. Bonaventure (1217–1274). In contrast, the great Christian thinkers of the previous two centuries, St. Anselm (1033/34–1109) and St. Bernard, were products of the monasteries.

Earlier Christian thinkers had sought wisdom by meditating on the Scriptures. Twelfth-and especially thirteenth-century Christian theologians confronting the challenge of Hellenism sought to supplement such wisdom with another kind of understanding. And so there emerged alongside the monk and the mystic the speculative theologian and the philosopher, just as the institution of the university was emerging alongside the institution of the monastery. This was a decisive moment in the history of Western Christian and secular thought.

When thirteenth-century Christian scholars read the philosophical works of Aristotle (384–327 B.C.), they were introduced to a new way of looking at the world and themselves. As Christians, they could not accept Greek assumptions or tenets about the eternity of matter and motion. Nor could they accept the position of Averroës (1126–1198) regarding the collective unicity of the human intellect, since such would entail denial of personal immortality. They could, of course, demonstrate from Scripture that one or another tenet of Hellenic thought or Arabic commentary was contrary to Christian faith. But Aristotle and his Arab commentators claimed to have demonstrated their positions by reason, and so Christian thinkers, unless they were to accept a double standard of truth (one from revelation, the other from reason), needed to use reason itself to refute what they deemed to be erroneous in the tenets of Greek and Arab philosophers. And to do that, Christian thinkers had to learn how to philosophize systematically: to know what reason could prove, and how; to know what reason could not prove; to know what reason could neither prove nor disprove.

ST. THOMAS AND ARISTOTLE

Although Plato (428?-348/47 B.C.) and Aristotle agreed on many things, they and their respective heirs offered radically different views of reality and the intellectual process. For the Platonist, abstract immaterial forms, the Ideas, are the only unqualifiedly real things and so the only objects of true understanding; material things, since they are in a persistent state of flux, are only shadowy symbols obscurely reflecting the pure forms, and so only objects of opinion, that is, uncertain knowledge. For the Aristotelian, on the other hand, concrete forms exist in material things, although particular forms come and go in the ongoing process of change. The human intellect has true understanding of these forms, although the intellect understands the forms abstractly, that is, as abstracted from the matter in which the forms concretely exist. And from systematized knowledge of the proximate causes of material things, in which knowledge Aristotle held the natural sciences to consist, the human intellect could ascend to systematized knowledge of the ultimate causes of every kind of reality, in which knowledge Aristotle held metaphysics to consist.

A Neoplatonist derivative of Platonic thought dominated Western Christian theology up to the time of St. Thomas, thanks to the influence of St. Augustine (354–430). St. Augustine adopted such a philosophical approach in his prodigious and profound theological works, and the theological faculty of the University of Paris in St. Thomas's time followed suit.

Augustinian traditionalists had good reason to be suspicious of the introduction of Aristotle's substantive philosophy into the framework of

Christian thought. Aristotle's *Physics* offended Christian sensibilities because, contrary to the Book of Genesis, the *Physics* assumed, if it did not assert, the eternity of matter and motion. Aristotle's *De anima* offended Christian sensibilities because, contrary to the teaching of the New Testament, the *De anima* at best contained no explicit affirmation of personal immortality. Aristotle's *Metaphysics* offended Christian sensibilities because, contrary to the teaching of both the Old and New Testaments, the *Metaphysics'* version of God, the ultimate final cause of all motion, had no providential concern about the affairs of human beings. And Aristotle's *Ethics* offended Christian sensibilities because, contrary to the heavenly bliss proclaimed by the New Testament, the *Ethics* considered the happiness of human beings in this life their ultimate end.

But it was not simply the historical Aristotle who was a problem for thirteenth-century theologians; Latin Averroists, Western exponents of Averroës's interpretation of Aristotle, radically compounded the problem. As Augustinian Neoplatonism dominated the faculty of theology at the University of Paris in the first half of the thirteenth century, so Averroist Aristotelianism was at that time gaining ascendancy in the university's faculty of arts. The classic and unambiguous tenets of Averroist Aristotelianism—the uncreated, necessary, and eternal character of the world, the absence of an immediate divine providence over the material world and human affairs, the collective unicity of the human intellect that implicitly denied personal immortality—were as abhorrent to St. Thomas as they were to traditional Christian theologians. Nor could St. Thomas accept the "double-truth" theory of the Latin Averroist Siger of Brabant (ca. 1240–1281/84), that is, the theory that reason might legitimately affirm the very same propositions that Christian revelation might legitimately deny, and vice versa. St. Thomas and traditional Christian theologians were of one mind in regarding such a theory as absurd.

St. Thomas, along with many of his contemporaries, found the basic philosophical approach of Aristotle attractive, especially in contrast to that of Plato. Unlike Plato, Aristotle did not disdain the reality of the sensible world, affirmed the unity of the body-soul composite, and distinguished the abstract status of forms as understood, from the concrete status of forms as belonging to things. From St. Thomas's point of view, Plato committed a fundamental error when he failed to distinguish the extramental actuality of forms as they partake of God's existing, from the intramental nonactuality of abstract forms in the human intellect. From this error, in St. Thomas's opinion, Plato was induced to deprive material things of their intrinsic causes (form and matter), to limit human knowledge to knowledge of abstract essences, to denigrate the reality of material things in their individuality, and to create an unbridgeable chasm between the world of sense perception and the world of intellectual conception.

St. Thomas was unwilling to accept either Avicenna (980-1037) or Averroës as the definitive interpreter of Aristotle. By refusing to accept Avicenna's rather Platonic interpretation of Aristotle, St. Thomas could be faithful to Aristotle's criticism of the Platonic theory of forms. And by refusing to accept Averroës's interpretation of Aristotle, St. Thomas could supplement Aristotle's *Physics* with the theory of creation, Aristotle's *De anima* with the theory of the soul's immortality, Aristotle's *Metaphysics* with the theory of God's comprehensive providence, and Aristotle's *Ethics* with the theory of a transtemporal human end. Nor did St. Thomas consider even Aristotle himself the definitive interpreter of philosophy.

St. Thomas, however much he preferred Aristotle's philosophical approach and substantive conclusions to those of Plato, did not reject all of the latter's teachings, as Aristotle himself did not. Indeed, some aspects of St. Thomas's synthesis, particularly regarding the doctrine of participation, seem to echo Platonic themes. Central to St. Thomas's philosophical theology was the view that God possesses, or, more precisely, is identical with, the fullness of existing, and that created things share existing in diverse, limited ways. And in the fourth of the ways that St. Thomas elaborated in the *Summa* to prove God's existence (I, Q. 2, A. 3), he adopted a favorite Platonic line of argument (although not necessarily one that Aristotle would reject): the hierarchy of beings of limited perfection is unintelligible apart from the existence of an exemplary cause of unlimited perfection.

Even St. Thomas's treatment of the human constitution reveals a significant departure from Aristotle's approach to the subject. In the prologue to this section of the Summa, St. Thomas states that "it belongs to the theologian to consider the human constitution from the perspective of the soul, not the body except insofar as the body is related to the soul." Accordingly, St. Thomas begins his treatment (I, Q. 75) with the immaterial, subsistent, and immortal nature of the human soul, and only then considers the soul as part of the human composite (I, QQ. 76–88). In other words, St. Thomas affirms the subsistent nature of the human soul in itself before he considers the soul's function in relation to the body. While St. Thomas devotes the bulk of his consideration of the human soul to its role and activities in the human composite, and in doing so follows Aristotle closely, St. Thomas's affirmation of the soul's subsistence at the very outset of his treatment indicates the priority that he attached to that theme and at least a divergence of emphasis from that of Aristotle. St. Thomas's concerns in this respect are more akin to those of Plato than to Aristotle's this-world concerns.

Aristotle and St. Thomas, on the one hand, and modern scientists, on the other, understand very different things by the word "science." For the former, the purpose of natural science is to explain observable phenomena by purely deductive reasoning, especially from formal and final causes, and the formal and final causes on which such deductive reasoning depends are "givens," products of intuition not subject to empirical verification. For modern scientists, the purpose of natural science is to explain the efficient causality of observable phenomena by hypothetical reasoning from postulated explanatory theories about the causality, and the theories, while intuitive, are subject to indirect verification by testing for observable consequences deducible from the theories.

No intelligent contemporary can doubt the vastly superior heuristic value of modern science to that of Aristotelian science, and modern science has conclusively disproved certain tenets of Aristotle's physics (e.g., that the earth is the center of the universe, that heavier objects as such tend toward lower places in the universe, that celestial bodies are substantial units). But however inadequate Aristotle's scientific method by modern standards, and however erroneous some of Aristotle's scientific conclusions, the philosophical components of his physics, and all of his metaphysics, should be judged on their own merits. And in the case of the human constitution, each of us can "test" some aspects of Aristotelian psychology (e.g., the processes of understanding, judging, and reasoning) by reflecting on our own internal experience.

From the modern perspective, Aristotelian science has proven weakest in its analysis and conclusions about inanimate matter. Modern science has been able to discover the intricate workings of atomic and subatomic matter, workings inaccessible to direct sense perception and philosophical reflection. Modern science has likewise discovered much about the inner workings and the origins and development of living material things. But modern science, for all its discoveries, has not explained, and in terms of its methodology cannot explain, the phenomenon of life itself. Indeed, in describing the most general characteristics of living material things, modern science has largely followed in the footsteps of Aristotle. For example, modern science, like Aristotle, associates nutrition, growth, and reproduction with all forms of living material things, and sense perception with all forms of animal life. Least of all can modern science explain the intellectual life of the human person. In short, modern science is at its best in explaining mechanical physical phenomena and at its weakest in explaining the phenomenon of life as such in all its gradations, and especially the phenomenon of human life as such. Here Aristotle's combination of philosophy and science may contribute to our understanding.

THE STRUCTURE AND METHOD OF THE *SUMMA*

As St. Thomas makes clear at the beginning of the *Summa*, the work is designed for "beginners" or "novices in the study of theology (although the *Summa* evidently presupposes substantial academic preparation on their part). The *Summa* is thus expressly theological, and its audience Christian believers, presumably clerics and aspiring clerics, interested in understanding their faith more deeply. Nonetheless, the *Summa* proposes many theses and arguments about God) human beings, and the world that do not rely on Scripture or the Church's teaching. Such theses and arguments merit study by believers and nonbelievers alike, by students of philosophy as well as by those of theology.

The *Summa* is divided into three parts. In the first part, St. Thomas considers God and the attributes we predicate about him, creation, the angels, human beings, and Adam's state before the Fall. The second part, itself divided into two parts) deals with the ultimate end of human beings, the nature of specifically human acts, sin, law, and the virtues. The third part deals with the role of Christ and the sacraments in the redemption and salvation of the human race. The *Summa* thus progresses cyclically: human beings proceed from God and, despite Adam's Fall, are destined to return to God if they freely cooperate with the graces won by Christ and communicated by the sacraments.

This volume of translations is from the first part of the *Summa* and deals with St. Thomas's view of the human constitution. St. Thomas poses a series of questions related to this topic, and the questions are divided into articles raising specific points of inquiry. Each article poses a problem in the form of a question (e.g., I, Q. 75, A. 3: "Is the Human Soul Subsistent?"). The article begins with objections to the position that St. Thomas will adopt. Each objection cites at least one Scriptural, patristic, theological, philosophical, or popular statement. St. Thomas then declares his contrary position. Next, St. Thomas elaborates one or more arguments in favor of his position. Lastly, St. Thomas answers each objection in turn. While many of the objections are superficial or plays on words, others provide the opportunity for him to make clarifications or distinctions that he deems important.

Why do the articles have this formal structure? The short answer lies in the academic conventions of the University of Paris and other medieval universities. Faculty masters and student degree-candidates would at appointed times defend theses against all comers, and the format resembled that of a modern debate. The first step in the process was to recapitulate an opponent's position in such a way that the opponent could agree that his position was correctly stated and interpreted. Only then would the master or student explain and defend his own position.

The longer explanation of the formal structure of the articles in the *Summa* is that the medieval thesis-defense format invited audience participation in a way similar to that of the Platonic dialogue. As Plato implicitly invites readers of the dialogues to become intellectually involved in the exchange of ideas between Socrates and his interlocutors, so St. Thomas and other medieval masters invited their audience, and implicitly continue to invite readers, to become intellectually involved in resolving the questions posed. The objections in the medieval format thus take on the role of Socrates's interlocutors in the Platonic dialogues. Unlike the Socrates represented in the Platonic dialogues, however, St. Thomas and other medieval masters clearly enunciated their own positions and directly distinguished the terms involved in the discussions. Where Plato progressively raised a series of questions to indicate the presuppositions of Socrates's interlocutors, and the need to go beyond conventional understanding of the world and human experience, St. Thomas gave explicit answers to clearly framed questions. In this respect, St. Thomas has more in common with modern academic conventions than Plato does, however much both want to involve their respective audiences.

St. Thomas's treatment of the human soul may serve to illustrate the logic of his method of inquiry. St. Thomas begins his inquiry with consideration of the soul's essence (I, Q. 75). He asks first whether the human soul is a material substance (A. 1). He responds negatively, explaining that the soul is the ultimate intrinsic source of life in human beings, and that no ultimate intrinsic source of life in material things is to be identified with the substance that it animates. St. Thomas then argues that the human soul is by reason of the immateriality of its activity subsistent, that is, not intrinsically dependent on anything for its existence; the capacity to understand the essences of material things transcends the limitations of matter and sense perception (A. 2). St. Thomas next inquires whether the souls of irrational animals as well are subsistent, and argues that they are not, since their cognition is limited to sense perception, and sense perception intrinsically depends on bodily organs (A. 3). If the human soul is subsistent, the question naturally arises whether it is the human being, and St. Thomas affirms that it is not; rather, the integral composite of soul and body constitutes the human being (A. 4). Because some contemporaries like St. Bonaventure maintained that the human soul itself is a composite of form and spiritual matter, St. Thomas considers and rejects this position (A. 5). St. Thomas argues that the human soul cannot pass away, that is, that it is intrinsically immortal (A. 6). The human soul, because it is subsistent, cannot pass away when its union with the body ceases, and because it has no parts, it cannot pass away by decomposition. Lastly, St. Thomas argues that the human soul differs specifically from angels because their respective intellectual activities differ specifically (A. 7).

Only after thus considering the essence of the human soul does St. Thomas proceed to consider the union of the soul with the body, the sensory and intellectual powers of the soul, its appetitive powers and the will's freedom, and how the intellect knows material things, itself, and immaterial things (I, QQ. 76-88).

CONCLUSION

The issues that concerned St. Thomas in the topics included in this volume of translations—the nature of the human soul, the relation of the human soul to the body, the functions of the external and internal senses, the activities of the intellect, free will, and how the intellectual soul knows the world, itself, and immaterial things—mirror the concerns of the intellectual climate in which he lived. The introduction of the corpus of Aristotle's philosophical works (and to a lesser extent, the introduction of Plato's) impelled Western philosopher-theologians to rethink the rational underpinnings of their beliefs. It is accordingly, of course, necessary to study St. Thomas in the context of his times, but it would be a mistake to regard his (or indeed the work of any first-rate thinker) as simply the product of a bygone age without significance for our world and ourselves. The questions that St. Thomas raised about the human constitution may need to be reformulated or nuanced, the answers he gave may need to be modified or rejected, and new questions may be pertinent, but one should not fail to recognize the importance of the topics, and the many insights that St. Thomas brings to them.

BIBLICAL ABBREVIATIONS

Cor.	Corinthians
Eccl.	Ecclesiastes
Eph.	Ephesians
Gen.	Genesis
Jer.	Jeremiah
Jn.	John
Mt.	Matthew
Phil.	Philippians
Prov.	Proverbs
Ps.	Psalms
Rom.	Romans
Sir.	Sirach
Tit.	Titus
Wis.	Wisdom

OTHER ABBREVIATIONS

A	Article
PG	J. P. Migne, *Patrologia Graeca*
PL	J. P. Migne, *Patrologia Latina*
Q	Question
ST	St. Thomas Aquinas, *Summa Theologiae*

WORKS CITED BY ST. THOMAS

Most titles are in Latin, according to common usage.

Aristotle
  De anima
  Categories
  De causa motus animalium
  De coelo
  De coelo et mundo
  De divinatione per somnia
  Epistolae
  Ethics (Nichomachean)
  Eudemian Ethics
  De generatione
  De generatione animalium
  Historia animalium
  De interpretatione
  De memoria et reminiscentia
  Metaphysics
  Meteorology
  Physics
  Politics
  Posterior Analytics
  Rhetoric
  De somno et vigilia
Augustine
  The City of God
  Confessions
  De doctrina Christiana
  Enchiridion
  Super Genesim ad litteram
  De libero arbitrio
  Octoginta trium quaestionum
  De origine animae
  De quantitate animae
  Retractationum
  Soliloquiorum

De Trinitate
De vera religione
Averroës
De animae beatudine
In libros De anima
In libros De coelo
In libros Metaphysicorum
De sensu et sensibilibus
Avicenna
De anima
De animalibus
Metaphysics
Basil
Homiliae in principium Proverborum
Bernard, St.
Tractatus de gratia et libero arbitrio
Boethius
On the Consolation of Philosophy
Damascene, St. John
De fide orthodoxa
Denis the Pseudo-Areopagite
De coelesti hierarchia
De divinis nominibus
Ecclesiae historia
De mystica theologia
Edmer
De similitudinibus (erroneously attributed by St. Thomas to St.
      Anselm)
Gennadius
De ecclesiasticis dogmatibus
Gilbert de la Porrée
In librum Quomodo substantiae bonae sint
Glossa ordinaria
Gregory the Great, Pope St.
Homiliarum in Evangelia
Jerome, St.
In Evangelium Matthaei
In Ezechielem
Liber de causis

Lombard, Peter
In Epistolam ad Romanos
Sentences
Nemesius
De natura hominis (erroneously attributed by St. Thomas to St. Gregory of Nyssa)
Origen
In Epistolam ad Romanos
Peri Archon
Plato
Alcibiades
The Laws
Meno
Phaedo
Phaedrus
Republic
Theatetus
Timaeus

AUTHORS CITED BY ST. THOMAS

Albumazar (A.D. 787–886)
Aristotle, "The Philosopher" (384–327 B.C.)
Augustine, St. (A.D. 354–430)
Avempace (A.D. ca. 1095–1138/39)
Averroës, "The Commentator" (A.D. 1126–1198)
Avicenna (A.D. 980–1037)
Basil, St. (A.D. 329?–379)
Bernard of Clairvaux, St. (A.D. 1090–1153)
Boethius (A.D. 480?–524?)
Damascene, St. John (A.D. 700?–754?)
Denis the Pseudo-Areopagite (early sixth century A.D.)
Edmer of Canterbury (A.D. 1060?–1128?)
Empedocles (490?–430 B.C.)
Gennadius of Marseilles (late fifth century A.D.)
Gilbert de la Porrée (A.D. 1075?–1154)
Gregory the Great, Pope St. (A.D. 540?–604)
Jerome, St. (A.D. 347?–419/20)
Lombard, Peter (A.D. 1100?–1160)
Nemesius (late fourth century A.D.)
Origen (A.D. 185?–254?)
Paul, St., "The Apostle" (first century A.D.)
Plato (428?–348/47 B.C.)
Themistius (fourth century A.D.)

ST I

Question 75

On Human Beings, Who Are Composite Spiritual and Material Substances, and First Concerning the Essence of the Soul

[This question is divided into seven articles, six of which are included here.]

First Article

Is the Soul a Material Substance?

I proceed in this way to the first article: it seems that the soul is a material substance.

Obj. 1. The soul moves the body. But the soul does not cause motion without itself being moved. First, this is so because nothing seems capable of causing motion without itself being moved, since nothing gives to something else what it does not possess; for example, nothing cold causes something else to become hot. Second, if something causes something else to move without itself being moved, it causes perpetual and uniform motion, as the *Physics* proves,[1] and there is no evidence of such motion in the motion of animals, which their souls cause. Therefore, the soul is itself moved when it causes motion. But everything that is moved when it causes motion is a material substance. Therefore, the soul is a material substance.

Obj. 2. Some likeness causes all knowledge. But material substances cannot be like immaterial things. Therefore, the soul, if it were not to be a material substance, could not know material things.

Obj. 3. Causes of motion necessarily have contact with the things they move. But only material substances have contact. Therefore, the soul, since it moves the body, seems to be a material substance.

On the contrary, Augustine says in his *De Trinitate* that the soul "is called simple in relation to the body because there is no mass to give the soul spatial extension."[2]

I answer that we necessarily presuppose for inquiry about the soul's nature that we affirm that the soul [*anima*] is the first source of life in the living things in the world, since we call living things animate, while we call nonliving things inanimate. And life is most evident in two kinds of action, namely, knowledge and movement. Ancient philosophers, however, were unable to rise above their imagination and held material substances to be the sources of such actions, saying that only material things are real, and that there are no immaterial substances. And they accordingly said that the soul is a material substance.

And although we can demonstrate the falsity of that opinion in many ways, we shall notwithstanding employ only one, one that both more generally and more surely shows that the soul is not a material substance. For it is evidently the case that not every source of vital activity is the soul; for example, the eye, since it is a source of sight, would then be the soul, and we would have to say the same about other instrumentalities of the soul. But we call the soul the *prime* source of life. And although some material substances can be certain sources of life, as, for example, the heart is a source of life in animals, yet no material substance can be the prime source of life. For being the source of life, or being alive, evidently does not belong to a material substance because it is such; otherwise, every material substance would be alive or a source of life. Therefore, it belongs to a material substance to be alive, or even a source of life, because the material substance is *a particular kind* of material substance. But the fact that a thing is actually such derives from a source that we call the thing's actuality. Therefore, the soul, that is, the prime source of life, is not a material substance but the actuality of a material substance, just as, for example, heat, which is the source of heating, is not a material substance but a certain actuality of a material substance.

Reply to Obj. 1. Since everything moved is moved by another, and there cannot be an infinite series of moved things moving other things, we need to affirm that not every cause of motion is itself moved. Since being moved is indeed going from potentiality to actuality, a cause of motion gives something it possesses to a moveable object, inasmuch as it causes the moveable object to be actually moved. But as the *Physics* demonstrates,[3] there is one kind of cause of motion that is completely unmovable, a cause of motion that is neither intrinsically nor by chance moved, and such a cause can cause perpetually uniform motion. And there is another kind of cause of motion that is moved by chance but not intrinsically, and so this kind of cause of motion does not cause perpetually uniform motion. And such a cause of motion is the soul. There is yet another kind of cause of motion that is moved intrinsically, and material substances are such causes. And the natural philosophers of antiquity, because they believed that only material substances exist, held that every cause of motion is moved, and that the soul is moved intrinsically, and that the soul is a material substance.

Reply to Obj. 2. The likeness of something known does not need to be actually in the natural condition of the one who knows. But assuming that something first potentially knows and then actually knows, the likeness of the thing known needs to be in the natural condition of the knowing subject only potentially, not actually. Just so, color is only potentially, not actually, in the pupil of an eye. And so the likenesses of material things do not need to be actually in the natural condition of the soul but to be only in the potentiality of the soul for such likenesses. But natural philosophers of antiquity, because they did not know how to distinguish between actuality and potentiality, held that the soul is a material substance in order that the soul might know material substances, and held that the soul needs to be composed of the sources of every material substance in order that the soul might know every material substance.

Reply to Obj. 3. There are two kinds of contact: one by way of extension, and the other by way of power. In the first way, only material substances have contact with material substances. In the second way, something immaterial that moves a material substance can have contact with it.

Second Article

Is the Human Soul Something Subsistent[4]?

I proceed in this way to the second article: it seems that the human soul is not a subsistent thing.

Obj. 1. We call something subsistent a particular thing. But the composite of soul and body, not the soul, is a particular thing. Therefore, the soul is not a subsistent thing.

Obj. 2. We can say that everything subsistent acts immanently. But we do not say that the soul acts immanently, since "to say that the soul sensibly perceives, or understands, is like saying that the soul constructs or builds," as the *De anima* says.[5] Therefore, the soul is not a subsistent thing.

Obj. 3. The soul, if it were something subsistent, would have some activity apart from the body. But the soul has no activity apart from the body, not even understanding, since the soul does not have understanding without a sense image, and there is no sense image apart from a body. Therefore, the human soul is not a subsistent thing.

On the contrary, Augustine says in his *De Trinitate:* "Whoever perceives that the nature of the mind is both a substance and immaterial, perceives that the error of those who hold that the mind is material, derives from the fact that they attribute to the mind the things apart from which they cannot think about any nature, namely, sense images of material substances."[6] Therefore, the nature of the human mind is both immaterial and a substance, that is to say, something subsistent.

I answer that the source of intellectual activity, which source we call the human soul, is an immaterial and subsistent source. For human beings by means of their intellects evidently can know the nature of every kind of material substance. And something that can know several kinds of material substances necessarily possesses no part of such substances in its own natural condition. This is so because what would be part of the knower by nature would prevent knowledge of other kinds of things. Just so, we observe that a sick person's tongue, poisoned by a bilious and bitter fluid, cannot perceive anything sweet; rather, everything seems bitter to such a tongue. Therefore, if the source of intellection were to have in itself the natural condition of a particular material substance, the source would be unable to know every material substance. But every material substance has a fixed nature. Therefore, the source of intellectual activity cannot be a material substance.

And it is likewise impossible that the source of intellectual activity understand by means of a bodily organ, since the fixed nature of such a bodily organ would also prevent knowledge of all material substances; for example, if a fixed color be both in the pupil of the eye and in a glass vase, liquid poured into the vase seems to be of the same color.

Therefore, the very source of intellection that we call the mind or intellect, intrinsically has an activity in which the body does not share. But nothing can intrinsically act unless it intrinsically subsists. For activity belongs only to actual beings, and so things act in the same way that they exist. Consequently, we do not say that heat heats, but that something hot does.

We conclude, therefore, that the human soul, which we will call the intellect or mind, is something immaterial and subsistent.

Reply to Obj. 1. We can understand in two ways what it means to be a particular thing: in one way, as something subsistent; in the other way, as something subsistent that is complete in a specific nature. In the first way, being a particular thing excludes the quality of inhering that belongs to accidents and material forms; in the second way, being a particular thing also excludes the incompleteness of parts. And so we could call hands particular things in the first way but not in the second way. Therefore, since the human soul is part of the human species, we can call the human soul a particular thing in the first way something subsistent, as it were, but not in the second way, for we in that way call the composite of soul and body a particular thing.

Reply to Obj. 2. Aristotle does not express those words as his own opinion but as the opinion of those who said that to understand is to be moved, as is clear from what he there previously states.[7]

Or we should say that activity as such belongs to existing as such. Now, we can sometimes say that something intrinsically exists when it does not inhere as an accident or material form, even though it be a part. On the other hand, we say that something neither inhering in the aforementioned way nor a part is subsistent in the proper sense and intrinsically. And we could not in the latter way call eyes or hands intrinsically subsistent, and neither, consequently, could we call them intrinsically active. And so also do we attribute the activity of parts to the whole by means of the parts. For we say that human beings see by means of their eyes and touch by means of their hands, in a different way than we say that something hot heats by means of heat, since heat, properly speaking, in no way heats anything. We can say, therefore, that the soul understands, just as we can say that the eye sees, but we say more properly that human beings understand by means of their soul.

Reply to Obj. 3. We need the body for intellectual activity by reason of the intellect's object, not as an instrument for the exercise of such activity, since sense images are related to the intellect as colors are to sight. And to need the body in this way does not take away the fact that the intellect is subsistent; otherwise, animals would not be subsistent things, since they need external sensible objects for sense perception.

Third Article

Are the Souls of Irrational Animals Subsistent?

I proceed in this way to the third article: it seems that the souls of irrational animals are subsistent.

Obj. 1. Human beings belong to the same genus as other animals. But the soul of a human being is something subsistent, as I have shown.[8] Therefore, the souls of other animals are also subsistent.

Obj. 2. Powers of sense perception are related to sensible objects as the power of understanding is to intelligible objects. But the intellect without the body understands intelligible objects. Therefore, the senses without the body also apprehend sensible objects. But the souls of irrational animals sensibly perceive. Therefore, the souls of irrational animals are subsistent for the same reason that the intellectual souls of human beings are.

Obj. 3. The souls of irrational animals move the animals' bodies. But animals' bodies, rather than moving anything else, are themselves moved. Therefore, the souls of irrational animals have some activity apart from the animals' bodies.

On the contrary, the work *De ecclesiasticis dogmatibus* says: "We believe that human beings alone have subsistent souls, while the souls of animals are not subsistent."[9]

I answer that ancient philosophers held that there was no distinction between the senses and the intellect, and they attributed both to a material source, as I have said.[10] And Plato, although he distinguished between the intellect and the senses, nonetheless attributed both to an immaterial source, holding that sense perception as well as understanding belong to the soul as such.[11] And he consequently held that even the souls of irrational animals are subsistent.

But Aristotle held that understanding alone among the activities of the soul acts apart from bodily organs.[12] Now, bodily changes evidently accompany sense perceptions and the resulting activities of sensory souls; in seeing, for example, the forms of color change the pupil of the eye, and the same is evident in the case of other senses. And so sensory souls evidently do not have any intrinsic activity of their own, but every activity of such souls belongs to the composites. And so we conclude that the souls of irrational animals, since they do not act intrinsically, are not subsistent, since each thing has a way of existing like its way of acting.

Reply to Obj. 1. Although human beings belong to the same genus as other animals, yet human beings differ specifically from other animals, and we note different species by different forms. Nor does every difference of form need to cause a difference of genus.

Reply to Obj. 2. Powers of sense perception are in one way related to sensible objects as the power of understanding is related to intelligible objects, namely, insofar as both have a potentiality for their objects. But powers of sense perception and the power of understanding are in another way dissimilarly related to their objects, insofar as sensible objects act upon sensory powers in conjunction with bodily changes, and so the excellence of sensible objects weakens the senses. And this does not happen in the case of the intellect, for the intellect after understanding the most intelligible objects can then better understand less intelligible objects.

But if, in the activity of understanding, the body should be wearied, this happens by chance, insofar as the intellect needs the activity of sensory powers, powers that provide the intellect with sense images.

Reply to Obj. 3. There are two kinds of powers causing motion. the first kind, namely, appetitive power, commands motion. And sensory souls have no activity of appetitive powers apart from the body; rather, bodily changes accompany hate and joy and all such like. The second kind of power causing motion executes motion, and this kind of power renders members of the body suitable to obey appetites, and acts of this kind of power consist in being moved rather than causing motion. And so causing motion is clearly not an act of sensory souls apart from the body.

Fourth Article

Is the Human Soul the Human Being?

I proceed in this way to the fourth article: it seems that the human soul is the human being.

Obj. 1. The Second Letter to the Corinthians says: "Although our outer human being decays, yet our inner human being is daily renewed."[13] But what is inner in human beings is the soul. Therefore, the human soul is the inner human being.

Obj. 2. The human soul is a certain substance. But the human soul is not substance in general. Therefore, the human soul is a particular substance. Therefore, the human soul is a hypostasis or person. But the human soul is nothing other than human. Therefore, the human soul is the human being, for the human person is the human being.

On the contrary, Augustine in the *City of God* praises Varro, who "thought that human beings are neither simply souls nor simply bodies but both souls and bodies."[14]

I answer that we can understand in two ways the proposition "The human soul is the human being." In one way, we can understand "human being" to be the soul but "this particular human being" (e.g., Socrates) to be a composite of soul and body rather than the soul. And I say this because certain thinkers held that the form alone belongs to the nature of the species, while the matter belongs to individuals and not to the species.[15]

But this indeed cannot be true. For the meaning of definitions belongs to species, and definitions in the case of things of nature signify form and matter, not simply form. And so matter is part of species in the case of things of nature. This matter is indeed not particular matter, which is the source of individuation; rather, it is general matter. For example, as it belongs to the nature of this particular human being to be composed of this particular soul and this particular flesh and these particular bones, so it belongs to the nature of being human to be composed of soul and flesh and bones. For whatever belongs generally to the substance of every individual in a species necessarily belongs to the substance of the species.

And we can understand in a second way the proposition "The human soul is the soul" in this way: that this particular human soul is this particular human being. And we could indeed maintain this if we were to suppose that the activities of sensory souls are proper to such souls apart from bodies, since all the activities that we attribute to human beings would belong to the human soul alone. And what effects the activities of each thing is the thing, and so what effects the activities of a human being is the human being.

I have shown, however, that sense perception is not an activity of the soul alone.[16] Therefore, since sense perception is a certain activity of human beings, albeit not their peculiar activity, the human being is evidently not the soul alone but the composite of soul and body.

Indeed, Plato, because he held that sense perception belongs to the soul, could hold that human beings are "souls using bodies."[17]

Reply to Obj. 1. What is chief in each thing seems chiefly to be the thing itself, according to the Philosopher in the *Ethics*.[18] For example, we say that the political community does what the ruler of the political community does. And we sometimes in this way call the chief characteristic in human beings the human being. We indeed sometimes so designate the intellectual part, which we call the "inner human being," according to the truth of the matter, while we sometimes so designate the sensory part together with the body, according to the evaluation of people completely occupied about sensible things. And we here speak of the "outer human being."

Reply to Obj. 2. Not every particular substance is a hypostasis or person, but only one that has the complete nature of the species. And so we cannot call hands or feet hypostases or persons. And likewise neither can we call the human soul a hypostasis or person, since the human soul is part of the human species.

Fifth Article

Is the Human Soul Composed of Matter and Form?

I proceed in this way to the fifth article: it seems that the human soul is composed of matter and form.

Obj. 1. We distinguish potentiality from actuality. But each and everything actual shares in the first actuality, which is God, and everything is good and a being and living by sharing in God, as the teaching of Denis in his work *De divinis nominibus* makes clear.[19] Therefore, everything potential shares in the first potentiality. But the first potentiality is prime matter.[20] Therefore, since the human soul is in one way potential—and this is evidenced by the fact that human beings sometimes understand potentially—it seems that the human soul shares in prime matter as part of itself.

Obj. 2. We find matter wherever we find properties of matter. But we find in the human soul properties of matter, namely, to be a subject and to be changed, for the human soul is a subject of knowledge and virtue, and is changed from ignorance to knowledge, and from vice to virtue. Therefore, there is matter in the human soul.

Obj. 3. Things without matter have no cause of their existing, as the *Metaphysics* says.[21] But the human soul, because God created it, has a cause of its existing. Therefore, the human soul has matter.

Obj. 4. What has no matter and is only a form, is pure and unlimited actuality. But such a state belongs to God alone. Therefore, the human soul has matter.

On the contrary, Augustine proves in his *Super Genesim* that the human soul is not made of either corporeal or spiritual matter.[22]

I answer that the human soul does not have matter. And we can consider this in two ways. In the first way, indeed, from the nature of the soul in general. For it belongs to the nature of the soul to be the form of a body. Therefore, the soul is either entirely or partially a form. If entirely, no part of it can be matter, assuming that we mean by matter purely potential being. This is because form as such is actuality, and something purely potential cannot be part of actuality, since potentiality, as distinguished from actuality, is incompatible with actuality. And if part of the soul be a form, we shall call that part the soul, and we shall call the matter which that part first actualizes, the first enlivened thing.

Second, we can consider specifically from the nature of the human soul as intellectual that the human soul does not have matter. For everything received in something else is evidently received in the recipient according to the recipient's condition. And each thing is known in the way in which its form is in the knower. And the intellectual soul knows a thing in its nature completely (for example, stone as such completely). Therefore, the form of a stone, regarding the stone's own formal nature, is completely in the intellectual soul. Therefore, the intellectual soul is a pure form and not something composed of matter and form.

For if the intellectual soul were composed of matter and form, the soul would receive in itself the forms of things as individual forms, and so it would know only singular things, as happens in the case of sensory powers, powers that receive the forms of things in bodily organs; this is so because matter is the source that individuates forms. Therefore, we conclude that the intellectual soul and every intellectual substance that knows forms completely, has no composition of form and matter.

Reply to Obj. 1. The first actuality is the universal source of all actualities, since it is unlimited, "containing everything beforehand" by its power, as Denis says.[23] And so things do not share in it as parts but by the outpouring of processions from itself. And potentialities, since they receive actualities, need to be proportioned to actualities. But received actualities, which proceed from the first, unlimited actuality and are certain sharings thereof, differ. And so there cannot be one potentiality that receives all actualities (as there is one actuality that flows into all shared actualities); otherwise, the receptive potentiality would equal the active power of the first actuality. And there is in the intellectual soul a receptive potentiality other than that of prime matter, as the diversity of actualities received makes apparent, for prime matter receives individual forms, while the intellect receives pure forms. And so such potentiality in the intellectual soul does not indicate that the soul is composed of matter and form.

Reply to Obj. 2. Being a subject and being changed belong to matter as potential. Therefore, as the potentiality of the intellect is one thing, and the potentiality of prime matter another, so there are different reasons why the intellect and prime matter are subjects and changed. For the intellect is accordingly a subject of knowledge and changed from ignorance to knowledge because the intellect has potentiality for intelligible forms.

Reply to Obj. 3. Forms and efficient causes cause matter to exist, and so efficient causes cause matter to exist inasmuch as they bring matter to the actuality of forms by processes of change. But if something is a subsistent form, it does not have existing from any formal source, nor does it have a cause that changes it from potentiality to actuality. And so, after the cited words, the Philosopher concludes that "the only cause" in composites of matter and form "is one that causes movement from potentiality to actuality, but each and every thing without matter is directly something truly a being."[24]

Reply to Obj. 4. Everything shared is related to the thing sharing as an actuality of the latter. And any created, intrinsically subsistent form that we suppose, necessarily shares in existing, because even "life itself" (or any such thing one might mention) "shares in existing itself," as Denis says in his *De divinis nominibus*.[25] But shared existing is limited to the capacity of the thing sharing. And so God alone, who is his very existing, is pure and unlimited actuality, while there is a composition of actuality and potentiality in intellectual substances, not indeed one of matter and form but one of form and shared existing. And so certain thinkers say that intellectual substances are composed of "that by which the substances exist" and "what the substances are,"[26] for the very act of existing is that by which something exists.

Sixth Article

Can the Human Soul Pass Away[27]?

I proceed in this way to the sixth article: it seems that the human soul can pass away.

Obj. 1. Things with a like source and a like course seem to have a like end. But there is a like source of the coming-to-be of human beings and beasts, since both are made out of the dust of the earth. Both also have a like course of life, since "they all breathe alike, and human beings possess nothing more than beasts do," as the Book of Ecclesiastes says.[28] Therefore, as the same text concludes, "human beings and beasts have one and the same dissolution, and the condition of both is the same." But the souls of irrational animals can pass away. Therefore, the human soul can also pass away.

Obj. 2. Everything that comes from nothing can revert to nothing, since the end of things needs to correspond to their beginning. But "we are produced out of nothing," as the Book of Wisdom says,[29] and this is true regarding the soul as well as the body. Therefore, as the same text concludes, "we shall be as if we were not to have been," even regarding the soul.

Obj. 3. Everything has its peculiar activity. But the peculiar activity of the soul (which is understanding with the aid of sense images) cannot exist apart from the body, since the soul cannot understand anything without a sense image, and there are no sense images apart from the body, as the *De anima* says.[30] Therefore, the soul cannot survive when the body is destroyed.

On the contrary, Denis says in his *De divinis nominibus* that God's goodness bestows on human souls that they be "intellectual" and possess a "substantial life that cannot pass away."[31]

I answer that the human soul, which we call the source of intellection, cannot pass away. For something passes away in two ways: in one way, intrinsically; in the other way, by chance. But nothing subsistent can come to be or pass away by chance, that is, when something else has come to be or passed away. For coming-to-be and passing away belong to something in the same way that existing does, and existing is acquired by the coming-to-be and lost by the passing away. And so things that have existing intrinsically can come to be or pass away only intrinsically, while we say that nonsubsistent things like accidents and material forms come to be and pass away by the coming-to-be and the passing away of composites.

I have shown before, moreover, that the souls of irrational animals are not intrinsically subsistent, and that only human souls are.[32] And so the souls of irrational animals pass away when irrational animals' bodies pass away, but human souls could not pass away unless they were to pass away intrinsically.

And it is indeed altogether impossible not only for the human soul to pass away but also for any subsistent pure form to do so. For what as such belongs to something, evidently cannot be separated from it. But existing belongs intrinsically to forms, which are actualities. And so matter acquires actual existing when it acquires form, and passing away happens in matter when form is separated from it. But form cannot be separated from itself. And so subsistent form cannot cease to exist.

Even granted that the human soul were to be composed of matter and form, as certain thinkers say, we would still need to hold that the human soul cannot pass away. For we do not find passing away except where we find contrariety, since comings-to-be and passings away are out of, and into, contraries. And so heavenly bodies, because they do not have any matter subject to contrariety, cannot pass away. And there cannot be any contrariety in intellectual souls. For intellectual souls receive in the way in which they exist, and the things received in them have no contrariety, since even the natures of contraries are not contraries in the intellect; rather, the intellect knows contraries simultaneously. Therefore, the intellectual soul cannot possibly pass away.

We can also take evidence of this matter from the fact that each thing by nature desires to exist in its own fashion. And desire, in things that know, is a consequence of knowledge. Now, while the senses know existing only under conditions of particular times and places, the intellect grasps existing unconditionally and regarding every point of time. And so everything with an intellect desires by nature to exist forever. But a desire from nature cannot be in vain. Therefore, no intellectual substance can pass away.

Reply to Obj. 1. Solomon introduces that argument out of the mouth of fools, as the Book of Wisdom expresses it.[33] The saying that human beings and other animals have a like source of their coming to be, therefore, is true regarding the body, since all animals are made out of the dust of the earth. But the saying is not true regarding the soul, since material powers produce the souls of irrational animals, while God produces human souls. And to indicate this, the Book of Genesis says regarding other animals that "the earth produces living souls,"[34] but regarding human beings that "he [God] breathed the breath of life into their faces."[35] And so the conclusion of the Book of Ecclesiastes says: "Dust reverts to its soil, whence it came, and the spirit returns to God, who gave it."[36]

In like manner, the course of life of human beings and other animals is similar regarding the body, and the saying of the Book of Ecclesiastes that "they all breathe alike,"[37] and the saying of the Book of Wisdom that "steam and breath are in our nostrils," and so forth,[38] pertain to this similarity. But there is no like course regarding the soul, since human beings understand, while irrational animals do not. And so the saying that "human beings possess nothing more than irrational animals do,"[39] is false.

And so there is like dissolution regarding the bodies of human beings and irrational animals but not regarding their souls.

Reply to Obj. 2. Passive power cannot create anything, but only the active power of the creator, who can produce something out of nothing, can create something. Just so, when we say that something can revert to nothing, we do not imply any potentiality in creatures not to exist, but we do imply power in the creator not to cause existing. And we do say that some things, by reason of potentiality not to exist, can pass away.

Reply to Obj. 3. Understanding with the aid of a sense image is the peculiar activity of the human soul insofar as the latter is united to the body. When separate from the body, however, the human soul will have another way of understanding, a way of understanding like other substances separate from bodies, as I shall later make more evident.[40]

Notes

1. Aristotle, *Physics* VIII, 6, 10. 259b32–260al, 267b11–17.
2. *De Trinitate* VI, 6. PL 42:929.
3. Aristotle, *Physics* VIII, 6. 259b32–260al.
4. I.e., something that is in matter in such a way that it does not depend on matter in existing.
5. Aristotle, *De anima* I, 4. 408b9–18.
6. *De Trinitate* X, 7. PL 42:979.

7. *De anima* I, 4. 408b1-9.

8. Q. 75, A. 2.

9. Gennadius of Marseilles, *De ecclesiasticis dogmatibus* 16, 17. PL 42:1216. Cf. PL 58:984, PL 83:1231.

10. Q. 75, A. 1.

11. *Theatetus* 29, 30. 185D–186.

12. *De anima* III, 4. 429a24–27.

13. 2 Cor. 4:16.

14. *The City of God* XIX, 3. PL 41:626.

15. See Averroës, *In libros Metaphysicorum* VII (VI in the Bekker notation), comm. 34.

16. Q. 75, A. 3.

17. *Alcibiades* I, 25. 123E–130. The Platonic authorship is generally regarded as spurious.

18. *Ethics* IX, 8. 1168b31–34.

19. *De divinis nominibus* 5. PG 3:816.

20. See Glossary, s.v. "matter."

21. Aristotle, *Metaphysics* VII, 6. 1045a36–b7.

22. *Super Genesim ad litteram* VII, 7–9. PL 34:359–60.

23. *De divinis nominibus* 5, PG 3:817.

24. *Metaphysics* VII, 6. 1045b21–23.

25. *De divinis nominibus* 5. PG 3:820.

26. Gilbert de la Porrée, *In librum Quomodo substantiae bonae sint,* on rule 8, PL 64:1321.

27. On coming to be and passing away, see Glossary, s.v. "Generation and Corruption."

28. Eccl. 3:19.

29. Wis. 2:2.

30. Aristotle, *De anima*, I, 1. 403a5–10.

31. *De divinis nominibus* 4. PG 3:696.

32. Q. 75, AA. 2, 3.

33. Wis. 2:1, 21.

34. Gen. 1:24.

35. Gen. 2:7.

36. Eccl. 12:7.

37. Eccl. 3:19.

38. Wis. 2:2.

39. Eccl. 3:19.
40. Q. 89, A. 1.

ST I

Question 76

On the Union of the Soul to the Body

[This question is divided into eight articles, six of which are included here.]

First Article

Is the Source of Intellection United to the Body as the Body's Form?

I proceed in this way to the first article: it seems that the source of intellection is not united to the body as the body's form.

Obj. 1. The Philosopher says in the *De anima* that the intellect is "separate," and that it is not the actuality of any material substance.[1] Therefore, the intellect is not united to the body as the body's form.

Obj. 2. Every form is limited by the nature of the matter of which it is the form; otherwise, no proportion between matter and form would be required. Therefore, if the intellect were to be united to the body as the body's form, the intellect would consequently have a limited nature, since every material substance has a limited nature. And so the intellect would not know every kind of thing, as is clear from what I have said before,[2] and this is contrary to the nature of the intellect. Therefore, the intellect is not united to the body as the body's form.

Obj. 3. Every potentiality that receives the actuality of a material substance, receives a form in a material and individual way, since things received are in recipients in the condition of the recipients. But the intellect receives the forms of understood things in an immaterial and universal way rather than in a material and individual way; otherwise, the intellect would know only singular things, as the senses do, and not know immaterial and universal things. Therefore, the intellect is not united to the body as the body's form.

Obj. 4. Powers and their activities belong to the same things, for it is one and the same thing that can and does act. But intellectual activity does not belong to any material substance, as is clear from what I have said before.[3] Therefore, neither is intellectual power the power of a material substance. But no capacity or power can be more abstract or more simple than the essence that is the source of the capacity or power. Therefore, neither is the intellectual substance the form of the body.

Obj. 5. What intrinsically possesses existing is not united to a body as the body's form, since a form is that by which something exists, and so the very existing of a form does not belong to the form itself as such. But the source of intellection as such possesses existing and is subsistent, as I have said before.[4] Therefore, the source of intellection is not united to the body as the body's form.

Obj. 6. What belongs to something as such, always belongs to it. But being united to matter belongs to forms as such. For something is by its essence and not by chance the actuality of matter; otherwise, matter and form would be one accidentally rather than substantially. Therefore, a form cannot exist without its own matter. But the source of intellection, since it cannot pass away, as I have shown before,[5] abides separate from the body after the body has dissolved. Therefore, the source of intellection is not united to the body as the body's form.

On the contrary, according to the Philosopher in the *Metaphysics*, we understand specific difference from the form of a thing.[6] But the constitutive, specific difference of being human is to be "rational," which we affirm of human beings on account of their intellectual source. Therefore, the source of intellection is the form of human beings.

I answer that we need to affirm that the intellect, which is the source of intellectual activity, is the form of the human body. For that whereby something acts, is the form of the thing to which we attribute the activity. Just so, that whereby the body is primarily made healthy, is health, and that whereby the soul primarily knows, is knowledge, and so health is a form of the body, and knowledge is a form of the soul. And this is so because nothing acts except insofar as it is actual, and so something acts by that whereby it is actual. Now, the primary thing whereby a body is alive is evidently the soul. And since the different kinds of activities in different grades of living things manifest life, that whereby we primarily perform each of these vital activities is the soul. For the soul is the primary thing whereby we nourish ourselves and sensibly perceive and move ourselves from place to place, and likewise that whereby we primarily understand. Therefore, the source whereby we primarily understand, whether we call that source the intellect or the intellectual soul, is the form of the body.

And this is Aristotle's argument in the *De anima*.[7]

And if anyone should choose to deny that the intellectual soul is the form of the body, such a person would need to find a way whereby the activity of understanding is the action of this particular human being, since all experience that they themselves are the ones who understand. Now, we attribute actions to things in three ways, as the Philosopher makes clear in the *Physics*.[8] For we say that things move something, or act either by their whole selves, as doctors heal, or by part of themselves, as human beings see by their eyes, or by chance, as we say that something white builds, since the builder happens to be white. When we say that Socrates or Plato understands, therefore, we evidently do not attribute understanding to him by chance, for we attribute to him as a human being what we predicate essentially of his very self. Therefore, either we need to say that Socrates understands by his whole self, as Plato supposed when he said that human beings are intellectual souls,[9] or we need to say that the intellect is a part of Socrates. And the former position cannot be maintained, as I have shown before,[10] because the very same human beings perceive that they both understand and sense. But there is no sense perception apart from the body, and so the body is necessarily a part of human beings. Therefore, we conclude that the intellect whereby Socrates understands, is a part of Socrates in such a way that the intellect is somehow united to his body.

Now, the Commentator says in his *In libros De anima* that this union of soul and body is by means of the intelligible form.[11] And the intelligible form in fact has a double substratum: one, namely, the potential intellect, and the other the sense images present in bodily organs. And so the intelligible form connects the potential intellect to the body of this or that human being.

But such a connection or union is not enough for the activity of the intellect to be the activity of Socrates. And comparison to the senses, whence Aristotle proceeds to consider what belongs to the intellect, makes this clear. For sense images are related to the intellect as colors are related to the sense of sight, as the *De anima* says.[12] Therefore, the forms of sense images are in the potential intellect in the same way that the forms of colors are in the sense of sight. But we obviously do not attribute the activity of seeing to a housewall because there are in the housewall the colors whose likenesses are in the sense of sight, for we do not say that the housewall sees, but rather that the housewall is seen. Therefore, it does not follow from the fact that the forms of sense images are in the potential intellect that Socrates, in whom the sense images are, understands, but that he himself or his sense images are understood.

And certain thinkers chose to say that the intellect is united to the body as the agent that moves the body, and so that the intellect and the body form a unit in such a way that we can attribute the activity of the intellect to the whole unit.[13]

But this explanation is groundless for many reasons. First, indeed, because the intellect moves the body only by appetite, whose motion presupposes the intellect's activity. Therefore, Socrates does not understand because the intellect moves him, but rather, conversely, the intellect moves Socrates because he understands.

Second, the explanation is groundless because Socrates is an individual in whose nature there is only one essence, one composed of matter and form, and consequently, if the intellect be not his form, it follows logically that the intellect is something added to his essence, and then the intellect will be related to the whole Socrates as something causing motion is to something moved. But understanding is an activity that rests in its active source, not an activity that affects something else, as heating does. Therefore, we cannot attribute understanding to Socrates because the intellect moves him.

Third, the explanation is groundless because we never attribute the activity of a cause of motion to the thing moved, except as a means to the end, as, for example, we attribute the activity of a carpenter to his saw. Therefore, if we should attribute understanding to Socrates because it is the activity of a cause moving him, it would logically follow that we attribute it to him as a means to an end. And this conclusion is contrary to the Philosopher, who is of the opinion that understanding is not the product of bodily instrumentalities.[14]

Fourth, the explanation is groundless because, although we attribute the activity of parts to the whole, as, for example, we attribute eyes' activity to human beings, yet we never attribute the activity of one part to another part (except, perhaps, by chance), for we do not say that hands see because eyes see. Therefore, if the intellect and Socrates form one unit in the asserted way, we cannot attribute the activity of the intellect to Socrates. And if Socrates is a whole composed of the union of the intellect to the other things belonging to him, and yet the intellect is only united to the other things belonging to him as a cause that moves them, it would follow logically that Socrates would not be one unconditionally. And so neither would Socrates be a being unconditionally, for something is a being in the same way that it is one.

Therefore, we conclude that the mode of union that Aristotle proposes, that a particular human being understands because the source of intellection is that very human being's form, is the only mode of union. Therefore, the very activity of the intellect evidences that the source of intellection is united to the body as the body's form.

The nature of the human species can also manifest the same thing. For the activity of each thing reveals its nature. But the characteristic activity of human beings as such is understanding, for human beings by this activity surpass all animals. And so also does Aristotle in the *Ethics* constitute the final happiness of human beings in such activity, as the characteristic activity of human beings.[15] Therefore, human beings need to share in the species by what is the source of such activity. But individuals share in a species by the form characteristic of the species. Therefore, we conclude that the source of intellection is the specific form of human beings.

And we should consider that the more excellent a form is, the more it controls corporeal matter, and the less it is immersed in corporeal matter, and the more it exceeds corporeal matter by its activity and power. And so we see that the form of a mixed material substance[16] has some activity that elementary qualities do not cause. And the more progressively excellent the forms, the more we find that the power of forms exceeds elementary matter; for example, the vegetative soul exceeds elementary matter more than the form of metals does, and the sensory soul exceeds elementary matter more than the vegetative soul does. But the human soul is the most excellent form. And so the human soul by its power exceeds corporeal matter insofar as it has an activity and power in which corporeal matter in no way shares. And we call this power the intellect.

We should note, moreover, that one could in no way say that the soul is the form of the body if one were to hold that the soul is composed of matter and form. For in no way can the whole composite of matter and form, as such, be the form of something else, since form is actuality, and matter only potential being. And if part of the soul should be a form, we call that part the soul, and we call the part of which it is the form the "first enlivened thing," as I have said before.[17]

Reply to Obj. 1. As the Philosopher says in the *Physics*, the most excellent natural form, at which the contemplation of the natural philosopher aims, namely, the human soul, is indeed separate but nonetheless in matter. And he proves the latter from the fact that "human beings and the sun beget human beings out of matter."[18] The soul is indeed separate regarding its power of intellection, since the power of intellection is not the power of any bodily organ, as the power of seeing is activity of the eyes. For understanding is activity that cannot be performed by a bodily organ, as seeing is. But the soul is in matter insofar as the soul itself, to which the power of intellection belongs, is the form of the body and the goal of human generation. Therefore, the Philosopher says in the *De anima* that the intellect is "separate," because it is not the power of any bodily organ.[19]

Replies to Objs. 2 and 3. And the foregoing response makes clear the responses to the second and third objections. For the fact that the power of intellection is not an actuality of the body suffices for human beings to be able by means of their intellect to understand all kinds of things, and for the intellect to understand immaterial and universal things.

Reply to Obj. 4. The human soul, because of its perfection, is not a form immersed in corporeal matter or wholly enclosed by such matter. And so nothing prevents one of the soul's powers not being an actuality of the body, although the soul is essentially the form of the body.

Reply to Obj. 5. The soul communicates to corporeal matter the existing in which the soul itself subsists, and the corporeal matter and the intellectual soul form one thing in such a way that the existing belonging to the whole composite also belongs to the soul itself. And this does not happen in the case of other forms, forms that are not subsistent. And for this reason, the human soul abides in its own existing when the body is destroyed, and other forms do not.

Reply to Obj. 6. Being united to the body belongs to the soul as such, just as being above belongs to a light material substance as such. And as a light material substance indeed remains light when it has been drawn from its characteristic place, still with a disposition and inclination for its characteristic place, so the human soul abides in its existing when it has been separated from the body, having a disposition and inclination from its nature for union with the body.

Second Article

Does Multiplicity of Bodies Multiply the Source of Intellection?

I proceed in this way to the second article: it seems that multiplicity of bodies does not multiply the source of intellection, but that there is only one intellect in all human beings.

Obj. 1. There is numerically only one immaterial substance in a species. But the human soul is an immaterial substance, since the human soul is not composed of matter and form, as I have shown before.[20] Therefore, there are not many human souls in a single species. But all human beings belong to one and the same species. Therefore, there is only one intellect that belongs to all human beings.

Obj. 2. Effects are eliminated when their causes are eliminated. Therefore, if to multiply bodies were to multiply human souls, it would seem to follow that, if bodies were taken away, only some one thing from all souls, not the multitude of souls, would abide, and this conclusion is heretical, since it would wipe out the distinction between rewards and punishments.

Obj. 3. If my intellect is other than yours, my intellect is a certain individual thing, and yours is also, since things that differ in number but agree in a species are individual. But everything received in something else is in the recipient in the way of the recipient. Therefore, the forms of things in my intellect and yours would be received in an individual way, and this is contrary to the nature of the intellect, which knows universals.

Obj. 4. What is understood is in the intellect that understands. Therefore, if my intellect is other than yours, I would necessarily understand one thing, and you another. And so what is understood will be reckoned in an individual way and understood only potentially, and a common concept will need to be abstracted from both, since something intelligible that is common may be abstracted from all things that differ. And this conclusion is contrary to the nature of the intellect, since the intellect would then not seem to differ from the power of imagination. Therefore, the conclusion seems to be that there is one intellect that belongs to all human beings.

Obj. 5. When pupils receive knowledge from teachers, we cannot say that the knowledge of teachers begets the knowledge in pupils, since then knowledge would also be a causative form like color, and this is clearly false. Therefore, the numerically identical knowledge in teachers seems to be communicated to pupils. And this can only be the case if there be one intellect belonging to both, and consequently one intellect belonging to all human beings.

Obj. 6. Augustine says in his work *De quantitate animae*: "If I were to say that there is simply a plurality of human souls, even I shall laugh at myself."[21] But the human soul seems especially to be one regarding the intellect. Therefore, there is only one intellect that belongs to all human beings.

On the contrary, the Philosopher says in the *Physics* that particular causes are related to particular things as universal causes are related to universal things.[22] But a soul specifically one cannot belong to specifically different kinds of animals. Therefore, an intellectual soul numerically one cannot belong to numerically different things.

I answer that it is absolutely impossible that there is only one intellect that belongs to all human beings. And this is indeed evidently the case if human beings are their very intellects, as Plato thought.[23] For if only one intellect belongs to Socrates and Plato, it would logically follow that the two would be one and the same human being, and that they would differ from one another only by something outside the essence of both. And then the only difference between Socrates and Plato would be one between one man wearing a tunic, and the other wearing a cloak. And this is completely silly.

It is also likewise evident that this is impossible if we should hold, as Aristotle held,[24] that the intellect is a part or power of the soul that is the form of human beings. For one form cannot belong to several numerically different things, just as one existing cannot belong to them, since form is the source of existing.

It is also likewise evident that this is impossible howsoever one should hold that the intellect is united to this or that particular human being. For if there be one chief efficient cause and two instruments, we could evidently speak of one efficient cause without qualification but of several actions; for example, if one human being should touch different things with each hand, there will be one human being who touches, but two acts of touching. And if, conversely, there be one instrument and different chief efficient causes, we shall indeed speak of several efficient causes but of only one action; for example, if many people pull a boat with one rope, there will be many who pull the boat, but only one rope pulled. And if there be only one chief efficient cause and only one instrument, we shall speak of one efficient cause and one action; for example, if a worker strikes with one hammer, there is one who strikes, and one stroke.

And it is evidently the case that, in whatever kind of way the intellect is united or joined to this or that human being, the intellect has primacy over other things that belong to human beings, since human beings' sensory powers obey and are at the service of the intellect. Therefore, if we were to suppose that several intellects and one set of sensory powers belong to two human beings (e.g., if two humans being were to have one set of eyes), there would indeed be several persons who see, but only one act of sight. But if there is one intellect, however much all the other things that the intellect uses as instruments, may differ, we could in no way speak of Socrates and Plato except as one human being who understands.

And if we should add that no instrument other than the intellect itself causes the very act of understanding, which is the intellect's activity, it will further follow that there is but one efficient cause and one action, that is, that all human beings constitute one subject of understanding and one act of understanding. And I say this regarding the same intelligible object.

Now, the diversity of sense images would be able to distinguish my intellectual activity from yours, since there is, of course, one sense image of a stone in me and another sense image of a stone in you, if the sense image itself, as one image in me and another in you, were to be the form of the potential intellect. This is so because the same efficient cause by different forms produces different actions; for example, there are different acts of vision in relation to the same eyes by the different forms of things. But intelligible forms abstracted from sense images, not the sense images themselves, are the forms of the potential intellect. Moreover, in one intellect, only one intelligible form is abstracted from different sense images of the same kind. This, for example, is evident in the case of a single human being, in whom there can be different sense images of stones, and yet only the one intelligible form of stone is abstracted from all of these images, by which form the intellect of that one human being in one act understands the nature of stone, despite the different sense images. Therefore, if one intellect were to belong to all human beings, different sense images in this and that human being could not cause the different intellectual activities of those human beings, as the Commentator imagines in his *In libros De anima*.[25]

Therefore, we conclude that it is altogether impossible and inappropriate to posit one intellect that belongs to all human beings.

Reply to Obj. 1. The intellectual soul, although it has no matter whereby it exists, as neither do angels, is nonetheless the form of particular matter, something inappropriate for angels. And so many human souls belong to one species by a division of matter, while it is completely impossible for many angels to belong to one species.

Reply to Obj. 2. Each thing has oneness in the way in which it has existing, and so we judge the same about things' multiplicity as we do about their existing. And it is evident that the intellectual soul, with respect to its existing, is united to the body as the body's form, and yet the intellectual soul abides in its existing after the body has been destroyed. And by the same reasoning, there are as many human souls as there are many bodies, and yet the souls remain multiple in their existing after the bodies have been destroyed.

Reply to Obj. 3. The individuality of the one who understands, and of the form by means of which one understands, does not exclude understanding universals; otherwise, separate intellects, since they are certain subsistent substances and so individual, could not understand universals. Rather, the materiality of the knower and of the forms by means of which the knower knows, obstructs knowledge of the universal. For as every action corresponds to the mode of the form by which an efficient cause acts, as, for example, heating corresponds to the mode of heat, so every knowledge corresponds to the mode of the form by which the knower knows. And individuating sources, which come from matter, evidently divide and multiply a common nature. Therefore, if the form that causes knowledge be material, not abstracted from the conditions of matter, there will be a likeness of the nature of a species or genus insofar as individuating sources divide and multiply that nature, and so a knower could not know the nature of a thing in its commonality. But if the form be abstracted from the conditions of individual matter, the form will be the likeness of a nature apart from the things that divide and multiply the very nature, and so one will know the universal. Nor does it matter in this respect whether there be one intellect or several, since, even if there were to be only one, that one itself would necessarily be an individual intellect, and the form by which that intellect understands would necessarily be an individual form.

Reply to Obj. 4. Whether the intellect be one or several, what it understands is one. For the thing that we understand exists in the intellect by its likeness, not as such, "for the form of stone, not the stone, exists in the soul," as the *De anima* says.[26] And yet stone is what we understand, and not the form of stone unless the intellect reflect on itself; otherwise, sciences would have intelligible forms, not things, for their objects. Moreover, different forms may make different things like the same thing. And because the process of making knowers like the things known causes knowledge, different knowers may consequently know the same thing, as is evident in the case of the senses, for several individuals see the same color by different likenesses. And several intellects likewise understand the one and same thing that they understand. But according to the opinion of Aristotle,[27] there is only this difference between the senses and the intellect, that the senses perceive things according to the arrangement that the things have outside the soul, in the things' individuality, while the natures of things understood indeed exist outside the soul but do not have outside the soul the way of existing in which the things are understood. For we understand natures as universal when individuating sources have been excluded, and natures do not have this way of existing outside the soul.

But according to Plato, things understood exist outside the soul in the same way in which they are understood, for Plato held that the natures of things are separate from matter.[28]

Reply to Obj. 5. There is one knowledge in the pupil, and another in the teacher. And I shall later show how this is caused.[29]

Reply to Obj. 6. Augustine understands that there is not simply a plurality of human souls without the souls being united in one and the same specific nature.

Third Article

Do Human Beings Have Other, Essentially Different Souls Besides the Intellectual Soul?

I proceed in this way to the third article: it seems that human beings, besides the Intellectual soul, have other, essentially different souls, namely, the sensory soul and the nutritive soul.

Obj. 1. What can pass away and what cannot pass away do not belong to one and the same substance. But the intellectual soul cannot pass away, while the other souls, namely, the sensory soul and the nutritive soul, can pass away, as is clear from what I have said before.[30] Therefore, the essence of the intellectual soul and the essence of the sensory soul and the essence of the nutritive soul cannot be one and the same.

Obj. 2. If one should say that the sensory soul in human beings cannot pass away, the answer would be: "What can pass away and what cannot pass away differ generically," as the *Metaphysics* says.[31] But the sensory soul in horses and lions and other irrational animals can pass away. Therefore, if the sensory soul in human beings cannot pass away, the sensory souls in human beings and irrational animals will not belong to the same genus. But we call something an animal because it has a sensory soul. Therefore, "animal" will not be a single genus common to human beings and other animals. And this conclusion is inappropriate.

Obj. 3. The Philosopher says in his *De generatione animalium* that the human embryo is an animal before it is a human being.[32] But this would not be possible if the same essence belonged to the sensory soul and the intellectual soul, for there is an animal by reason of the sensory soul, and a human being by reason of the intellectual soul. Therefore, there is not one essence that belongs to the sensory soul and the intellectual soul.

Obj. 4. The Philosopher says in the *Metaphysics* that we understand genera from matter, while we understand specific differences from forms.[33] But we understand "rational," which is the constitutive specific difference of human beings, from the intellectual soul, while we call something "animal" because it has a body animated by a sensory soul. Therefore, the intellectual soul is related to the body animated by a sensory soul as a form is related to matter. Therefore, in human beings, the intellectual soul is not essentially the same as the sensory soul; rather, the intellectual soul presupposes the sensory soul as its material substratum.

On the contrary, the book *De ecclesiasticis dogmatibus* says: "Nor do we say that there are two souls in one and the same human being, as James and other Syrians write, one the animal soul, which animates the body and is mingled with the blood, and the other the spiritual soul, which serves reason; rather, we affirm that one and the same soul in human beings both vivifies the body by its partnership and disposes its very self by its power of reason."[34]

I answer that Plato held that there are different souls in one body, souls distinct even as to bodily organs, and he attributed different vital activities to organs, saying that the nutritive power is in the liver, the power of desire in the heart, the power of knowing in the brain.[35]

And Aristotle in the *De anima* indeed rejected this opinion regarding the parts of the soul that in their activities make use of bodily organs. He rejected the opinion because we find different activities of the soul, such as those of the senses and the appetites, in every part of animals that continue to live after they have been cut up.[36] Now, this would not be so if different sources of the soul's activities, as if essentially different, were to be parceled out to different parts of the body. But concerning the intellectual soul, he seems to remain in doubt whether that part of the soul is separate from other parts "only conceptually or locally as well."[37]

Still, the opinion of Plato could indeed be maintained if we were to hold, as he did, that the soul is not united to the body as the body's form but as the agent that moves the body. For nothing inappropriate results if different agents causing motion move the same moveable object, especially regarding its different parts. But if we should hold that the soul is united to the body as the body's form, it seems to be completely impossible that there be several essentially different souls in one body. And we can indeed demonstrate this by three arguments.

First, indeed, because an animal would not be unconditionally one thing if several souls were to belong to the animal. For nothing is unconditionally one thing except by one form, by which the thing has existing, since a thing has being and oneness from the same source, and so things designated by different forms are not unconditionally one, as, for example, a white human being is not. Therefore, if human beings were to have life from one form, namely, the vegetative soul, and animality from another form, namely, the sensory soul, and humanity from another form, namely, the rational soul, human beings would consequently not be unconditionally one thing. And Aristotle similarly argues in the *Metaphysics* against Plato that a two-footed animal would not be unconditionally one thing if the form of animal were to be distinct from the form of two-footed.[38] And for this reason, against those who maintained that there are several souls in the body, Aristotle asks in the *De anima*: "What would contain the several souls?" that is, what would unify them?[39] And we cannot say that the unity of the body unites several souls, since the soul contains the body and makes the body itself one thing, rather than the converse.

Second, multiplicity of souls seems by our way of predication to be impossible. For we predicate things understood by different forms of one another either by chance or intrinsically. They are predicated by chance if the forms are not related to one another, as when we say that something white is sweet. Or if the forms are related to one another, things understood by the different forms will be predicated intrinsically in the second way of predicating "intrinsically,"[40] since we posit the subject in the definition of the predicate. For example, surface is a prerequisite for color; therefore, there will be the second way of predicating "intrinsically" if we should say that a surfaced material substance is colored.

Therefore, if there be one form by which we call something an animal, and another form by which we call the thing a human being, one of two consequences would logically follow: we could only predicate animal or human being of the other by chance if the two forms have no relation to one another, or there may be a predication in the second way of predicating "intrinsically" if one soul be a prerequisite for the other. But both of these consequences are evidently false, since we predicate "animal" of human beings intrinsically, not by chance, and we do not posit "human being" in the definition of animal, but we posit "animal" in the definition of human being. Therefore, the form by which something is an animal, and the form by which it is a human being, are the same; otherwise, human beings would not be truly animals in such a way that we may predicate "animal" of human beings intrinsically.

Third, multiplicity of forms seems to be impossible because one activity of the soul, when intense, obstructs a different activity. And such would in no way happen unless the source of the activities were to be essentially one.

Therefore, we need to say that the sensory soul and the intellectual soul and the nutritive soul in human beings are numerically the same soul. Moreover, one can easily consider how this may be if we should note the differences among species and forms. For we find that the species and forms of things differ from one another by the more perfect and the less perfect. For example, in the rank of things, living things are more perfect than nonliving things, and animals more perfect than plants, and human beings more perfect than irrational animals, and there are different grades in each of these genera. And so Aristotle in the *Metaphysics* likens the species of things to numbers, which differ specifically by adding or subtracting units.[41] And in the *De anima*, he compares different kinds of souls to species of shapes, of which one contains another;[42] for example, a pentagon contains and exceeds a tetragon.

Therefore, the intellectual soul in its power contains whatever the sensory soul of irrational animals and the nutritive soul of plants possess. Therefore, as a surface having the shape of a pentagon is not a tetragon by one shape and a pentagon by another shape, since the shape of a tetragon, as contained in the shape of a pentagon, would be superfluous, so neither is Socrates a human being by one soul, and an animal by another soul, but he is a human being and an animal by one and the same soul.

Reply to Obj. 1. The sensory soul, because it is sensory, does not have an incapacity to pass away, but the incapacity to pass away belongs to the soul because it is intellectual. Therefore, when a soul is only sensory, it can pass away, but when the soul possesses intellectual powers along with sense powers, the soul cannot pass away. For although sense powers do not bestow freedom from destruction, yet the sense powers cannot take freedom from destruction away from the intellectual power.

Reply to Obj. 2. Composites, not forms, are posited in genera and species. But human beings can pass away just like other animals. And so the difference regarding what can pass away and what cannot, which difference is on the part of forms, does not cause human beings to differ from other animals generically.

Reply to Obj. 3. The human embryo first has a soul that is only sensory, and when that soul has been laid aside, a more perfect soul comes to the embryo, a soul that is at the same time sensory and intellectual, as I shall later show more fully.[43]

Reply to Obj. 4. We do not need to understand that there are differences in natural things according to the different notions or logical concepts that result from our way of understanding, since reason can understand one and the same thing in different ways. Therefore, reason can consider separately what belongs to the power of the sensory soul, as something imperfect and material, as it were, since, as I have said,[44] the intellectual soul by its power contains what the sensory soul possesses, and still more. And because reason finds what belongs to the sensory soul something common to human beings and other animals, reason forms from it the notion of the genus. And reason understands as something formal and perfective, as it were, that wherein the intellectual soul surpasses the sensory soul, and reason thereby fashions the specific difference of human beings.

Fourth Article

Is There Any Other Form in Human Beings Besides the Intellectual Soul?

I proceed in this way to the fourth article: it seems that there is in human beings some other form besides the intellectual soul.

Obj. 1. The Philosopher says in the *De anima* that "the soul is the actuality of a physical body that potentially possesses life."[45] Therefore, the soul is related to the body as form is to matter. But the body has a substantial form by which it is a body. Therefore, there is some substantial form in the body before there is a soul.

Obj. 2. Human beings and every animal cause their own motion. But everything that moves itself is divided into two parts, one of which causes the motion, and the other of which is moved, as the *Physics* proves.[46] And the part causing motion is the soul. Therefore, the other part needs to be such that it can be moved. But prime matter cannot be moved, as the *Physics* says,[47] since it is only a potential being; on the contrary, everything moved is a material substance. Therefore, there needs to be in human beings and every animal another substantial form by which their bodies are constituted.

Obj. 3. We note the rank of forms by their relationship to prime matter, for we speak of first and second in relation to some starting point. Therefore, if human beings were to have no other substantial form besides the rational soul, and the rational soul were to inhere directly in prime matter,[48] the rational soul would consequently be in the rank of the most imperfect forms, forms that inhere directly in matter.

Obj 4. The human body is a mixed material substance.[49] But matter alone does not produce the mixture, since then only passing away would result. Therefore, the forms of elements necessarily remain in a mixed material substance, and such forms are substantial forms. Therefore, there are in the human body other substantial forms besides the intellectual soul.

On the contrary, one substantial existing belongs to one thing. But substantial forms bestow substantial existing. Therefore, only one substantial form belongs to one thing. But the soul is the substantial form of human beings. Therefore, there cannot be in human beings any other substantial form than the intellectual soul.

I answer that, if we were to hold, as the Platonists did,[50] that the intellectual soul is not united to the body as the body's form but only as the agent moving the body, we would need to say that there is in human beings another substantial form that constitutes the body in its own existing as moveable by the soul. But if the intellectual soul is united to the body as the body's substantial form, as we have already said before,[51] we cannot find in human beings any other substantial form besides the intellectual soul.

And to show this, we need to consider that substantial forms differ from accidental forms because accidental forms bestow existing in a particular way rather than existing in an absolute sense, as, for example, heat causes something subject to it to be hot rather than simply to exist. And so, when an accidental form comes to something, we do not say that the thing is made or comes to be in an unqualified way, but we say that the thing is made such or disposed in a particular way. And similarly, when an accidental form leaves something, we do not say that the thing passes away without qualification, but we say that the thing passes away in a particular respect. But substantial forms bestow existing without qualification, and so we say that their coming causes things to come to be without qualification, and that their departure causes things to pass away without qualification. And it was for this reason that the natural philosophers of antiquity, who held that prime matter is an actual being (for instance, fire or air or some such thing), said that nothing comes to be or passes away without qualification, and "they considered every coming-to-be an alteration," as the *Physics* says.[52]

Therefore, if, in addition to the intellectual soul, there were to pre-exist any other substantial form in matter, by means of which form the soul's substratum would be an actual being, the soul would consequently not bestow existing without qualification, and so not be a substantial form. And the soul's arrival would consequently not bring about coming-to-be in an unqualified sense, nor would the soul's departure consequently bring about passing away in an unqualified sense, but only coming-to-be and passing away in a particular respect. And these consequences are clearly false.

And so we need to say that the only substantial form in human beings is the intellectual soul, and that that very soul by means of its power contains all the lower forms, just as it by means of its power contains the sensory soul and the nutritive soul, and that only the intellectual soul itself does whatever the less perfect forms do in other things. And we should say the like about the sensory soul in irrational animals, and about the nutritive soul in plants, and universally about all more perfect forms in relation to less perfect forms.

Reply to Obj. 1. Aristotle does not say that the soul is just "the actuality of a body," but that the soul is "the actuality of an organic, physical body that possesses life potentially," and that such potentiality "does not dispense with the soul."[53] And so the soul is also evidently included in the living thing whose actuality we call the soul, in the same way of speaking as we say that heat is the actuality of something hot, and light the actuality of something luminous; we say that light is the actuality of something, not to mean that something is separately luminous apart from light, but that something is luminous by means of light. And we say in like manner that the soul is "the actuality of a body," and so forth, because, by means of the soul, the body is a body, and is organic, and possesses life potentially. But we call the first actuality potential in relation to the second actuality, that is, activity. For such potentiality "does not dispense with," that is, exclude, the soul.

Reply to Obj. 2. The soul does not move the body by the soul's existing, by which the soul is united to the body as the body's form, but by the soul's power to move the body. And the acts of this power presuppose that the soul has already made the body actual, so that the soul by its power to move the body is the part that causes bodily movement, and the enlivened body is the part that is moved.

Reply to Obj. 3. We are considering in matter the different grades of perfection, such as existing, living, sensing, and understanding. But something is always more perfect by what is added to the first grade of perfection. Therefore, the form that bestows only the first grade of perfection to matter is the most imperfect form, while the form that bestows the first and the second and the third grades, and so one added to another, is the most perfect form and yet the direct form of matter.

Reply to Obj. 4. Avicenna held that the substantial forms of elements abide undiminished in a mixed material substance, and that the mixture comes about as the contrary qualities of the elements are brought to a mean.[54]

But this is impossible, since the different forms of elements can exist only in different parts of matter, and we need to understand spatial dimensions, without which matter is indivisible, in order for the parts to be different. And we find the matter underlying spacial dimensions only in material substances. But different material substances cannot be in the same place. And so it follows logically that the elements in a mixed material substance are separated by their position. And so there will not be a real mixture, that is, one regarding the whole, but a mixture in relation to the senses, that is, one regarding the smallest juxtaposed parts.

And Averroës in his *In libros De coelo* held that the forms of elements, because of their imperfection, are in between accidental and substantial forms, and so can be greater or lesser. And so they are diminished in the mixture and brought to a mean, and a single form is forged out of them.[55]

But this is even less possible. For the substantial existing of anything consists of something indivisible, and every addition and subtraction changes the species, as, for example, in the case of numbers, as the *Metaphysics* says.[56] And so no substantial form can possibly be greater or lesser.

Nor is it any more possible for something to be in between substance and accident.

And so we need to say, as the Philosopher says in the *De generatione et corruptione*, that the forms of elements remain in a mixed material substance virtually, not actually.[57] For the special qualities of elements, although diminished, abide, and the power of the forms of elements is in these qualities. And the quality of such a mixture is a special disposition toward the substantial form of the mixed material substance, for instance, the form of stone or the form of any kind of soul.

Fifth Article

Is the Intellectual Soul Suitably United to the Body?

I proceed in this way to the fifth article: it seems that the intellectual soul is unsuitably united to such a body.

Obj. 1. Matter ought to be proportioned to form. But the intellectual soul is a form that cannot pass away. Therefore, the intellectual soul is unsuitably united to a body that can pass away.

Obj. 2. The intellectual soul is the most immaterial form, and this is indicated by the fact that the intellectual soul has an activity in which corporeal matter does not share. But the simpler the body, the less matter it has. Therefore, the soul ought to be united to the simplest material substance, for instance, fire, and not to a mixed and more earthly material substance.

Obj. 3. One form cannot produce different species, since form is the source of species. But the intellectual soul is one form. Therefore, the intellectual soul ought not to be united to a body composed of parts proper to dissimilar species.

Obj. 4. A more perfect form should have something more perfect receiving it. But the intellectual soul is the most perfect kind of soul. Therefore, since nature has implanted covering on the bodies of other animals (e.g., fur instead of clothes, and hooves instead of shoes), and since nature has given other animals weapons (e.g., claws, teeth, and horns), so it seems that the intellectual soul ought not to be united to an imperfect body deprived of such means, as it were.

On the contrary, the Philosopher says in the *De anima* that the soul is "the actuality of a physical, organic body that possesses life potentially."[58]

I answer that, since form does not exist by reason of matter, but rather matter exists by reason of form, reason needs to understand from form why matter is of such a kind, and not the converse. And the intellectual soul by the order of nature holds the lowest rank among intellectual substances, as I have previously maintained.[59] This is so inasmuch as intellectual souls, unlike angels, do not have their knowledge of truth implanted in them by nature, but they need to acquire knowledge of truth from composite things by way of the senses, as Denis says in his *De divinis nominibus*.[60] But nature does not fail to provide everything with what it needs, and so intellectual souls necessarily have not only the power of understanding but also sensory powers. And sensory activities do not occur without bodily instruments. Therefore, the intellectual soul needed to be united to such a body as could be a suitable instrument of the senses.

Moreover, all the other senses are based on the sense of touch. And the organs of touch require that there be a mean between contraries (i.e., hot and cold, wet and dry, and the like), and the sense of touch perceives these contraries, since it in this way has potentiality for the contraries and can sensibly perceive them. And so the more the organs of touch have been brought to a harmonious composition, the more the sense of touch will be able to perceive. And the intellectual soul possesses sensory power more completely, since what belongs to something inferior pre-exists more completely in something superior, as Denis says in his work *De divinis nominibus*.[61] And so the body to which the intellectual soul is united, needed to be a mixed material substance, one brought to a harmonious composition more than any other material substance.

And for this reason, human beings, of all animals, have the best sense of touch. And among human beings themselves, those with a better sense of touch have a better intellect. And this is indicated by the fact that "we see that those supple of flesh are mentally well-equipped," as the *De anima* says.[62]

Reply to Obj. 1. One might perhaps wish to avoid this objection by saying that the body of human beings, before sin, could not pass away. But this answer does not seem to be sufficient, since the body of human beings, before sin, was not immortal by nature but by the gift of divine grace; otherwise, sin would not have taken away the body's immortality, as sin did not take away the immortality of the devil.

And so we need to respond in another way, that we find two conditions in matter: one that is chosen in order that the matter be suitable to the form; the other that results from the necessity of a prior disposition. For example, a craftsman chooses matter made of iron, matter suitable for cutting hard things, to form a saw, but a necessity of the matter causes the teeth of the saw to become dull and collect rust. So also the intellectual soul requires a body of harmonious composition, but the fact that the body can pass away results from a necessity of its matter.

And if one should assert that God could avoid this necessity, we need to say that we do not consider in the constitution of natural things what God could do, but what is suitable for the nature of things, as Augustine says in his *Super Genesim*.[63] Still, God provides an additional remedy against death by the gift of grace.

Reply to Obj. 2. The body is not owed to the intellectual soul because of intellectual activity itself as such, but because of sense powers, which require a harmoniously composed instrument. And so the intellectual soul needed to be united to such a body, and not to simple elements—or to a mixed material substance in which fire would be quantitatively excessive, since, owing to the excessive causal power of fire, there could be no harmonious composition in the body. And the actual, harmoniously composed body has a certain merit in that it is removed from contraries, and in this respect made somehow like heavenly bodies.

Reply to Obj. 3. The parts of animals, for example, eyes, flesh and bones, and the like, do not belong to species, but whole animals do, and so we cannot, properly speaking, say that the parts belong to different species, but that they belong to different arrangements. And it belongs to the intellectual soul that, though essentially one, it is nonetheless by reason of its perfection multiple in power, and so needs for different activities different arrangements in the parts of the body to which it is united. And for this reason we see that there is greater diversity of parts in perfect animals than in imperfect animals, and greater diversity of parts in imperfect animals than in plants.

Reply to Obj. 4. The intellectual soul, because it comprehends universals, has power for countless things. And so nature could not determine for the intellectual soul either fixed judgments relating to nature or even fixed means, whether of defense or of covering the body, as nature did for other animals, whose souls have knowledge and power for some particular fixed things. But instead of all of the latter, nature endows human beings with reason—and with hands, which are "the instruments of instruments,"[64] since human beings can by means of their hands prepare for themselves instruments of countless kinds, and for doing countless things.

Eighth Article

Is the Whole Soul in Every Part of the Body?

I proceed in this way to the eighth article: it seems that the whole soul is not in every part of the body.

Obj. 1. The Philosopher says in the *De causa motus animalium*: "The soul does not need to be in each part of the body, but the rest need to live in some existing bodily source, so that they by nature at once sprang forth to produce their own motion."[65]

Obj. 2. The soul is in the body of which it is the actuality. But the soul is the actuality of an organic body. Therefore, the soul is only in the organic body. But not every part of the body is the organic body. Therefore, the whole soul is not in every part of the body.

Obj. 3. The *De anima* says that the whole soul is related to the whole body of an animal as parts of the soul are related to parts of the body,[66] as, for example, the power of sight is related to the pupil of the eye. Therefore, if the whole soul is in every part of the body, it follows logically that every part of the body is an animal.

Obj. 4. Every power of the soul is grounded in the very essence of the soul. Therefore, if the whole soul is in every part of the body, it follows logically that all powers of the soul are in every part of the body, and so there will be power of sight in ears, and power of hearing in eyes. And this conclusion is inappropriate.

Obj. 5. Every part of the body would directly depend on the soul if the whole soul were to be in every part of the body. Therefore, one part of the body would not depend on another part, nor would one part be more important than another, and these conclusions are clearly false. Therefore, the whole soul is not in every part of the body.

On the contrary, Augustine says in his *De Trinitate* that "the whole soul is in every body and is entirely in the whole of the body and is entirely in every part of the body."[67]

I answer, as I have already said elsewhere,[68] that, if the soul were to be united to the body only as the agent that moves the body, we could say that the soul would not be in every part of the body but in only one part, the part by which the soul would move the other parts.

But because the soul is united to the body as the body's form, the soul needs to be in the whole body and in every part of the body. For the soul is the substantial, not the accidental, form of the body, and a substantial form is the perfection both of the whole and of every part of the body. For, since a whole consists of parts, a form of the whole that does not bestow existing on individual parts of the body is a form that composes and orders, as, for example, the form of a house does. And such a form is an accidental form. On the other hand, the soul is a substantial form and so needs to be the form and actuality both of the whole body and of every part of the body. And so, as we speak of animals and human beings only equivocally when their souls depart (as we also speak of painted or stone animals), so it is in the case of hands and eyes, or flesh and bones, as the Philosopher says.[69] And this is indicated by the fact that no part of the body has a special function when the soul departs, while everything that retains its form still retains the activity of the form. And an actuality is in the thing of which it is the actuality, and so the soul needs to be in the whole body and in every part of the body.

And we can consider that the whole soul is in every part of the body from the fact that, since a whole is divided into parts, there are three kinds of totality by three kinds of division. For instance, there is one kind of whole, for example, a whole line or a whole material substance, that is divided into quantitative parts. There is also another kind of whole that is divided into logical and essential parts; for example, a defined term is divided into the parts of its definition, and a composite is divided into matter and form. And the third kind of whole is potential, one that is divided into kinds of power.

Now, the first kind of totality does not belong to forms, except perhaps by chance, and only to those forms that have an undifferentiated relationship to the quantitative whole and its parts. For example, whiteness, insofar as its nature is concerned, is equally disposed to be in an entire surface and in every part of the surface, and so whiteness is divided by chance when the surface is divided. But forms that require differentiated parts, forms like the soul and especially the souls of perfect animals, are not equally related to the whole and the parts, and so a quantitative division does not by chance divide such forms. Therefore, we cannot attribute a quantitative totality to the soul either intrinsically or by chance.

On the other hand, the second kind of totality, which we note by logical and essential perfections, belongs properly and intrinsically to forms. And so too does the totality of power, since forms are sources of activity.

Therefore, if we were to ask if the entire whiteness is in the whole surface and every part of the surface, we would need to distinguish. For the entire whiteness would not be in every part of the surface if we should be talking about the quantitative totality, which the whiteness has by chance. And we need to speak in a like manner about the totality of power, for the whiteness in the whole surface can cause vision more than the whiteness of some particular part of the surface can. But if we are talking about the totality of form and essence, the entire whiteness is in every part of the surface.

And because the soul has no quantitative totality, whether intrinsically or by chance, as I have said, it suffices to say that the whole soul is in every part of the body with respect to the totality of the soul's perfection and essence but not with respect to the totality of the soul's power. For the soul is not in every part of the body regarding every one of its powers, but in eyes regarding sight, in ears regarding hearing, and similarly in the case of other powers.

Nevertheless, we should note that, because the soul needs diversity in the body's parts, the soul is not related to the whole body in the same way that the soul is related to the body's parts; rather, the soul is indeed primarily and intrinsically related to the whole body as what the soul can specially and proportionately perfect, while the soul is secondarily related to parts of the body insofar as the latter are ordered to the whole body.

Reply to Obj. 1. The Philosopher is speaking about the power of the soul to move the body.

Reply to Obj. 2. The soul is the actuality of an organic body as the actuality of what the soul can primarily and proportionately perfect.

Reply to Obj. 3. An animal is composed of its soul and its whole body, which body is what the soul can primarily and proportionately perfect. And so an animal's soul is not in parts of the animal's body. And so it is not necessary that parts of animals be animals.

Reply to Obj. 4. Certain powers of the soul, namely, the intellect and the will, are in the soul insofar as the soul surpasses the entire capacity of the body, and so we say that such powers are in no part of the body. But other powers are common to the soul and the body, and so it is not necessary that any such power be wherever the soul is, but only that the power be in the part of the body that is proportioned to the activity of such a power.

Reply to Obj. 5. We call one part of the body more important than another part by reason of the different powers of which the parts of the body are the instruments. For the part that is the instrument of a more important power, or even that more importantly serves the same power, is a more important part of the body.

Notes

1. *De anima* III, 4. 429a24–27.
2. Q. 75, A. 2.
3. Ibid.
4. Ibid.
5. Ibid., A. 6.
6. *Metaphysics* VII, 2. 1043a2–12.
7. *De anima* II, 2. 414a4–19.
8. *Physics* V, 1. 224a21–34.
9. *Alcibiades* I, 25. 129E–130.
10. Q. 75, A. 4.
11. Averroës, *In libros De anima* III, comm. 5, digression, part 5.
12. Aristotle, *De anima* III, 5. 430a10–17. Also: III, 7. 431a14–17.
13. See Plato, *Alcibiades* I, 25. 129E–130. Also: *Phaedrus* 30. 250C; Timaeus 15. 44–44; *The Laws* X, 8–9. 898–99.
14. *De anima* III, 4. 429a24–27.
15. *Ethics* X, 7. 1177a12–19.
16. A "mixed" material substance is one that has powers beyond those of elementary matter, for example, vegetative and sense powers.

17. Q. 75, A. 5.

18. *Physics* II, 2. 194b8–15.

19. See n. 1, *supra.*

20. Q. 75, A. 5.

21. *De quantitate animae* 32. PL 32:1075.

22. *Physics* II, 3. 195b25–28.

23. *Alcibiades* I, 25. 129E–130.

24. *De anima* II, 2–3. 414a4–19, 29–32.

25. Averroës, *In libros De anima* III, comm. 5, digression, part 5.

26. Aristotle, *De anima* III, 8. 431b28–432a3.

27. *De anima* III, 8. 432a3–14.

28. *Timaeus* 18. 52A.

29. Q. 117, A. 1.

30. Q. 75, A. 6.

31. Aristotle, *Metaphysics* IX, 10. 1058b26–29.

32. *De generatione animalium* II, 3. 736b2–5.

33. *Metaphysics* VII, 2. 1043a2–12.

34. Gennadius of Marseilles, *De ecclesiasticis dogmatibus* 15. PL 42:1216. Cf. PL 58:984, PL 83:1231.

35. *Timaeus* 31, 32. 69–72B.

36. *De anima* II, 2. 413b15–24.

37. *De anima* II, 2. 413b24–29.

38. *Metaphysics* VII, 6. 1045a15–20.

39. *De anima* I, 5. 411b6–14.

40. The first way of predicating "intrinsically" posits the predicate in the definition of the subject. The second way, as indicated, posits the subject in the definition of the predicate.

41. *Metaphysics* VII, 3. 1043b36–1044a2.

42. *De anima* II, 3. 414b19–32.

43. Q. 118, A. 2, *ad* 2.

44. In the body of the article.

45. *De anima* II, 1. 412a15–b6.

46. Aristotle, *Physics* VIII, 5. 257b6–13.

47. Aristotle, *Physics* V, 1. 225a20–31.

48. See Glossary, s.v. "matter."

49. See n. 16, *supra.*

50. See Q. 76, A. 1, and n. 13, *supra.*

51. Q. 76, A. 1.

52. Aristotle, *Physics* I, 4. 187a26–31.

53. *De anima* II, 1. 412b.

54. Avicenna, *De anima*, part 4, chap. 5. Also: *Sufficientia* I, 6.

55. Averroës, *In libros De coelo*, comm. 67.

56. Aristotle, *Metaphysics* VII, 3. 1043b36–1044a2.

57. *De generatione et corruptione* I, 10. 327b29–31.

58. *De anima* II, 1. 412a15–b6.

59. Q. 55, A. 2.

60. *De divinis nominibus* 7. PG 3:868.

61. *De divinis nominibus* 5. PG 3:820–21.

62. Aristotle, *De anima* II, 9. 421a16–26.

63. *Super Genesim ad litteram* II, 1. PL 34:263.

64. Aristotle, *De anima* III, 8. 431b28–432a3.

65. *De causa motus animalium [De animalium motione]* 10. 703a36–b2.

66. Aristotle, *De anima* II, 1. 412b17–413a10.

67. *De Trinitate* VI, 6. PL 42:929.

68. Q. 76, A. 1.

69. *De anima* II, 1. 412b9–17.

ST I

Question 78

On the Powers of the Soul in Particular

[This question is divided into four articles, all of which are included here.]

First Article

Should We Distinguish Five Kinds of Powers of the Soul?

I proceed in this way to the first article: it seems that we should not distinguish five kinds of powers of the soul, namely: the vegetative, sensory, appetitive, locomotive, and intellectual powers.

Obj. 1. We call the soul's powers parts of the soul itself. But we universally assign three parts of the soul, namely, the vegetative, the sensory, and the rational. Therefore, there are only three kinds of powers of the soul and not five.

Obj. 2. Powers of the soul are sources of vital activities. But we say in four ways that things are living. For the Philosopher says in the *De anima*: "We say that things are living, with the word "living" predicated in many different ways—for example, understanding, sense perception, local motion and rest, and ongoing change by nourishment, both decrease and increase—even though only one of these ways is present."[1] Therefore, there are only four kinds of powers of the soul, since appetitive power is excluded.

Obj. 3. To what is common to all the soul's powers we ought not assign some particular kind of soul. But desiring belongs to every power of the soul. For example, the power of sight desires the visible things proper to it, and so the Book of Sirach says: "Eyes will desire charm and beauty, and green fields more than these."[2] And by the same reasoning, every other power desires the object proper to it. Therefore, one ought not to hold that appetitive power is one special kind of power of the soul.

Obj. 4. The sources causing movement in animals are the senses or the intellect or the appetites, as the *De anima* says.[3] Therefore, in addition to the aforementioned sources, we ought not posit the power to cause movement in animals as a special kind of power of the soul.

On the contrary, the Philosopher says in the *De anima*: "And we call the powers vegetative, sensory, appetitive, locomotive, and intellectual."[4]

I answer that there are the five kinds of powers of the soul that we have enumerated. And we call three kinds of these powers souls. And we call four kinds of these powers ways of being alive.

And the reason for so differentiating powers of the soul is because we distinguish different souls as the soul's activities surpass, in different ways, the activities of our material nature, for our whole material nature is subject to the soul and related to the soul as the soul's matter and instrument. Therefore, there is one kind of activity of the soul that so far surpasses our material nature that the activity is not even performed by means of a bodily organ. And such is the activity of the rational soul.

And there is another activity, an activity inferior to rational activity, that is indeed performed by means of bodily organs but not by means of any bodily property. And such is the activity of the sensory soul, because, although hot and cold, and wet and dry, and other such material properties are required for the activity of the senses, yet the properties are needed only for the requisite disposition of the organs, not so that the activity of the sensory soul results from the properties' power.

And the lowest of the soul's activities is one that is performed by means of bodily organs and by the power of material properties. Nonetheless, such activities surpass the activity of our material nature, since such activities of the soul are produced by an intrinsic source, while the movements of material substances are produced by an extrinsic source. For an intrinsic source is common to every activity of the soul, since an enlivened thing in some way moves itself. And such is the activity of the vegetative soul; for example, the body's heating action instrumentally causes digestion and the results of digestion, as the *De anima* says.[5]

And we distinguish kinds of powers of the soul by the powers' objects. For the higher the power, the more universal is the object that belongs to the power, as I have said before.[6] And we can consider the objects of the soul's activities in three ranks. For the only object of some powers of the soul is the body united to the soul. And we call this kind of power of the soul vegetative, since the vegetative power acts only on the body to which the soul is united.

And there is another kind of power of the soul, a kind to which a more universal object belongs, namely, every sensibly perceptible material substance and not only the body united to the soul. And there is another kind of power of the soul, a kind that to which an object still more universal belongs, namely, every being without exception and not only sensibly perceptible material substances. And so it is evident that the latter two kinds of power of the soul have activities not only with respect to something conjoined but also with respect to something external.

And since an active subject needs to be in some way joined to the object of its activity, we need to relate the external thing that is the object of the soul's activity to the soul in two ways. In one way, as the external thing is constituted to be joined to the soul and to be in the soul by the thing's likeness. And as to this way, there are two kinds of powers, namely, sense powers with respect to the less universal object, that is, sensibly perceptible material substances, and intellectual powers with respect to the most universal object, that is, being without exception.

And in the second way, we relate an external thing to the soul as the soul itself is inclined and tends toward the external thing. And regarding this relation also, there are two kinds of powers of the soul: indeed one kind, namely, appetitive powers, as we relate the soul to external things as ends, which are the first thing in strivings, and the other kind locomotive powers, as we relate the soul to external things as the termini of activity and movement, since every animal is moved in order to gain something desired and striven for.

And we distinguish ways of being alive by the grades of living things. For there are certain kinds of living things, like plants in which there are only vegetative powers. And there are certain kinds of living things in which there are sense powers as well as vegetative powers but no locomotive power; for example, there are immobile animals like shellfish. And there are certain kinds of living things that have locomotive power as well, as do perfect animals, which need many things for their life, and so need movement in order to seek necessities of life situated at a distance from them. There are still other kinds of living things, namely, human beings, in which there are intellectual powers as well. But appetitive powers do not constitute a particular grade of living things, since everything with sense also has appetites, as the *De anima* says.[7]

Replies to Objs. 1 and 2. And this analysis resolves the first two objections.

Reply to Obj. 3. A natural appetite is the inclination of every thing, by its nature, toward something, and so every power by a natural appetite desires something proper to itself.

But an animal appetite results from the perception of a form. Moreover, a special power of the soul is required for this kind of appetite, and perception alone does not suffice. For a thing is desired as it is in its nature, and it is in a power of perception by its likeness, not by its nature. And so it is clear that the sense of sight by nature desires a visible object only for the power's act, namely, in order to see, but the animal by its appetitive power desires the thing seen not only in order to see but also for other uses.

Moreover, if the soul were to need the things perceived by their senses only for the sake of the activities of the senses, namely, for the sake of perceiving the things, we would not need to suppose that appetitive power is a special kind of power of the soul, since the natural appetite of the soul's powers would suffice.

Reply to Obj. 4. Although sense powers and appetites are sources causing movement in perfect animals, yet sense powers and appetites as such do not suffice to cause movement unless another power is added to them, for there are sense powers and appetites in immobile animals, but such animals do not have the power to move. Rather, this power to move consists not only in the sense powers and appetites as they command movement, but also in the body's parts themselves, that the parts be suitable to obey appetites of the soul that are moving them. And this is indicated by the fact that the body's members do not obey appetites for movement when the members are removed from their natural arrangement.

Second Article

Do We Suitably Assign the Vegetative Parts of the Soul,
Namely, Powers of Nutrition, Growth, and Generation?

I proceed in this way to the second article: it seems that we unsuitably assign the vegetative parts of the soul, namely, powers of nutrition, growth, and generation.

Obj. 1. We call the powers of nutrition, growth, and generation natural powers. But powers of the soul surpass natural powers. Therefore, we ought not posit the powers of nutrition, growth, and generation as natural powers.

Obj. 2. We ought not assign a power of the soul to what is common to living and nonliving things. But generation is common to everything that can come to be and pass away, both living and nonliving. Therefore, we ought not posit the power of generation as a power of the soul.

Obj. 3. The soul is more powerful than a material nature. But a material gives form and requisite size by the same active power. Therefore, much more does the soul. Therefore, the soul has no power of growth different from the power of generation.

Obj. 4. Each thing is preserved in existing by that whereby it has existing. But the power of generation is the power whereby a living thing acquires existing. Therefore, a living thing is preserved by the same power. But the power of nutrition is ordained for the preservation of living things, as the *De anima* says,[8] for the power of nutrition is "the power capable of preserving the subject of the very power."[9] Therefore, we ought not distinguish the power of nutrition from the power of generation.

On the contrary, the Philosopher says in the *De anima* that the activities of the vegetative soul are "to generate and to use food,"[10] and also "to produce growth."[11]

I answer that there are three powers of the vegetative part of the soul. For vegetative power has for its object the very body that is a living body by means of the soul, as I have said,[12] and three activities of the soul are indeed necessary for such a body. There is indeed one activity by which the living body acquires existing, and the power of generation is ordained for this purpose. And there is a second activity by which the body that is alive acquires its requisite size, and the power of growth is ordained for this purpose. And there is a third activity by which the body of a living thing is preserved both in its existing and in its requisite size, and the power of nutrition is ordained for this purpose.

We should, however, note a certain difference between these powers. For the powers of nutrition and growth have their effects in that in which the powers exist, since the very body united to the soul grows and is preserved by the powers of growth and nutrition existing in the same soul. But the power of generation has its effect in another body, not in the same body, since nothing generates itself.

And so the power of generation approaches the rank of the sensory soul, which has activities in relation to external things (albeit in a more excellent and more universal way), for what is highest in a lower nature borders on what is lowest in a higher nature, as Denis makes clear in his *De divinis nominibus.*[13]

And so the power of generation is the ultimate and most important and most perfect of these three powers, as the *De anima* says,[14] for it belongs to something perfect "to produce something just like itself."[15] Moreover, both the power of growth and the power of nutrition assist the power of generation, and the power of nutrition assists the power of growth.

Reply to Obj. 1. We call the powers of nutrition, growth, and generation natural both because they have effects like nature, which also bestows existing and size and preservation (although these powers have their effects in a higher way), and because the powers perform their activities instrumentally, by means of the active and passive properties that are the sources of natural actions.

Reply to Obj. 2. The generation in nonliving things is entirely by something external. But the generation of living things is in a higher way, by part of living things themselves, that is, the seed, in which is the formative source of the body. And so living things need to have some power that prepares the seed, and this power is the power of generation.

Reply to Obj. 3. Since the generation of living things is from some seed, it is necessary that quantitatively small animals be initially generated. And for this reason, living things need to have a power of the soul that brings them to their requisite size. But nonliving material substances are generated from matter determined by external efficient causes, and so nonliving material substances receive their form and size at the same time, according to the condition of the matter.

Reply to Obj. 4. As I have already said,[16] the activities of the vegetative source are executed by means of heat, which has the property of consuming moisture. And so, in order to restore lost moisture, the vegetative source needs to have the power of nutrition, whereby food is converted into the substance of the body. And this is also necessary for activities of the powers of growth and generation.

Third Article

Do We Suitably Distinguish the Five External Senses?

I proceed in this way to the third article: it seems that we unsuitably distinguish the five external senses.

Obj. 1. The senses know accidents. But there are many kinds of accidents. Therefore, since we distinguish powers by their objects, it seems that there are numerically as many senses as there are kinds of accidents.

Obj. 2. Size and shape and the other things that we call "things perceptible by several senses"[17] are not "things perceptible by chance," and the *De anima* distinguishes the former from the latter.[18] But the intrinsic differences of powers' objects distinguish powers. Therefore, since size and shape differ more from color than sound does, it seems that there ought much more to be a different sense power cognitive of size and shape than there ought to be different sense powers cognitive of color and sound.

Obj. 3. The object of each sense is one set of contraries; for example, the object of sight is white and black. But the sense of touch knows several sets of contraries, namely, hot and cold, wet and dry, and suchlike. Therefore, there are several senses of touch, not one. Therefore, there are more than five senses.

Obj. 4. We do not distinguish a species from its genus. But tasting is a kind of touching. Therefore, we ought not regard taste as a distinct sense in addition to the sense of touch.

On the contrary, the Philosopher says in the *De anima* that "there are only five senses."[19]

I answer that certain thinkers chose to understand the reason for distinguishing and numbering the external senses from the sense organs, in which one or another element predominates, whether water or air or some such thing.

And certain other thinkers chose to understand the reason for distinguishing and numbering the external senses from the media by which the senses perceive, whether a medium is conjoined or external, and whether the latter is air or water or some such thing.

And still others chose to understand the reason for distinguishing and numbering the external senses from the different natures of perceptible properties insofar as the properties belong to simple material substances or result from a combination of the same.

But none of these explanations is suitable. For sense powers do not exist because of sense organs but sense organs because of sense powers, and so there are not different sense powers because there are different sense organs; rather, nature constituted the diversity of the sense organs so that they might correspond to the diversity of the sense powers. And nature similarly assigned different media to different senses according to what was suitable for activities of the sense powers. And to know the natures of perceptible properties belongs to the intellect, not to the senses.

Therefore, we should understand the reason for numbering and distinguishing the external senses by what properly and intrinsically belongs to each sense. But the senses are certain passive powers that are constituted to be affected by external perceptible things. Therefore, external perceptible things are what the senses intrinsically perceive, and we distinguish sense powers by the diversity of those things.

Moreover, there are two kinds of change: one natural and the other immaterial. There is indeed a natural change as the form of something causing change is received in the thing changed according to the form's natural existing; for example, heat is received in the thing heated. And there is an immaterial change as the form of something causing change is received in the thing changed according to the form's immaterial existing; for example, the form of color is received into an eye's pupil, which does not thereby become colored. And an immaterial change, which produces the representation of a perceptible form in a sense organ, is required for activities of the senses. Otherwise, if a natural change alone were to suffice for perceiving, every natural material substance would perceive when it is changed.

But while we find in some of sense perceptions immaterial changes, as in the sense of sight, we find in other sense perceptions both immaterial changes and natural changes, and the natural changes are either only on the part of the objects or on the part of sense organs as well. And we find a natural change on the part of the object, indeed one regarding place, in sound, which is the object of the sense of hearing, since percussion and disturbance of air cause sound. And we find a natural change on the part of the object by alteration in odor, which is the object of the sense of smell, since something hot needs to change a material substance in some way in order that the substance emit an odor. And there is a natural change on the part of the sense organs in the senses of touch and taste, since both the hand that touches hot things becomes hot, and the tongue becomes moistened by the moisture of flavors. But no natural changes alter the organs of the senses of smell and hearing in the course of perception, except by chance.

Moreover, the sense of sight, since it has no natural change, whether of its organ or of its object, is the most immaterial and the most perfect and most universal of all the senses. And the next most immaterial and the most perfect and the most universal is the sense of hearing, and the next the sense of smell, both of which senses have natural changes on the part of their objects. (Locomotion, however, is more perfect than, and by nature prior to, the motion of change, as the Philosopher proves in the *Physics*.[20]) And the senses of touch and taste are the most material, and I shall speak later of their difference.[21] And so the senses of sight, hearing, and smell are not executed by conjoined media, so that no natural change affects their sense organs, as happens in the case of the senses of touch and taste.

Reply to Obj. 1. Not every accident as such has the power to cause change, but only properties of the third kind do,[22] and such properties bring about change. And so only such properties are objects of the senses, since "the same things that affect nonliving material substances, affect the senses," as the *Physics* says.[23]

Reply to Obj. 2. Size and shape and suchlike, which Aristotle calls "things perceptible by several senses," are in between "things perceptible by chance" and "things peculiarly perceptible by one sense," which are the objects of the senses.[24] For things peculiarly perceptible by one sense primarily and intrinsically affect the senses, since such things are properties that cause change.

On the other hand, we trace all the things perceptible by several senses to quantity. And it is indeed evident that size and number are forms of quantity. And shape is a property that concerns quantity, since the essence of shape consists in the limitation of size. And we perceive motion and rest as the subject of motion and rest is, in one or several ways, disposed regarding the subject's size (as to the motion of growth) or regarding the magnitude of the subject's spatial distance (as to the motion of locomotion) or also regarding perceptible properties (as in the motion of change). And so to perceive motion and rest is in a way to perceive one thing and many things. But quantity is the proximate subject of the properties that cause change; for example, surfaces are the proximate subjects of colors. And so the things perceptible by several senses do not affect the senses primarily and intrinsically, but do so by reason of perceptible properties; for example, surfaces by reason of their color affect the sense of sight.

Still, neither are the things perceptible by several senses things perceptible by chance, since things perceptible by several senses produce different alterations of the senses. For example, large and small surfaces affect the senses in different ways, since we call even whiteness itself large or small, and thus distinguish it according to the subject to which it belongs.

Reply to Obj. 3. The sense of touch is generically one sense but specifically many different senses, as the Philosopher seems to say in the *De anima*,[25] and different sets of contraries are for this reason the object of the sense of touch. And yet the different sets of contraries are not separate from one another with respect to sense organs; rather, the different sets of contraries accompany one another throughout the body, and so there is no apparent distinction between them. (On the other hand, the sense of touch, which perceives sweet and bitter, accompanies the sense of touch in the tongue but not throughout the body, and so we easily distinguish the sense of taste from the sense of touch.)

Nevertheless, we could say both that each of these sets of contraries belongs to one proximate genus, and that all of them belong to one common genus, which by a common aspect is the object of the sense of touch. There is, however, no name for this common genus, just as there is no name for the proximate genus of hot and cold.

Reply to Obj. 4. The sense of taste is a certain kind of touch that is only in the tongue, as the Philosopher says.[26] And we do not distinguish the sense of taste from the sense of touch in general but as to the kinds of touch diffused throughout the body.

But if touch be only one sense, because of the one common aspect of its object, we will need to say that we distinguish the sense of taste from the sense of touch by the different nature of the changes in them. For the sense of touch is affected not only by immaterial changes but also by natural changes respecting the organ of touch, by reason of the property that is the proper object of touch. The organ of taste, on the other hand, is not necessarily affected by natural changes respecting the property that is the proper object of taste, namely, such that the tongue become sweet or bitter, but by reason of the prefatory property on which flavor is based, namely, moisture, which is the object of touch.

Fourth Article

Do We Suitably Distinguish the Internal Senses?

I proceed in this way to the fourth article: it seems that we unsuitably distinguish the internal senses.

Obj. 1. We do not distinguish the common from the proper.[27] Therefore, we ought not reckon the common sense among the internal sense powers in addition to the proper external senses.[28]

Obj. 2. We ought not posit an internal cognitive power to accomplish purposes for which the proper and external senses suffice. But proper and external senses suffice for us to judge about perceptible things, since each sense judges about its own object. Likewise, the proper and external senses also seem to suffice for the purpose of perceiving their own acts, since, because activities of the senses are in a way in between the sense powers and the powers' objects, the sense of sight would seem to be much more able to perceive its act of sight, as more closely related to itself, than to perceive color, and the same seems to be true in the case of the other senses. Therefore, it was unnecessary for these purposes to posit the internal power that we call the common sense.

Obj. 3. The powers of imagination and memory are passive properties of the first sense powers, according to the Philosopher.[29] But we do not distinguish passive properties from their subject. Therefore, we ought not regard memory and imagination as distinct powers in addition to the external senses.

Obj. 4. The intellect depends less on the external senses than any power of the sensory part of the soul does. But the intellect knows only by receiving things from the external senses, and so the *Posterior Analytics* says that "those who lack one sense, lack one way of knowing."[30] Therefore, we ought much less to posit a power of the sensory part of the soul to perceive imports that the external senses do not perceive, a power that proponents call the estimative power.

Obj. 5. Acts of the cogitative power, acts that compare and compose and divide, and acts of the power of recall, acts that use a kind of syllogism for inquiring, do not differ less from acts of the estimative power and the power of memory than acts of the estimative power differ from acts of the power of imagination. Therefore, we ought either to hold the cogitative power and the power of recall to be distinct powers besides the estimative power and the power of memory, or not to hold the estimative power and the power of memory to be distinct powers besides the power of imagination.

Obj. 6. Augustine in his *Super Genesim* posits three kinds of vision, namely: bodily vision, which the external sense produces, and immaterial vision, which the power of imagination or fancy produces, and intellectual vision, which the intellect produc es.[31] Therefore, the power of imagination is the only internal power in between the external senses and the intellect.

On the contrary, Avicenna in his work *De anima* posits five internal sense powers, namely: "the common sense, the power of fancy, the power of imagination, the estimative power, and the power of memory."[32]

I answer that, since nature is not wanting in necessary things, there need to be as many activities of the sensory soul as suffice for the life of a perfect animal. And whichever of these activities we cannot trace to one source require different powers, since powers of the soul are simply proximate sources of the soul's activities.

And we should consider that, for the life of a perfect animal, the animal needs to perceive things not only when sensibly perceptible things are present, but also when they are not. Otherwise, since an animal's movement and activity result from perception, the animal would not be moved to seek things that are not present. And the opposite of this is most apparent in the case of perfect animals, which have forward motion, since they are moved to seek something absent that they have perceived. Therefore, animals through their sensory souls need not only to receive the forms of perceptible things when those things are currently affecting the animals, but also to retain and preserve such forms. But in the case of material things, we trace receiving and retaining to different sources; wet things, for example, take things in well and retain them poorly, while the opposite is true of dry things. And so, since sense powers are actualities of bodily organs, there needs to be one power that receives the forms of perceptible things, and another power that preserves the forms.

We should also consider that, if animals were to be moved only on account of what is agreeable or disagreeable to the external senses, we would need to posit in animals only perception of the forms that the external senses perceive, forms in which external senses delight, or at which they shudder. But animals need to seek after, or flee from, some things, not only because the things are suitable or unsuitable for external sense perception, but also because of some other advantages and benefits, or some detriments; for example, sheep flee when they see a wolf coming, not because of the uncomeliness of the wolf's color or shape but because the wolf is by nature their enemy, as it were, and similarly, a bird gathers straw, not because straw delights the bird's senses but because straw is useful for building a nest. Therefore, animals need to perceive such imports, imports that the external senses do not perceive. And there needs to be another source of such perceptions, since perceptions of perceptible forms derive from the changes that perceptible things cause, while perceptions of the aforementioned imports do not.

Therefore, the proper [external] senses and the common [internal] sense are ordained to receive perceptible forms, and I shall speak later of the difference between the proper senses and the common sense.[33] And fancy or imagination—and they are the same thing—is ordained to retain and preserve the perceptible forms, since fancy or imagination is a kind of storehouse, as it were, of the forms received by the external senses. And the estimative power is ordained to perceive imports that the external senses do not receive. And the power of memory, which is a kind of storehouse of such imports, is ordained to preserve those imports. And the latter is indicated by the fact that the source of remembering comes from some such import, for example, the import that something is harmful or suitable. And the very aspect of the past, which memory notes, is counted among such imports.

And we should consider that there is no difference between human beings and animals as to perceptible forms, since external perceptible things similarly affect human beings and animals. But there is a difference with respect to the aforementioned imports, since nonhuman animals perceive such imports only by a certain instinct from nature, while human beings perceive such imports by a process of comparison. And so what we call the natural power of estimation, we call the cogitative power of human beings, which power by a process of comparison discovers such imports. And so we also call the cogitative power "particular reason" (to which doctors assign a fixed organ, namely, the midsection of the brain), since the cogitative power compares individual imports just as reason understands universal imports. Moreover, on the part of the power of memory, human beings have not only, like other animals, memory in the unexpected recollection of things from the past, but also recall regarding the particular imports of things from the past, by almost dialectically seeking to remember things from the past.

Avicenna, however, posits a fifth power in between the estimative power and the power of imagination,[34] a power that composes and divides forms imagined by us; for example, it is evident that we compose the one form of a gold mountain, which we have never seen, from the forms of gold and mountain imagined by us. But such activity does not show itself in animals other than human beings, in whom the power of imagination suffices for this purpose. And Averroës in one of his works, *De sensu et sensibilibus*, also attributed such activity to the power of imagination.[35]

And so we need to posit only four internal powers of the sensory part of the soul, namely: the common sense, the power of imagination, the estimative power, and the power of memory.

Reply to Obj. 1. We do not call the internal common sense common by predication as a genus but as the common root and source of the external senses.

Reply to Obj. 2. The proper senses judge about the perceptible things proper to them by distinguishing those very things from other perceptible things that fall within the power of the same senses, for example, by distinguishing white from black or green. But neither the sense of sight nor the sense of taste can distinguish white from sweet, since the sense that distinguishes between several perceptible things needs to know each of them. And so the judgment that distinguishes between several perceptible things needs to belong to the common sense, to which, as a common terminus, all perceptions of the external senses are referred, and by which the imports of external sense perceptions are perceived, as when individuals perceive that they see. For the proper sense of sight, which knows only the form of the perceptible thing affecting it, cannot do this. And the act of seeing is completed in that alteration of the sense of sight, and from that alteration results another alteration in the common sense, which perceives the act of seeing.

Reply to Obj. 3. As one power originates from the soul by means of another power, as I have said before,[36] so also is the soul the subject of one power by means of another power. And we accordingly call the powers of imagination and memory passive qualities of the first sense powers.

Reply to Obj. 4. Although the activity of the intellect originates from the external senses, yet the intellect knows in the things perceived by the senses many things that the external senses cannot perceive. And similarly, the estimative power knows many things that the external senses do not perceive, although in a lesser way.

Reply to Obj. 5. The cogitative power and the power of memory in human beings have that excellence, not by a property of the sensory soul but by an affinity and proximity to universal reason, by a kind of overflow. And so the cogitative power and the power of memory are not different powers but the same as the powers in other animals, more perfect powers than exist in other animals.

Reply to Obj. 6. Augustine calls immaterial the vision that the likenesses of material substances produce in the absence of such substances. And so it is evident that such vision is common to all internal perceptions.

Notes

1. *De anima* II, 2. 413a20–25.
2. Sir. 40:22.
3. Aristotle, *De anima* III, 10. 433a9–13.
4. *De anima* II, 3. 414a29–32.
5. Aristotle, *De anima* II, 4. 416b23–31.
6. Q. 77, A. 3, *ad* 4.
7. Aristotle, *De anima* II, 3. 414a29–32.
8. Aristotle, *De anima* II, 4. 416b23–25.
9. Aristotle, *De anima* II, 4. 416b17–23.
10. *De anima* II, 4. 415a22–26.
11. *De anima* II, 2. 413a25–31.
12. Q. 78, A. 1.
13. *De divinis nominibus* 7. PG 3:872.
14. Aristotle, *De anima* II, 4. 416b23–25.
15. Aristotle, *De anima* II, 4. 415a26–b7.
16. Q. 78, A. 1.
17. That is, the things that several senses can perceive, together with the things that each sense peculiarly perceives. Cf. Q. 17, A. 2.
18. Aristotle, *De anima* II, 6. 418a17–25.
19. *De anima* III, 1. 424b22–24.
20. Aristotle, *Physics* VIII, 7. 260a26–b7.
21. In the responses to the third and fourth objections.

22. Cf. I-II, Q. 49, A. 2. Note that the third type of quality listed there is "passion," that is, the capacity to be acted upon, while the present text refers to "action," that is, the capacity to cause change. The latter type is listed as the second in I–II, Q. 49, A. 2.

23. Aristotle, *Physics* VII, 2. 244a27–245a22.

24. That is, the objects that each sense uniquely perceives. Cf. Q. 17, A. 2.

25. *De anima* II, 11. 422b17–424a16.

26. *De anima* II, 9, 11. 421a16–22, 423a17–21.

27. That is, we do not distinguish genera from the species belonging to them. For example, we do not distinguish "animal" from "rational animal."

28. See Glossary, s.v. "Senses."

29. *De memoria et reminiscentia* 1. 450a9–14.

30. Aristotle, *Posterior Analytics* I, 18. 81a38–39.

31. *Super Genesim ad litteram* XII, 6, 7, 24. PL 34:458, 459, 474–75.

32. *De anima*, part 4, chap. 1.

33. Replies to Objs. 1 and 2.

34. That is, the power of fancy. Cf. the quotation from Avicenna in the section "On the contrary," supra.

35. *De sensu et sensibilibus* 8.

36. Q. 77, A. 7.

ST I
Question 79
On the Intellectual Powers of the Soul

[This question is divided into thirteen articles, eight of which are included here.]

First Article

Is the Intellect a Power of the Soul?

I proceed in this way to the first article: it seems that the intellect is not a power of the soul but the soul's very essence.

Obj. 1. The intellect seems to be the same thing as the mind. But the mind is the soul's essence, not one of its powers, since Augustine says in his *De Trinitate*: "We do not predicate mind and spirit in relation to the soul; rather, mind and spirit signify the soul's essence."[1] Therefore, the intellect is the soul's very essence.

Obj. 2. Different kinds of powers of the soul are united in the soul's essence, not in a particular power of the soul. But appetitive and intellectual powers are different kinds of powers of the soul, as the *De anima*, says,[2] and yet the two powers are united in the mind, for Augustine in his *De Trinitate* posits understanding and willing in the mind.[3] Therefore, the mind and intellect is the soul's very essence and not one of its powers.

Obj. 3. According to Gregory in his homily on the Ascension, "Both human beings and angels understand."[4] But we call angels "minds" and "intellects."[5] Therefore, the mind and intellect of human beings is the soul itself, not one of the soul's powers.

Obj. 4. It belongs to a particular substance to be intellectual because it is immaterial. But the soul is by its essence immaterial. Therefore, it seems that the soul is by its essence intellectual.

On the contrary, the Philosopher posits an "intellectual" power of the soul, as the De anima makes clear.[6]

I answer that, as I have said before,[7] we need to say that the intellect is one of the soul's powers and not the soul's very essence. For only when activity itself is the existing of the thing that acts, is the direct source of activity the very essence of that thing, since essence is related to existing as powers are related to activities as actualities of the powers. But only in the case of God are understanding and his existing identical. And so only in the case of God is his intellect his essence, while the intellect is in the case of intellectual creatures other than God a particular power of the one who understands.

Reply to Obj. 1. We sometimes understand "senses" to mean sense powers, and we sometimes understand "senses" to mean the sensory soul itself, since the sensory soul derives its name from its chief powers, which are the sense powers. And we likewise sometimes call the intellectual soul the intellect by reason of its chief power, as it were; for example, the *De_anima* says that "the intellect is a certain substance."[8] And Augustine also says in this way that the mind is "spirit" or "essence."[9]

Reply to Obj. 2. The appetitive and intellectual powers, by reason of the different natures of their objects, are different kinds of powers of the soul. But appetitive power belongs partially with the intellectual powers and partially with the sense powers, depending on whether the appetitive power acts by means of, or apart from, a bodily organ, since appetite results from apprehension. And Augustine accordingly posits the will in the mind, and the Philosopher the will in reason.[10]

Reply to Obj. 3. Angels have only the powers of intellect and will, and will results from intellect. And so we call angels "minds" or intellects," since the totality of angels' power consists in such. But the human soul has many other powers, such as sense powers and the power of nutrition, and so the cases of angels and human beings are dissimilar.

Reply to Obj. 4. The very immateriality of a created intelligent substance is not its intellect; rather, a created intelligent substance has the power to understand by reason of its immateriality. And so the intellect does not need to be the soul's substance but only the soul's characteristic excellence and power.

Second Article

Is the Intellect a Passive Power?

I proceed in this way to the second article: it seems that the intellect is not a passive power.

Obj. 1. Everything is acted upon by reason of its matter but acts by reason of its form.   But the intellect's power results from the immateriality of an intelligent substance. Therefore, it seems that the intellect is not a passive power.

Obj. 2. The intellect's power cannot pass away, as I have said before.[11] But "the intellect can pass away if it is passive," as the *De anima* says.[12] Therefore, the intellect's power is not passive.

Obj. 3. "What acts is more excellent than what is acted upon," as Augustine says in his *Super Genesim*,[13] and Aristotle says in the *De anima*.[14] But all the powers of the soul's vegetative part are active powers, and yet they are the lowest powers of the soul. Therefore, much more are all the intellect's powers, which are the highest powers of the soul, active powers.

On the contrary, the Philosopher says in the *De anima* that "understanding is a way of being acted upon."[15]

I answer that we speak about "being acted upon" in three ways. In one way, in the most proper sense, namely, when something is taken away from what belongs to it by nature or its own tendency, as when water loses coldness by being heated, and when human beings become sick or sad. In a second way, we say in a less proper sense that one is acted upon because something, whether suitable or not, is cast off from the person. And we say accordingly not only that a sick person but even a healthy person is acted upon, not only a sad person but even a joyful person, or in whatever way one is altered or moved. In a third way, we say in a general sense that something is acted upon solely by reason of the fact that something with a potentiality for something receives that for which the thing had potentiality, without anything being cast off. And we can in the latter way say that everything going from potentiality to actuality is acted upon, even when it is perfected. And it is in this way that our understanding consists of being acted upon.

And this is indeed evident by the following consideration. For the intellect has activity regarding being in general, as I have said before.[16] Therefore, we can consider whether the intellect is actual or potential by considering how the intellect is related to all being. For we find one intellect that is related to all being as the actuality of all being, and such is the divine intellect, that is, the essence of God, in the source and power of which essence, as first cause, the totality of being pre-exists. And so the divine intellect has no potentiality but is pure actuality.

But no created intellect can be related as actuality with respect to the totality of all being, since such an intellect would then need to be an infinite being. And so no created intellect, by the very fact that it exists, is the actuality of all intelligible things but is related to intelligible things themselves as potentiality to actuality.

And potentiality is related to actuality in two ways. For there is one kind of potentiality that is always perfected by actuality, as we have said about the matter of heavenly bodies.[17] And there is another kind of potentiality that is not always actual but goes from potentiality to actuality, as we find in the case of things that come to be and pass away.

Therefore, angels' intellects are always actual with respect to the things that they can understand, because of their intellects' approximation to the first intellect, which, as I have said above, is pure actuality. But the human intellect, the lowest in the rank of intellects and the most remote from the perfection of the divine intellect, is potential with respect to the things that it can understand, and initially "like an empty tablet on which nothing is written," as the Philosopher says in the *De anima*.[18] And this is manifestly evidenced by the fact that we understand initially only potentially but are subsequently brought to understand actually.

Therefore, it is clear that our understanding consists of being acted upon in a certain way, in the third way of being acted upon. And so our intellect is a passive power.

Reply to Obj. 1. The thrust of this objection concerns the first and second ways of being acted upon, which ways belong to prime matter. But the third way of being acted upon belongs to anything existing potentially that is brought to actuality.

Reply to Obj. 2. Certain thinkers call sense appetites, in which the emotions of the soul are situated, the passive intellect, and the *Ethics* also calls sense appetites "rational by participation," because "they obey reason."[19] And other thinkers call the cogitative power, which we call "particular reason,"[20] the passive intellect. And either way, we can understand "passive" by the first two ways of being acted upon, insofar as such a so-called intellect is the actuality of a bodily organ.

But the intellect with potentiality for the things that it can understand, which Aristotle for this reason calls the "potential intellect,"[21] is only passive in the third way of being acted upon, since that intellect is not the actuality of a bodily organ. And so the intellect cannot pass away.

Reply to Obj. 3. What acts is more excellent than what is acted upon if the acting and the being acted upon are related to the same thing, but what acts is not always more excellent than what is acted upon if the acting and the being acted upon are related to different things. Now, the intellect is a passive power with respect to the totality of all being, while the vegetative power is active with respect to a particular kind of being, namely, the body united to the soul. And so nothing prevents such a passive power being more excellent than such an active power.

Third Article

Should We Posit an Active Intellect?

I proceed in this way to the third article: it seems that we should not posit an active intellect.

Obj. 1. As the senses are ordered to perceptible things, so is our intellect ordered to intelligible things. But we posit only passive senses, not active senses, since the senses are potential regarding perceptible things. Therefore, since our intellect is potential regarding intelligible things, it seems that we ought to posit only a potential intellect, not an active one.

Obj. 2. If one should say that there is also in sense perception something active, such as light, the answer would be: light is necessary for seeing, inasmuch as light makes the medium actually luminous, since color itself as such affects something luminous. But we do not posit in the activity of the intellect any medium that needs to become actual. Therefore, we do not need to posit an active intellect.

Obj. 3. The likeness of the thing acting is received in the thing acted upon in the way of the thing acted upon. But the potential intellect is an immaterial power. Therefore, the immateriality of the potential intellect suffices for forms to be received immaterially in that intellect. But forms are actually intelligible because they are immaterial. Therefore, we do not need to posit an active intellect in order to make forms actually intelligible.

On the contrary, the Philosopher says in the *De anima* that "as in every nature, so also in the soul, there is something whereby the soul becomes all things, and something whereby the soul makes all things [actually intelligible]."[22] Therefore, we need to posit an active intellect.

I answer that, according to the opinion of Plato, we had no need to posit an active intellect to make things actually intelligible, except perhaps to furnish the light of intelligibility to one who understands, as

I shall explain later.[23] For Plato held that the forms of natural things subsist apart from matter, and so that they are intelligible, since things are actually intelligible because they are immaterial.[24] And he called such intelligible things "Forms" or "Ideas." And he said that, by sharing in these Forms or Ideas, even corporeal matter is formed to constitute individual things by nature in their special genera and species, and that our intellects are formed to possess knowledge about the genera and species of things.

But because Aristotle did not hold that the forms of natural things subsist apart from matter, and because forms existing in matter are not actually intelligible,[25] the natures or forms of perceptible things, which natures or forms we understand, would consequently not be actually intelligible. And only actual beings bring things from potentiality to actuality; actual perceptible things, for example, actualize the senses. Therefore, we needed to posit on the part of the intellect a power that would make things actually intelligible by abstracting forms from material conditions. And this is why we need to posit an active intellect.

Reply to Obj. 1. We find that perceptible things are actual outside the soul, and so we do not need to posit active sense powers. And so it is clear that all the powers of the nutritive part of the soul are active, and that all the powers of the sensory part of the soul are passive, but that there is partially something active and partially something passive in the intellectual part of the soul.

Reply to Obj. 2. There are two views about the effect of light. For certain thinkers say that light is necessary for seeing in order to make colors actually visible. And in this view, an active intellect is necessary for understanding in like manner and for the same reason that light is necessary for seeing.

In the view of other thinkers, however, light is not necessary for seeing in order to make colors actually visible, but is necessary for seeing in order to make the medium actually luminous, as the Commentator says in his *De anima*.[26] And we in this way take note of Aristotle's comparison[27] likening the active intellect to light with respect to light being necessary for understanding as light is necessary for seeing—but not for the same reason.

Reply to Obj. 3. Given an active cause, its likeness may fittingly be received in different ways in different things because of the things' different dispositions. But if the active cause does not pre-exist, the disposition of the recipient will do nothing with respect to receiving the cause's likeness. And things actually intelligible are not things existing in the world, as regards the world of perceptible things, which do not subsist apart from matter. And so the immateriality of the potential intellect would not be enough for understanding without the presence of an active intellect that by means of abstraction would make things actually intelligible.

Fourth Article

Is the Active Intellect Something Belonging to Our Soul?

I proceed in this way to the fourth article: it seems that the active intellect is not something belonging to our soul.

Obj. 1. The effect of the active intellect is to illumine things for understanding. But something loftier than the soul produces this effect, as the Gospel of John says: "He [Christ] was the true light that enlightens every human being who comes into this world."[28] Therefore, it seems that the active intellect is not something belonging to our soul.

Obj. 2. The Philosopher in the *De anima* ascribes to the active intellect that "it does not sometimes understand and sometimes not understand."[29] But our soul does not always understand; rather, it sometimes understands and sometimes does not understand. Therefore, the active intellect is not something belonging to our soul.

Obj. 3. The thing acting and the thing acted upon are enough for acting. Therefore, if the potential intellect, which is a passive power, and likewise the active intellect, which is an active power, are things belonging to our soul, it would logically follow that human beings would always be able to understand whenever they wished to do so. But this conclusion is evidently false. Therefore, the active intellect is not something belonging to our soul.

Obj. 4. The Philosopher says in the *De anima* that the active intellect is "a substantially actual being."[30] But nothing is actual and potential with respect to the same thing. Therefore, if the potential intellect, which is potential with respect to everything intelligible, is something belonging to our soul, it seems to be impossible that the active intellect be something belonging to our soul.

Obj. 5. The active intellect, if it belongs to the soul, must be a power of the soul. For the active intellect is neither a characteristic of being acted upon nor a habit, since habits and characteristics of being acted upon do not have the nature of efficient causes with respect to the soul's characteristics of being acted upon; rather, the characteristic of being acted upon is the very activity of a passive power, and habits are the products of acts. But all of the soul's powers flow from the soul's essence. Therefore, it would follow that the active intellect would come from the soul's essence. And so the active intellect would not be in the soul by reason of sharing in intellectual power from a higher intellect. And such a conclusion is inappropriate. Therefore, the active intellect is not something belonging to our soul.

On the contrary, the Philosopher says in the *De anima* that "these different elements," namely, the potential intellect and the active intellect, "need to be in the soul."[31]

I answer that the active intellect about which the Philosopher is speaking is something belonging to our soul. And for evidence of this, we should consider that we need to posit a higher intellect superior to the human intellectual soul, an intellect from which the human soul would obtain the power of understanding. For what shares in something and is changeable and is imperfect requires antecedent to itself something that is essentially such and unchangeable and perfect. And we call the human soul intellectual by reason of its sharing in intellectual power. And the fact that one part and not the whole of the human soul is intellectual indicates this. The human soul also arrives at understanding of truth by a discursive process and mental movement, by reasoning. And the human soul also has imperfect understanding, both because the human soul does not understand everything, and because the human soul advances from potentiality to actuality in understanding the things that the soul does understand. Therefore, there needs to be a higher intellect that helps our soul to understand.

Therefore, certain thinkers held that this substantially distinct intellect is the active intellect, which makes sense images actually intelligible by illumining them, as it were.[32] But granted that there is some such separate active intellect, we nevertheless still need to posit in the human soul itself a power shared from that higher intellect, by which power the human soul makes things actually intelligible. So also in the case of other perfect natural things, each is endowed with its own powers, which are derived from universal causes and supplement them; the sun, for example, does not alone beget human beings, but human beings have power to beget human beings, and the like is true of other perfect animals. And nothing in things here below is more perfect than the human soul. And so we need to say that the human soul has a power derived from a higher intellect that enables the soul to illumine sense images.

And we know this from our experience when we realize that we abstract universal forms from conditions of particularity, that is, make things actually intelligible. But activity belongs to something only by reason of a source formally inhering in it, as I have said before when I treated of the potential intellect.[33] Therefore, a power that is the source of such activity needs to belong to our soul. And so Aristotle compared the active intellect to light, which is something received in air.[34] And Plato compared the separate intellect impressed on our souls to the sun, as Themistius says in his commentary on the *De anima*.[35]

But the separate intellect, according to the teachings of our faith, is God himself, who is the creator of the soul, and in whom alone is the soul made happy, as I shall make clear later.[36] And so the human soul shares in intellectual light from himself, as the Psalm says: "The light of your countenance, O Lord, is stamped on us."[37]

Reply to Obj. 1. That true light illumines things as the universal cause, from which the human soul shares a particular power, as I have said.[38]

Reply to Obj. 2. The Philosopher is not speaking those words about the active intellect but about the intellect actually understanding. And so, before the cited text, he premises the following about the intellect actually understanding: "And the intellect as actual and knowledge of something are identical."[39]

Or if we should understand the cited text to refer to the active intellect, Aristotle so speaks because it is on the part of the potential intellect, not the active intellect, that we sometimes understand and sometimes do not understand.

Reply to Obj. 3. If we were to relate the active intellect to the potential intellect as we relate the active object of a power to the power (e.g., an actually visible thing to the power of sight), it would logically follow that we would understand everything immediately, since the active intellect is that whereby all things are made [actually intelligible]. But we are not now relating the active intellect as an object of the intellect but as what makes the objects of the intellect actually intelligible. And to do this, we need, in addition to the presence of the active intellect, the presence of sense images, and the fit disposition of sense powers, and practice in such activity. For the understanding of one thing causes other things to be understood; for example, the understanding of terms causes propositions to be understood, and the understanding of first principles causes conclusions to be understood. And in this respect, it does not matter whether the active intellect is something belonging to, or separate from, the soul.

Reply to Obj. 4. The intellectual soul is indeed actually immaterial, but it is potential with respect to the fixed forms of things. And conversely, sense images are indeed actually likenesses of certain forms, but they are potentially immaterial. And so nothing prevents one and the same soul, as actually immaterial, from having one power by which it makes things actually immaterial by abstracting from the conditions of individual matter (and we indeed call this power the active intellect), and from having another power that receives such forms (and we call this power the potential intellect insofar as it is potential with respect to such forms).

Reply to Obj. 5. Since the soul's essence is immaterial, created by the highest intellect, nothing prevents a power shared from the highest intellect, a power by which the soul abstracts from matter, from flowing from the essence of the soul itself, just as the soul's other powers do.

Sixth Article

Is there Memory in the Intellectual Part of the Soul?

I proceed in this way to the sixth article: it seems that there is no memory in the intellectual part of the soul.

Obj. 1. Augustine says in his *De Trinitate* that things not "common to human beings and beasts" belong to the higher part of the soul.[40] But memory is common to human beings and beasts, for he says in the same place that "beasts can by their bodily senses perceive material things and commit the latter to memory."[41] Therefore, memory does not belong to the intellectual part of the soul.

Obj. 2. There is memory of past things. But we speak of the past by reference to a fixed point of time. Therefore, memory knows things subject to a fixed point of time, and that is to know things under the conditions of "here" and "now." But such belongs to the senses, not to the intellect. Therefore, there is memory only in the sensory part of the soul, not in the intellectual part of the soul.

Obj. 3. Memory preserves the forms of things that we are not actually thinking about. But this cannot happen in the intellect, since the reception of intelligible forms in the intellect actualizes the intellect, and the intellect as actual consists in actual understanding itself. And so the intellect actually understands all the things of which it contains forms. Therefore, there is no memory in the intellectual part of the soul.

On the contrary, Augustine says in his *De Trinitate* that "memory, understanding, and will are one mind."[42]

I answer that, since it belongs to the nature of memory to preserve the forms of things that are not actually being apprehended, we should first consider whether intelligible forms can be so preserved in the intellect. Avicenna, for example, held that intelligible forms cannot be preserved in the intellect.[43] For he said that forms can be preserved in the sensory part of the soul with respect to some of its powers, inasmuch as there are acts of bodily organs in which some forms can be preserved apart from actual perception. But things exist only in an intelligible way in the intellect, which has no bodily organ. And so the things whose likenesses exist in the intellect, need to be actually understood.

Therefore, according to Avicenna, a thing's form ceases to exist in the intellect once one ceases to understand that thing actually. But if one wishes to understand that thing again, one needs to turn one's attention to the active intellect (which he holds to be a separate substance), so that intelligible forms may flow from the active intellect into the potential intellect. And from the practice and acts of turning one's attention to the active intellect, there abides in the potential intellect, according to him, a certain aptitude to turn one's attention to the active intellect, and he called this aptitude habitual knowledge.

Therefore, according to this position, nothing not actually under-stood is preserved in the intellectual part of the soul. And so, in this way, we would be unable to posit memory in the intellectual part of the soul.

But this opinion is clearly contrary to the position of Aristotle. For Aristotle says in the *De anima* that "we call" the potential intellect "actual," since, "by reason of its knowing, it becomes each thing," and that "this happens because it can act by its own activity. Accordingly, even then, it is indeed potential in one way but not in the same way as before learning and discovering."[44] And we say that the potential intellect becomes each thing as it receives the form of each thing. Therefore, because the potential intellect receives the forms of intelligible things, it has the capacity to act whenever it will have chosen to do so. But the potential intellect does not have the power to be ever active, since it is even with intelligible forms potential in one way (although otherwise than before understanding), namely, in the way in which habitual knowledge is potential with respect to actual consideration.

The aforementioned position is also contrary to reason. For what is received in something is received in the way of the recipient. But the intellect has a more stable nature, and is more unchangeable than corporeal matter. Therefore, if corporeal matter possesses the forms that it receives not only while it is actually acting by reason of them, but also after it has ceased to act by reason of them, much more firmly does the intellect without change or loss receive intelligible forms, whether the forms are received from perceptible things or also come from a higher intellect. Therefore, if we understand memory to mean only the power of preserving forms, we need to say that there is memory in the intellectual part of the soul.

But if it should belong to the nature of memory that its object be something past as past, there will be no memory in the intellectual part of the soul but memory only in the sensory part of the soul, which part perceives individual things. For the past as past, since it means being subject to a fixed point of time, belongs to the condition of something individual.

Reply to Obj. 1. Memory, in preserving forms, is not common to us and beasts. For forms are preserved not only in the sensory part of the soul but rather in the composite, since the power of memory is the actuality of some bodily organ. On the other hand, the intellect as such, in addition to the bodily organ accompanying it, conserves forms. And so the Philosopher says in the *De anima* that "the soul is the site of the forms, not the whole soul but the intellect."[45]

Reply to Obj. 2. We can relate the pastness of time to two things, namely, the object that we know, and the act of knowing. And these two things are indeed joined together in the sensory part of the soul, and the sensory part of the soul perceives something because something currently perceptible is affecting it. And so animals remember simultaneously that they have hitherto perceived in the past, and that they have perceived a particular past perceptible thing.

But as pertains to the intellectual part of the soul, although there may be pastness on the part of the object of the intellect, pastness as such does not belong to that object. For the intellect understands human beings as human beings, and human beings as human beings may exist either in the present or in the past or in the future. On the other hand, the intellect can intrinsically understand pastness on the part of the intellect's act, just as the senses intrinsically perceive pastness on the part of their acts. This is so because the understanding of our soul is an individual act that exists in this or that point of time, since we say that human beings are understanding now or have understood yesterday or will understand tomorrow. And this is not contrary to the character of the intellect, since such understanding, although something individual, is nonetheless an immaterial act, as I have said before about the intellect.[46] And so the intellect understands its understanding, which is an individual act that has taken place in the past or is taking place in the present or will take place in the future, just as the intellect, although an individual intellect, understands itself.

Therefore, the nature of memory as concerning things of the past is preserved in the intellect insofar as the intellect understands that it has previously understood, but not insofar as the intellect understands something past as being here and now in the intellect.

Reply to Obj. 3. Intelligible forms are sometimes only potential in the intellect, and then we say that the intellect is potential. And intelligible forms are sometimes in the intellect by the final completion of the act of the intellect, and then the intellect actually understands. Intelligible forms are sometimes in a mode in between potentiality and actuality, and then we say that the intellect is habitual. And the intellect in this way preserves forms even when it is not actually understanding.

Eighth Article

Is Reason a Different Power from the Intellect?

I proceed in this way to the eighth article: it seems that reason is a different power from the intellect.

Obj. 1. The work *De spiritu et anima* says: "When we wish to climb from lower things to higher things, the external senses assist us first, then imagination, then reason, then the intellect."[47] Therefore, reason is a different power from the intellect, just as imagination is a different power from reason.

Obj. 2. Boethius says in his work *On the Consolation of Philosophy* that the intellect is related to reason as eternity is related to time.[48] But it does not belong to the same power to be in eternity and to be in time.

Therefore, reason and the intellect are not the same power.

Obj. 3. Human beings share with angels in the power of the intellect, and with irrational animals in sense powers. But reason, which belongs to human beings and is the reason why we call them rational animals, is a different power from the senses. Therefore, by like argument, reason is a different power from the intellect, which in the proper sense belongs to angels, and so we also call angels intellectual.

On the contrary, Augustine says in his *super Genesim* that "that whereby human beings excel irrational animals, is reason or mind or the ability to understand, or whatever we may more appropriately call it by whatever other word."[49] Therefore, reason and the intellect and mind are one and the same power.

I answer that reason and the intellect in human beings cannot be different powers. And we clearly recognize this if we happen to consider their respective acts. For understanding consists of apprehending intelligible truth in an unqualified way. But reasoning consists of proceeding from one understood thing to another, in order to know intelligible truth. And so angels, who by the mode of their nature perfectly possess knowledge of intelligible truth, have no need to progress from one understood thing to another; rather, they apprehend the truth about things in an unqualified way and without argument, as Denis says in his *De divinis nominibus.*[50] But human beings come to know intelligible truth by progressing from one understood thing to another, as Denis says in the same place, and so we call human beings rational. Therefore, it is evident that reasoning is related to understanding as being moved is related to being at rest, or as acquiring is related to possessing, and one of these belongs to something complete, and the other to something incomplete.

And so, since movement always proceeds from something immoveable and ends in something at rest, human reasoning progresses by way of inquiry and discovery from certain things understood in an unqualified way, that is, from first principles. And also, human reasoning in the course of judgment returns by analysis to the first principles, and it considers the things discovered in relation to them.

Moreover, it is evident that, even in the case of things of nature, we do not trace being at rest and being moved to different powers; rather, we trace being at rest and being moved to one and the same power, since the same nature causes something to be moved toward a place and to be at rest in that place. Therefore, much more do we understand and reason by the same power. And so it is clear that reason and intellect in human beings are the same power.

Reply to Obj. 1. That enumeration is by reason of the rank of the acts, not by reason of different powers. But the cited work does not have great authority.[51]

Reply to Obj. 2. The response is clear from what I have said.[52] For eternity is related to time as something immoveable is to something moveable. And so Boethius compared the intellect to eternity, and reason to time.

Reply to Obj. 3. Other animals are so far inferior to human beings that they cannot arrive at knowing the truth that reason seeks. And human beings arrive at knowing the intelligible truth that angels know, but human beings arrive at such truth imperfectly. And so the angels' power of knowing is not of a different kind than reason's power of knowing, but angels' power of knowing is related to reason's power of knowing as something perfect to something imperfect.

Twelfth Article

Is Synderesis[53] a Special Intellectual Power Distinct from the Others?

I proceed in this way to the twelfth article: it seems that *synderesis* is a special intellectual power distinct from the others.

Obj. 1. Things that fall within one and the same class seem to belong to one and the same genus. But a gloss of Jerome on Ezechiel distinguishes *synderesis* from the irascible and the concupiscible and the rational, which are particular powers.[54] Therefore, *synderesis* is a particular power.

Obj. 2. Opposites belong to one and the same genus. But *synderesis* and sensuality seem to be opposites, since *synderesis* always tends toward something good, and sensuality always tends toward something evil. (And it is by reason of the latter tendency that the serpent symbolizes sensuality, as Augustine makes clear in his *De Trinitate.*[55]) Therefore, it seems that *synderesis*, just like sensuality, is a power.

Obj. 3. Augustine says in his *De libero arbitrio* that there are in the natural power of judgment certain "rules and sources of virtue that are both true and invariable,"[56] and we call these rules and sources of virtue *synderesis.* Therefore, since the invariable rules by means of which we judge belong to reason regarding its higher part, as Augustine says in his *De Trinitate*,[57] it seems that *synderesis* is the same as reason. And so *synderesis* is a particular power.

On the contrary, "Powers of reason are related to opposites," according to the Philosopher.[58] But *synderesis* is not related to opposites; rather, *synderesis* tends only to what is good. Therefore, *synderesis* is not a power. For if *synderesis* were to be a power, it would need to be a power of reason, since it is not found in irrational animals.

I answer that *synderesis* is a characteristic disposition rather than a power, notwithstanding the fact that certain thinkers held *synderesis* to be a power higher than reason, and other thinkers said that *synderesis* is reason itself, not as reason but as nature.

And to prove this, we need to consider that, as I have said before,[59] human reasoning, since it is a certain movement, progresses from an understanding of some things (namely, things known by nature without inquiry by reason) as from an unmovable source. And human reasoning also terminates in understanding, inasmuch as it is by naturally self-evident principles that we judge about the things that we discover by reasoning. Moreover, it is evident that practical reason reasons about practical things in the same way that theoretical reason reasons about theoretical things. Therefore, as nature needs to implant in us the principles about theoretical things, so also does nature need to implant in us the principles about practical things.

But the first principles about theoretical things, principles implanted in us by nature, do not belong to any special power but to a special characteristic disposition, which we call "the understanding of principles," as the *Ethics* makes clear.[60] And so the principles about practical things, principles implanted in us by nature, also do not belong to a special power but to a special characteristic disposition from nature, which disposition we call *synderesis*. And so we also say that *synderesis* incites to good and complains about evil, since it is by first principles that we progress to discovery and judge about the things that we have discovered. Therefore, it is clear that *synderesis* is not a power but a characteristic disposition from nature.

Reply to Obj. 1. We note Jerome's classification with respect to different acts, not different powers. And different acts can belong to one and the same power.

Reply to Obj. 2. Similarly, we note the opposition between sensuality and *synderesis* by the opposition of acts, not the opposition of different species belonging to a single genus.

Reply to Obj. 3. Such invariable considerations are the first principles about practical things, about which principles there can be no error, and we attribute such considerations to reason as power, and to *synderesis* as characteristic disposition. And so also do we judge by nature by both, namely, by reason and *synderesis*.

Thirteenth Article

Is Conscience a Power?

I proceed in this way to the thirteenth article: it seems that conscience is a power.

Obj. 1. Origen says that conscience is "the correcting spirit and companion teacher of the soul, by which the soul is dissociated from evil things and clings to good things."[61] But "the spirit" in the soul designates a power: either the very power of the mind (according to the words of the Letter to the Ephesians, "Be renewed in the spirit of your minds"[62]) or the very power of imagination (which is also why we call the sight of imagination "spiritual," as Augustine makes clear in his *Super Genesim*[63]). Therefore, conscience is a power.

Obj. 2. Only powers of the soul are subjects of sin. But conscience is a subject of sin, since the Letter to Titus says of certain individuals that "their minds and consciences are defiled."[64] Therefore, it seems that conscience is a power.

Obj. 3. Conscience needs to be either an act or a characteristic disposition or a power. But conscience is not an act, since conscience would thereby not always abide in human beings. Nor is conscience a characteristic disposition, for conscience would thereby be many things rather than one thing, since many cognitive characteristic dispositions guide us in practical things. Therefore, conscience is a power.

On the contrary, conscience can be laid aside, but a power cannot be. Therefore, conscience is not a power.

I answer that conscience, properly speaking, is an act, not a power. And this is evident both from the meaning of the word and from the things that we in our ordinary way of speaking attribute to conscience. For conscience, according to the proper meaning of the word, implies a relation of knowledge to something, since we define "con-science" as "knowledge with something else." But acts connect knowledge to things. And so it is clear from this meaning of the word that conscience is an act.

And the same conclusion is evident from the things that we attribute to conscience. For we say that conscience bears witness, binds or incites, and also accuses or disquiets or reproves. And all these things result from connecting some knowledge of ours to what we do. And this connection arises in three ways. In one way as we recognize that we have done or not done something, as the Book of Ecclesiastes says: "Your conscience knows" that you have "very often" spoken evil "of others."[65] And we accordingly say that conscience bears witness. In the second way, we connect our knowledge to something as we by our conscience judge that we should or should not do something. And we accordingly say that conscience incites or binds. In the third way, we connect our knowledge to something as we by our conscience judge that we have or have not done some deed worthily. And we accordingly say that conscience excuses or accuses or disquiets. But all three of these ways clearly result from the actual connection of knowledge to what we do. And so, properly speaking, conscience designates an act.

Nevertheless, because characteristic dispositions are the sources of acts, we sometimes apply the word "conscience" to the initial characteristic disposition from nature, namely, *synderesis*. For example, Jerome in a gloss on Ezechiel calls conscience *synderesis*, and Basil calls it "the natural power of judgment,"[66] and Damascene calls it "the law of our intellect."[67] For we customarily designate causes and effects by one another.

Reply to Obj. 1. Because conscience is an utterance of the mind, we call conscience a spirit insofar as we equate spirit and mind.

Reply to Obj. 2. We do not say that there is defilement in conscience as in a subject, but we say that there is defilement in conscience as something known is in knowledge, namely, inasmuch as one knows that one is defiled.

Reply to Obj. 3. Although acts in themselves do not always abide, they nonetheless abide in their causes, which are powers and characteristic dispositions. But all the characteristic dispositions that shape conscience, however many, nonetheless have their efficacy from one that is primary, namely, the characteristic disposition of first principles, which we call *synderesis*. And so we sometimes in a special way call this characteristic disposition conscience, as I have said before.[68]

Notes

1. *De Trinitate* IX, 2. PL 42:962.

2. Aristotle, *De anima* II, 3. 414a29–32.

3. *De Trinitate* X, 11. PL 42:983.

4. *Homiliarum in Evangelia* II, *homilia* 29. PL 76:1214.

5. Cf. Q. 54, A. 3, Obj. 1.

6. See n. 2, supra.

7. Q. 54, A. 3. Q. 77, A. 1.

8. Aristotle, *De anima* I, 4. 408b18–31.

9. *De Trinitate* IX, 2. PL 42:962. Also: XIV, 16. PL 42:1053.

10. *De anima* III, 9. 432b3–7.

11. Q. 75, A. 6.

12. Aristotle, *De anima* III, 5. 430a23–25.

13. *Super Genesim ad litteram* XII, 16. PL 34:467.

14. *De anima* III, 5. 430a17–19.

15. *De anima* III, 4. 429b22–26.

16. Q. 78, A. 1.

17. Q. 58, A. 1.

18. *De anima* III, 4. 429b29–430a2.

19. Aristotle, *Ethics* I, 13. 1102b25–1103a3. Cf. Q. 81, A. 3.

20. Cf. Q. 78, A. 4.

21. *De anima* III, 4. 429a13–18.

22. *De anima* III, 5. 430a10–17.

23. Q. 79, A. 4.

24. *Timaeus* 18. 49–52.

25. *Metaphysics* II, 4. 999a24–b20.

26. Averroës, *In libros De anima* II, comm. 67.

27. *De anima* III, 5. 430a10–17.

28. Jn. 1:7.

29. *De anima* III, 5. 430a19–22.

30. *De anima* III, 5. 430a10–17.

31. Ibid.

32. Avicenna, *De anima*, part 5, chap. 5. Averroës *In libros De anima* III, comm. 18.

33. Q. 76, A. 1.

34. *De anima* III, 5. 430a10–17.

35. *In libros De anima* III, 32. Cf. Plato, *Republic* VI, 19. 508.

36. Q. 90, A. 3. I–II, Q. 3, A. 7.

37. Ps. 4:6.

38. In the body of the article.

39. *De anima* III, 5. 430a19–22.

40. *De Trinitate* XII, 2, 3, 8. PL 42:999, 1005.

41. *De Trinitate* XII, 2, PL 42:999.

42. *De Trinitate* X, 11. PL 42:983.

43. *De anima*, part 5, chap. 6.

44. *De anima* III, 4. 429b5–10.

45. *De anima* III, 4. 429a27–29.

46. Q. 76, A. 1.

47. Anonymous, *De spiritu et anima* 11. PL 40:786.

48. *On the Consolation of Philosophy* IV, 6 (prose). PL 63:817.

49. *Super Genesim ad litteram* III, 20. PL 34:292.

50. *De divinis nominibus* 7. PG 3:868.

51. The work is by an anonymous author, probably Alcher of Clairvaux.

52. In the body of the article.

53. See Glossary, s.v. "*Synderesis.*"

54. *In Ezechielem* I, 1 (on 1:6). PL 25:22. On the irascible, concupiscible, and rational appetites, see Glossary, s.v. "Appetite," "Concupiscible," and "Irascible."

55. *De Trinitate* XII, 12, 13. PL 42:1007, 1009.

56. *De libero arbitrio* II, 10. PL 32:1256.

57. *De Trinitate* XII, 2. PL 42:999.

58. *Metaphysics* VIII, 2. 1046b4–7.

59. Q. 79, A. 8.

60. Aristotle, *Ethics* VI, 6. 1140b31–1141a8.

61. *In Epistolam ad Romanos* II, 9 (on 2:15). PG 14:893.

62. Eph. 4:23.

63. *Super Genesim ad litteram* XII, 7, 24. PL 34:459, 475.

64. Tit. 1:15.

65. Eccl. 7:23.

66. *Homiliae in principium Proverborum, homilia* 12. PG 31:405.

67. *De fide orthodoxa* IV, 22. PG 94:1200.

68. In the body of the article.

ST I
Question 80
On the Appetitive Powers in General

[This question is divided into two articles, both of which are included here.]

First Article

Are Appetites Special Powers of the Soul?

I proceed in this way to the first article: it seems that appetites are not special powers of the soul.

Obj. 1. We should not ascribe any special power of the soul to what is common to living and nonliving things. But seeking is common to living and nonliving things, since good is "what all things seek," as the *Ethics* says.[1] Therefore, appetites are not special powers of the soul.

Obj. 2. We distinguish powers by their objects. But what we know, and what we seek, are the same thing. Therefore, there need not be distinct appetitive powers besides cognitive powers.

Obj. 3. We do not contradistinguish the common from the proper. But every power of the soul seeks a particular kind of desirable thing, namely, its own proper object. Therefore, with respect to such generally desirable objects, we do not need to understand any so-called appetitive powers distinct from other powers.

On the contrary, the Philosopher in the *De anima* distinguishes appetitive powers from other powers.[2] And Damascene in his work distinguishes appetitive powers from cognitive powers.[3]

I answer that we need to posit certain appetitive powers of the soul. And for evidence of this, we should consider that some tendency results from every form; for example, fire's form gives fire the tendency to rise and to produce its like. And we find that the forms in things that share in knowledge, exist in a higher way than do the forms in things that lack knowledge. For we find in things that lack knowledge only forms that determine each to its characteristic way of existing, that is, to the way of existing that also belongs to each as something from nature. Therefore, natural tendencies, which we call natural appetites, result from such forms of nature. But in things that possess knowledge, forms from nature thus determine each to its characteristic way of existing, but each nonetheless receives the forms of other things. For example, the senses take in the forms of every perceptible thing, and the intellect takes in the forms of every intelligible thing, so that the human soul by means of the senses and the intellect is somehow everything. And in this respect, things possessing knowledge somehow approximate likeness to God, "in whom everything pre-exists," as Denis says.[4]

Therefore, as the forms in things possessing knowledge exist in a way superior to the way of the forms of nature, so things possessing knowledge need to have tendencies superior to the way of natural tendencies, tendencies that we call natural appetites. And these superior tendencies belong to the appetitive powers of the soul, powers by which animals can seek the things they perceive, in addition to the things toward which the forms of nature incline them. Therefore, we need to posit some appetitive powers of the soul.

Reply to Obj. 1. We find that things possessing knowledge have appetites superior to the general way in which we find all things have appetites, as I have said.[5] And so other powers of the soul need to be constituted for this purpose.

Reply to Obj. 2. What is known, and what is sought, are the same for the subject that knows and seeks, but the two things differ conceptually. For we know something as a perceptible or intelligible being, but we seek it as suitable or good. And diversity of aspects and not diversity of subject matter is required for diversity of powers.

Reply to Obj. 3. Each power of the soul is a certain form of nature, and has a natural tendency toward something. And so each power by an appetite from nature seeks the object that befits it. And above such appetites are animal appetites, which result from knowledge, appetites whereby things are sought because they unconditionally befit animals, not because they befit acts of this or that power, as, for example, sight befits the power of sight, and hearing befits the power of hearing.

Second Article

Are Sense and Intellectual Appetites Different Powers?

I proceed in this way to the second article: it seems that sense and intellectual appetites are not different powers.

Obj. 1. Accidental differences do not differentiate powers, as I have said before.[6] But it is by accident that the senses or the intellect apprehend something desirable. Therefore, sense and intellectual appetites are not different powers.

Obj. 2. Universals are the object of intellectual knowledge, and we thereby distinguish intellectual knowledge from sense knowledge, whose object is singular. But there is no room for this distinction on the part of appetitive powers, for the object of every appetite seems to be something singular, since appetites are movements by the soul toward things, which are singular. Therefore, we ought not distinguish the intellectual appetite from sense appetites.

Obj. 3. As appetitive powers, being lower powers, are subordinate to cognitive powers, so also are powers to cause motion. But there is in human beings no power to cause motion as a consequence of their intellect different from such powers in other animals as a consequence of the animals' senses. Therefore, by like reasoning, neither do human beings have any other appetitive power than that of the senses.

On the contrary, the Philosopher in the *De anima* distinguishes two kinds of appetite[7] and says that the higher appetite moves the lower.[8]

I answer that we need to affirm that the intellectual appetite is a different power from the sense appetites. For appetitive powers are passive powers that are constituted to be moved by known things, and so desirable things when known cause motion without themselves being moved, while appetites cause motion with themselves being moved, as the *De anima*[9] and the *Metaphysics*[10] say. But we distinguish passive and moveable things by distinguishing the things that are active and cause motion, since what causes motion needs to be proportioned to what is moveable, and what is active to what is passive. And passive powers themselves derive their characteristic nature from the relation they have to what acts on them. Therefore, since things understood by the intellect and things perceived by the senses belong to different genera, it follows that the intellectual appetite is a different power from the sense appetites.

Reply to Obj. 1. It is not by accident that the senses or the intellect apprehends desirable things, but it intrinsically belongs to desirable things to be apprehended, since desirable things do not move appetites except insofar as desirable things are apprehended. And so differences in things apprehended are intrinsically differences in things desirable.

And so we distinguish appetitive powers by the different things apprehended, as the powers' characteristic objects.

Reply to Obj. 2. The intellectual appetite, although borne toward things that exist as singular things outside the soul, is nonetheless borne toward those things regarding a universal aspect, as when the intellectual appetite seeks something because it is good. And so the Philosopher in his *Rhetoric* says that the object of hatred can be something universal, as, for example, "we hold in hatred every kind of robber."[11]

Similarly, the intellectual appetite can also seek immaterial goods (e.g., knowledge, virtue, and the like), and the senses do not apprehend such goods.

Reply to Obj. 3. As the *De anima* says, universal opinions move us only by means of particular opinions.[12] And similarly, the higher appetite moves us by means of lower appetites. And so there are not different powers to cause motion as a consequence of the intellect and the senses.

Notes

1. Aristotle, *Ethics* I, 1. 1094a2–3.

2. *De anima* II, 3. 414a29–32.

3. *De fide orthodoxa* II, 22. PG 94:941.

4. *De divinis nominibus* 5. PG 3:817.

5. In the body of the article.

6. Q. 77, A. 3.

7. *De anima* III, 9, 10. 432b3–7, 433b5–10.

8. *De anima* III, 11. 434a12–15.

9. Aristotle, *De anima* III, 10. 433a13–26.

10. Aristotle, *Metaphysics* XI, 7. 1072a26–30.

11. *Rhetoric* II, 4. 1382a5–7.

12. Aristotle, *De anima* III, 11. 434a16–21.

ST I
Question 81
On Sensuality

[This question is divided into three articles, all of which are included here.]

First Article

Is Sensuality only Appetitive?

I proceed in this way to the first article: it seems that sensuality is both appetitive and cognitive.

Obj. 1. Augustine says in his *De Trinitate* that "sensual movements of the soul, which are directed toward the bodily senses, are common to us and beasts."[1] But bodily senses are included in cognitive powers. Therefore, sensuality is a cognitive power.

Obj. 2. Things that fall within one class seem to belong to one and the same genus. But Augustine in his *De Trinitate* distinguishes sensuality from higher and lower reason,[2] and sensuality and reason belong to knowledge. Therefore, sensuality is also a cognitive power.

Obj. 3. In human temptations, sensuality stands for the serpent. But the serpent in the temptation of our first parents presented himself as one announcing and proposing sin, and such functions belong to a cognitive power. Therefore, sensuality is a cognitive power.

On the contrary, we define sensuality as "the appetite for things belonging to the body."[3]

I answer that we seem to derive the word "sensuality" from sensual movement (about which Augustine speaks in his *De Trinitate*[4]), just as we take the name of powers from their acts; for example, the power of sight from the act of seeing. But sensual movements are appetites resulting from sense powers. For we do not call acts of cognitive powers movements in as strict a sense as we call appetitive activities movements, since the activity of cognitive powers is completed in known things being in a knower, while the activity of appetitive powers is completed in desires tending toward desirable things. And so we liken the activity of cognitive powers to rest, while we rather liken the activity of appetitive powers to movement. And so we understand by sensual movements the activity of appetitive powers. And so sensuality is the name we give sense appetites.

Reply to Obj. 1. When Augustine says that sensual movements of the soul are directed to the bodily senses, he does not give us to understand that the bodily senses are included in sensuality, but rather that movements of sensuality are certain inclinations to the bodily senses, namely, inclinations while we are desiring what the bodily senses are perceiving. And so the bodily senses belong to sensuality as preambles, as it were.

Reply to Obj. 2. Augustine distinguishes sensuality from higher and lower reason inasmuch as sensuality and reason participate in acts of movement. For cognitive powers, to which higher and lower reason belong, as well as appetitive powers, to which sensuality belongs, cause motion.

Reply to Obj. 3. The serpent not only manifested and proposed sin but also incited our first parents to commit sin. And in this respect, the serpent signifies sensuality.

Second Article

Do We Distinguish Sense Appetites into Distinct Irascible and Concupisciple Powers?

I proceed in this way to the second article: it seems that we do not distinguish sense appetites into distinct irascible and concupiscible powers.

Obj. 1. Contraries of the same contrariety are objects of the same power of the soul; white and black, for example, are objects of the same power of sight, as the *De anima* says.[5] But suitable and harmful are contraries. Therefore, since the suitable is the object of the concupiscible power, and the harmful is the object of the irascible power, it seems that the same power of the soul is irascible and concupiscible.

Obj. 2. Only sensibly agreeable things are the objects of sense appetites. But sensibly agreeable things are the object of the concupiscible appetite. Therefore, there is no sense appetite other than the concupiscible.

Obj. 3. Hatred is in the irascible power, for Jerome says in his commentary on the Gospel of Matthew: "Let us in our irascible power have hatred of vice."[6] But hatred, since it is contrary to love, is in the concupiscible power. Therefore, the same power is concupiscible and irascible.

On the contrary, Gregory of Nyssa[7] and Damascene[8] posit two powers, the irascible and the concupiscible, as parts of sense appetite.

I answer that sense appetite is one generic power, which we call sensuality, but is divided into two specific powers, namely, the irascible and the concupiscible, which are kinds of appetitive power. And for evidence of this, we need to consider that the destructible things of nature need not only to have inclinations to acquire suitable things and to flee from harmful things but also to resist destructive and contrary things that are hindrances to suitable things and impose harms. For example, fire has tendencies from nature not only to retreat from lower places, which are unsuitable for it, and to strive for higher places, which are suitable for it, but also to resist destructive and impeding things.

Therefore, because sense appetites are tendencies resulting from sense perceptions, just as natural appetites are tendencies resulting from the forms of nature, there need to be two appetitive powers in the sensory part of the soul. One power is the appetitive power whereby the soul unconditionally tends to gain sensibly agreeable things and to flee from harmful things, and we call this power the concupiscible power. And the second power is the appetitive power whereby animals resist hostile forces that attack suitable things, and that inflict harms, and we call this power the irascible power. And so we say that the object of the irascible power is the difficult, namely, because the power strives to conquer and overcome contrary things.

And we do not trace these two tendencies to one source, since the soul, contrary to the tendency of the concupiscible power, sometimes imposes itself on harsh things, as the soul by the tendency of its irascible power fights against contrary things. And so also emotions of the irascible power seem to be repugnant to emotions of the concupiscible power; for example, inflamed desire in most cases diminishes anger, and inflamed anger in most cases diminishes desire. It is also clear from this that the irascible power is, as it were, the champion and defender of the concupiscible power when the irascible power rises up against hindrances to the suitable things that the concupiscible power seeks, and presses against the harmful things from which the concupiscible power shrinks. And for this reason, all the emotions of the irascible power arise from the emotions of the concupiscible power and are terminated in them; for example, anger arises on the occasion of melancholy, and ends in joy when it brings deliverance. Also for this reason, fights between animals are about desirable things, namely, food and things related to sex, as the *Historia animalium* says.[9]

Reply to Obj. 1. Both the suitable and the unsuitable are objects of the concupiscible power. But the object of the irascible power is to resist the unsuitable things that attack.

Reply to Obj. 2. As there is in cognitive powers in the sensory part of the soul an estimative power, namely, a power that perceives things that the senses do not alter, as I have said before,[10] so also there is in sense appetites a power that seeks suitable things, not as the things are pleasurable to the senses, but as the things are useful to an animal for its defense. And the latter power is the irascible power.

Reply to Obj. 3. Hatred, absolutely speaking, belongs to the concupiscible power, but hatred can belong to the irascible power by reason of the struggle that arises from hatred.

Third Article

Do the Irascible and Concupiscible Powers Obey Reason?

I proceed in this way to the third article: it seems that the irascible and concupiscible powers do not obey reason.

Obj. 1. The irascible and concupiscible powers are part of sensuality. But sensuality does not obey reason, and so the serpent signifies sensuality, as Augustine says in his *De Trinitate.*[11] Therefore, the irascible and concupiscible powers do not obey reason.

Obj. 2. Nothing resists what it obeys. But the irascible and concupiscible powers resist reason, as the Apostle says in his Letter to the Romans: "I see another law in my members, a law that resists the law of my mind."[12] Therefore, the irascible and concupiscible powers do not obey reason.

Obj. 3. As appetitive power is inferior to the rational part of the soul, so also are sense powers. But the sensory part of the soul does not obey reason; for example, we do not hear or see whenever we wish to do so. Therefore, in like manner, neither do the powers of sense appetite, namely, the irascible and concupiscible powers, obey reason.

On the contrary, Damascene says that "the parts of the soul obedient and subject to reason are divided into desire and anger."[13]

I answer that the irascible and concupiscible powers in two ways obey the superior part of the soul, in which are intellect or reason, and will: in one way, indeed, regarding reason, and in the second way regarding will.

The irascible and concupiscible powers indeed obey reason regarding their very acts. And this is because sense appetite in other animals is indeed constituted to be moved by the estimative power; for example, sheep appraise wolves as enemies and fear them. But human beings have in place of the estimative power the cogitative power, as I have said before,[14] and some call the latter power "particular reason, since it compares individual imports. And so sense appetite in human beings is constituted to be moved by particular reason. But particular reason itself is constituted to be moved and directed by universal reason, and that is why we in syllogisms draw conclusions about particular things from universal propositions. And so it is clear that universal reason governs sense appetite, which we distinguish by the concupiscible and irascible powers, and that this appetite obeys universal reason.

And because drawing universal principles to particular conclusions is not the work of the simple intellect but of the power of reason, so we say that the irascible and concupiscible powers obey reason rather than the intellect.

Each one of us can experience this in ourselves; for example, anger or fear or some such thing is lessened (or also incited) by applying certain universal considerations.

Sense appetite is also subject to the will regarding execution, which is accomplished by powers causing movement. For in other animals, movements result immediately from appetites of the concupiscible and irascible powers, since nonhuman animals do not have any higher contrary appetite; for example, sheep, fearing wolves, immediately flee. But human beings are not immediately moved by appetites of the irascible and concupiscible powers; rather, they await a command of the will, that is, the higher appetite. For in all interrelated powers causing movement, the second cause moves only by the power of the first, and so lower appetites do not suffice to cause movement unless the higher appetite consents. And the Philosopher in the *De anima* says that "the higher appetite moves lower appetites just as higher spheres move lower ones."[15]

Therefore, the irascible and concupiscible are subject to reason in this way.

Reply to Obj. 1. The serpent signifies sensuality regarding what is proper to sensuality as sensory. But the irascible and concupiscible powers rather designate sense appetite regarding the acts to which reason brings the powers, as I have said.[16]

Reply to Obj. 2. As the Philosopher says in the *Politics*, "We should indeed consider carefully both the despotic and political principles of governance in animals; for example, the soul indeed rules the body by a despotic principle of governance, but the intellect rules appetites by a political and kingly principle of governance."[17] For we call despotic the principle of governance whereby one person rules slaves lacking the capacity in anything to resist the orders of the one who commands, since slaves possess nothing of their own. But we call political and kingly the principle of governance whereby one person rules free persons subject to the governance of the ruler but possessing things of their own whereby they can withstand the orders of the one who commands.

Therefore, we say that the soul rules the body by a despotic principle of governance, since in nothing can members of the body resist commands of the soul, and hands and feet, and every member of the body constituted to be moved by voluntary movement, are immediately moved at the soul's desire. But we say that the intellect, or reason, rules the irascible and concupiscible powers by a political principle of governance, since sense appetites have things of their own whereby they can withstand the orders of reason. For sense appetites are constituted to be moved not only by the estimative power in the case of other animals, and the cogitative power in the case of human beings, which universal reason directs, but also by the power of imagination and the senses. And so we experience that the irascible and concupiscible powers resist reason, in that we perceive or imagine things to be pleasant that reason forbids, or things to be harsh that reason commands. And so the irascible and concupiscible powers are not excluded from obeying reason because they resist reason in some things.

Reply to Obj. 3. The external senses need for their acts external, perceptible things, which alter the senses, and whose presence is not in the power of reason. But internal powers, both appetitive and cognitive, do not need external things. And so internal powers are subject to the commands of reason, which can not only incite or lessen emotions of appetitive power but also fashion sense images of the power of imagination.

Notes

1. *De Trinitate* XII, 12. PL 42:1007.
2. Ibid.
3. Peter Lombard, *Sentences* II, dist. 24, 6. PL192:702.
4. *De Trinitate* XII, 12, 13. PL 42:1007, 1009.
5. Aristotle, *De anima* II, 11. 422b23–27.
6. *In Evangelium Mattaei* II, 13 (on 13:33). PL 26:94.
7. Nemesius, *De natura hominis* 16, 17. PG 40:672, 676. St. Thomas erroneously attributes this work to Gregory of Nyssa.
8. *De fide orthodoxa* II, 12. PG 94:928.
9. Aristotle, *Historia animalium* VIII, 1. 589a2–5.
10. Q. 78, A. 2.
11. *De Trinitate* XII, 12, 13. PL 42:1007, 1009.
12. Rom. 7:23.
13. *De fide orthodoxa* II, 12. PG 94:928.
14. Q. 78, A. 4.
15. *De anima* III, 11. 434a12–15.
16. In the body of the article.
17. *Politics* I, 2. 1254.

ST I
Question 82
On the Will

[This question is divided into five articles, four of which are included here.]

First Article

Does the Will Desire Anything Necessarily?

I proceed in this way to the first article: it seems that the will desires nothing necessarily.

Obj. 1. Augustine says in *The City of God* that nothing necessary is voluntary.[1] But everything desired by the will is voluntary. Therefore, nothing desired by the will is desired necessarily.

Obj. 2. According to the Philosopher, rational powers are disposed toward opposites.[2] But the will is a rational power, since the will is part of the power of reason, as the *De anima* says.[3] Therefore, the will is disposed toward opposites. Therefore, the will is not determined to anything necessarily.

Obj. 3. We are the masters of our actions by means of our will. But we are not masters of what exists necessarily. Therefore, no action of the will can be of necessity.

On the contrary, Augustine says in his *De Trinitate* that "all human beings desire happiness with the same desire."[4] But if this statement were to be contingent rather than necessary, it would fail to be true, at least in quite a few cases. Therefore, the will wills something necessarily.

I answer that we speak about necessity in many ways. For the necessary is what cannot not be. And this befits things in one way by an internal source, whether material, as, for example, when we say that everything composed of contrary things necessarily passes away, or formal, as, for example, when we say that triangles necessarily have three angles equal to two right angles. And this is a natural and absolute necessity.

In another way, it belongs to something to be necessary by reason of an external source, either an end or an efficient cause. Something is indeed necessary by reason of an end, as when one cannot attain, or readily attain, an end without it; for example, we say that food is necessary for life, or a horse for a journey. And we call this the necessity of an end, and also sometimes utility. And it belongs to something to be necessary by reason of an efficient cause, as when a cause so compels someone that the person cannot do the contrary. And we call this the necessity of coercion.

Therefore, this necessity of coercion is altogether repugnant to the will. For we say that such is violent, that is, contrary to the inclination of something. And the very movement of the will is an inclination toward something. And so, as we call something natural because it is by an inclination of nature, so we call something voluntary because it is by an inclination of the will. Therefore, as it is impossible that something be simultaneously violent and natural, so it is impossible that something be, in an absolute sense, coerced or violent, and voluntary.

But the necessity of an end is not repugnant to the will when the will can arrive at its end in only one way; for example, from the will to cross a sea, there arises in the will the necessity to choose a ship.

In like manner also, neither is natural necessity repugnant to the will. Rather, indeed, just as the intellect necessarily adheres to first principles, so the will necessarily adheres to our last end, which is happiness, since the end is posited in practical matters as the principles are posited in theoretical matters, as the *Physics* says.[5] For what by nature and immutably belongs to things needs to be the foundation and source of everything else belonging to them, since the nature of things is first in each of them, and every movement proceeds from something immutable.

Reply to Obj. 1. We should understand the words of Augustine about the necessary to refer to the necessity of coercion. But natural necessity "does not take away the will's freedom," as he himself says in the same work.[6]

Reply to Obj. 2. The will, insofar as it wills something by nature, corresponds to the intellect understanding the principles from nature rather than to reason, which is disposed toward contrary things. And so, in this respect, the will is a power of the intellect rather than a power of reason.

Reply to Obj. 3. We are masters of our actions insofar as we can choose this or that. But choice does not concern the end but "the means to the end," as the *Ethics* says.[7] And so the appetite for the last end does not concern the things of which we are the masters.

Second Article

Does the Will Will Necessarily Everything that It Wills?

I proceed in this way to the second article: it seems that the will wills necessarily everything that it wills.

Obj. 1. Denis says in his *De divinis nominibus* that "evil is beyond the power of the will."[8] Therefore, the will tends necessarily toward the good set before it.

Obj. 2. We relate the object of the will to the will itself as we relate causes of movement to moveable objects. But the movement of moveable objects results necessarily from causes of movement. Therefore, it seems that the object of the will moves the will itself necessarily.

Obj. 3. As things perceived by the senses are the objects of sense appetites, so things understood by the intellect are the object of the intellectual appetite, which we call the will. But things perceived by the senses move sense appetites necessarily, for Augustine says in his *Super Genesim* that "animals are moved by the things they see."[9] Therefore, it seems that things understood by the intellect move the will necessarily.

On the contrary, Augustine says that "it is the will by which we sin and live rightly,"[10] and so the will is disposed toward contrary things. Therefore, the will does not will necessarily whatever it wills.

I answer that the will does not will necessarily whatever it wills. And for evidence of this, we need to consider that, as the intellect by nature and necessarily adheres to first principles, so the will by nature and necessarily adheres to our last end, as I have already said.[11] But there are some intelligible things with no necessary connection to first principles, for example, contingent propositions, whose negation implies no negation of first principles. And the intellect does not assent necessarily to such propositions. And there are some necessary propositions, propositions with a necessary connection to first principles, for example, demonstrable conclusions, whose negation implies negation of first principles. And the intellect assents necessarily to demonstrable conclusions when it knows by deductive demonstration the necessary connection of the conclusions to the principles, but does not assent necessarily before it knows by demonstration the necessity of such a connection.

It is also in like manner on the part of the will. For there are some particular goods that do not have a necessary connection to happiness, since one can be happy without them, and the will does not of necessity adhere to such goods. And there are some goods that have a necessary connection to happiness, namely, the goods whereby human beings adhere to God, in whom alone true happiness consists. But, nonetheless, the will does not adhere necessarily to God or the things of God before the certitude of the vision of God shows the necessity of such a connection. (But the will of those who see God by his essence of necessity adhere to him, just as we presently will necessarily to be happy.) Therefore, it is clear that the will does not will necessarily whatever it wills.

Reply to Obj. 1. The will can tend toward something only under the aspect of good. But because there are many kinds of good, the will is for this reason not determined necessarily to one of them.

Reply to Obj. 2. A cause of movement necessarily causes movement in a moveable object when the power of the cause is superior to the moveable object, so that the latter's whole potentiality is subject to the cause. But since the potentiality of the will regards the universal and complete good, the whole potentiality of the will is not subject to any particular good. And so no particular good moves the will necessarily.

Reply to Obj. 3. Sense powers do not compare different things, as reason does, but each sense power perceives only one particular thing. And so each sense power moves a sense appetite in a fixed way by that one thing. But reason compares several things, and so several things can, and not one thing by necessity does, move the intellectual appetite, namely, the will.

Third Article

Is the Will a Higher Power than the Intellect?

I proceed in this way to the third article: it seems that the will is a higher power than the intellect.

Obj. 1. Good and ends are the object of the will. But ends are the first and highest causes. Therefore, the will is the first and highest power.

Obj. 2. We find that things of nature progress from the imperfect to the perfect. And this is also apparent in the case of the soul's powers; for example, there is a progression from the senses to the intellect, which is more excellent than the senses. But there is a natural progression from acts of the intellect to the will. Therefore, the will is a more perfect and more excellent power than the intellect.

Obj. 3. Characteristic dispositions are proportioned to powers as perfections are proportioned to things perfectible. But the characteristic disposition whereby the will is perfected, namely, the virtue of charity, is more excellent than the characteristic dispositions whereby the intellect is perfected, for the First Letter to the Corinthians says: "If I should know all mysteries and have complete faith but not have charity, I am nothing."[12] Therefore, the will is a higher power than the intellect.

On the contrary, the Philosopher holds in the *Ethics* that the highest power of the soul is the intellect.[13]

I answer that we can in two ways consider the eminence of one thing over another: in one way, absolutely; in the second way, in some respect. And we consider something to be such absolutely as it is such in itself, while we consider something to be such in some respect as we call it such in relation to something else.

Therefore, if we consider the intellect and will as such, then we find the intellect more eminent. And this is evident by comparing their objects to one another. For the object of the intellect is simpler and more absolute than the object of the will, since the object of the intellect is the very nature of a desirable good, while the desirable good whose nature the intellect possesses, is the object of the will. But the simpler and more abstract something is, the more excellent and superior it is. And so the object of the intellect is superior to the object of the will. Therefore, since a power's own nature is in relation to its object, it follows that the intellect as such and absolutely is higher and more excellent than the will.

But we sometimes find the will to be higher than the intellect in some respect and in relation to something else, namely, because we find the object of the will is in something higher than the object of the intellect is. Such, for example, would be the case if I were to say that the power of hearing is more excellent than the power of sight in one respect, inasmuch as something to which sound belongs is more excellent than something to which color belongs, although color is more excellent and simpler than sound. For, as I have said before,[14] the action of the intellect consists in the nature of the thing understood being in the one who understands, while the act of the will is accomplished in the will being inclined to the very thing as it is in itself. And so the Philosopher says in the *Metaphysics* that "good and evil," which are the object of the will, "are in things"; "true and false," which are the object of the intellect, "are in the mind."[15] Therefore, when the thing in which there is good is more excellent than the soul itself, in which there is the understood nature, the will is superior to the intellect in relation to such a thing. But when the thing in which there is good is inferior to the soul, then the intellect is superior to the will, also in relation to such a thing. And so love of God is better than knowledge about him, while, conversely, knowledge of material things is better than love of them. Nonetheless, in an absolute sense, the intellect is more excellent than the will.

Reply to Obj. 1. We learn the nature of causes by relating one thing to another, and we discover in such relations that the nature of good is more important, but we predicate the true more absolutely, and the true signifies the nature of good itself. And so the good is also something true. But, conversely, the true itself is also some good, insofar as the intellect is a certain thing, and the true is the end of the intellect itself. And this end is more excellent than other ends; just so the intellect is more excellent than other powers.

Reply to Obj. 2. What is prior in coming to be and temporally is less perfect, since, in one and the same thing, potentiality temporally precedes actuality, and imperfection perfection. But what is prior in an absolute sense, and by the order of nature, is more perfect, since actuality is in this way prior to potentiality. And the intellect is in the latter way prior to the will, as a cause of movement is prior to a moveable object, and something active is prior to something passive, for it is the understood good that moves the will.

Reply to Obj. 3. The argument of this objection is valid about the will in relation to what is superior to the soul. For the virtue of charity is the virtue by which we love God.

Fourth Article

Does the Will Move the Intellect?

I proceed in this way to the fourth article: it seems that the will does not move the intellect.

Obj. 1. Causes of movement are more excellent, and prior to, the things they move, since causes of movement act, and "acting" is "more excellent than being acted upon," as Augustine says in his *Super Genesim*,[16] and the Philosopher says in the *De anima*.[17] But the intellect is prior to, and more excellent than, the will, as I have said before.[18] Therefore, the will does not move the intellect.

Obj. 2 Except perhaps by chance, moved things do not move the causes of their movement. But the intellect moves the will, since the desirable things understood by the intellect cause movement of the will without themselves being moved, and appetite causes movement with appetite itself being moved. Therefore, the will does not move the intellect.

Obj. 3. We can will only something understood. Therefore, if the will by willing to understand moves the intellect to understand, it will be necessary that another act of understanding also precede that act of willing, and that another act of willing precede that act of understanding, and so on endlessly. And such an infinite regress is impossible. Therefore, the will does not move the intellect.

On the contrary, Damascene says that "it is in our power to learn, or not to learn, any skill we desire."[19] But something is in our power by our will, and we learn skills by our intellect. Therefore, the will moves the intellect.

I answer that we say in two ways that things cause movement. In one way as an end, as we say that ends move efficient causes to act. And this is the way that the intellect moves the will, since understood goods are the object of the will and move the will as ends.

We say in a second way that things cause movement as efficient causes, as what causes change moves what is changed, and what pushes moves what is pushed. And this is the way that the will moves the intellect and every power of the soul, as Anselm says in his *De similitudinibus*.[20] And this is because, in all cases of ordered active powers, the power whose object is a general end moves the powers whose objects are particular ends. And this is evident both in the case of natural things and in the case of political matters. For the heavens, which act for the general preservation of things that can come to be and pass away, move all lower material substances, each one of which acts for the preservation of its own species or even the individual. Similarly, a king, who strives for the common good of his whole kingdom, by his rule moves the individuals in charge of local communities, those who lay out the business of governance for individual local communities. And the object of the will is the good and end in general. And every power is related to a characteristic good befitting itself; for example, the power of sight is related to perceiving color, the power of the intellect to knowing the true. And so the will as efficient cause moves all powers of the soul to their acts, aside from the natural powers of the vegetative part of the soul, which powers are not subject to our authority.

Reply to Obj. 1. We can consider the intellect in two ways: in one way as the intellect understands being and the true in general; in the second way as the intellect is a particular thing and a particular power having determined activity. And similarly, we can consider the will in two ways: in one way regarding the generality of its object, namely, as the will desires good in general; in the second way as the will is a particular fixed power having a determined activity.

Therefore, if we should compare the intellect and will regarding the nature of the generality of the objects of each, then the intellect is without qualification superior to, and more excellent than, the will, as I have said before.[21]

And if we should consider the intellect regarding the generality of its object, and the will as it is a particular fixed power, then the intellect is again superior and prior to the will, since the will itself and its acts and the object of the will itself are included in the notion of being and the true. And so the intellect understands the will and the will's acts and the object of the will itself, just as the intellect understands the other particular things that it understands (e.g., stone and wood) and are included in the general notion of being and the true.

But if we should consider the will regarding the general nature of its object (i.e., the good), and the intellect as it is a particular thing and a particular power, then both the intellect itself and its very acts of understanding and its object (i.e., the true), everyone of which is a particular good, are included as particular things in the general concept of the good. And the will in this way is higher than the intellect and can move the intellect itself.

Therefore, it is evident from these considerations why these powers by their activities include one another, since the intellect understands that the will wills, and the will wills that the intellect understand. And by like reasoning, the good in included in the true, inasmuch as the good is something true that is understood, and the true is included in the good, inasmuch as the true is a good that is desired.

Reply to Obj. 2. The intellect moves the will in a different way than the will moves the intellect, as I have said.[22]

Reply to Obj. 3. It is not necessary to regress endlessly; rather, the process starts in the intellect. For cognition needs to precede every movement of the will, whereas a movement of the will does not precede every cognition. But the source of deliberating and understanding is an intellectual source superior to our intellect (i.e., God), as Aristotle also says in the *Eudemian Ethics,*[23] and he thereby shows that there is no infinite regress.

Notes

1. *The City of God* V, 10. PL 41:152.
2. *Metaphysics* VIII, 2. 1046b4–7.
3. Aristotle, *De anima* III, 9. 432b4–7.
4. *De Trinitate* XIII, 4. PL 42:1018.
5. Aristotle, *Physics* II, 9. 200a15–34.
6. See n. 1, supra.
7. Aristotle, *Ethics* III, 2, 4. 1111b26–29, 1113a15.
8. *De divinis nominibus* 4. PG 3:732.
9. *Super Genesim ad litteram* IX, 14. PL 34:402.
10. *Retractationum* I, 9. PL 32:596.
11. Q. 82, A. 1.
12. 1 Cor. 13:2.
13. Aristotle, *Ethics* X, 7. 1177a12–17.
14. Q. 16, A. 1; Q. 27, A. 4.
15. *Metaphysics* V, 4. 1027b25–29.
16. *Super Genesim ad litteram* XII, 16. PL 34:467.
17. *De anima* III, 5. 430a17–19.
18. Q. 82, A. 3.
19. *De fide orthodoxa* II, 26. PG 94:960.
20. *De similitudinibus* 2. PL 159:605. Edmer of Canterbury is the actual author of the work.
21. Q. 82, A. 3.
22. In the body of the article.
23. *Eudemian Ethics* VII, 14. 1248a24–29.

[This question is divided into four articles, three of which are included here.]

First Article

Do Human Beings Have Free Choice?

I proceed in this way to the first article: it seems that human beings do not have free choice.

Obj. 1. All who have free choice, do what they will. But human beings do not do what they will, for the Letter to the Romans says: "I do not do the good that I will; rather, I do the evil that I detest."[1] Therefore, human beings do not have free choice.

Obj. 2. It belongs to whoever has free choice to will or not to will, to act or not to act. But such does not belong to human beings, for the Letter to the Romans says: "It," namely, willing, "does not belong to those who will, nor does it," namely, activity, "belong to those who are active."[2] Therefore, human beings do not have free choice.

Obj. 3. "To be free is to cause oneself to act," as the *Metaphysics* says.[3] Therefore, whatever is moved by something else is not free. But God moves the will, for the Book of Proverbs says: "The king's heart" is "in the hands" of God, and God directs "it" in whatever way "he wills."[4] And the Letter to the Philippians says: "God is the one who works in us our willing and accomplishing."[5] Therefore, human beings do not have free choice.

Obj. 4. All who have free choice are masters of their actions. But human beings are not masters of their actions, since, as Jeremiah says, "The path" of human beings "is not in their power, nor does it belong to them to direct their steps."[6] Therefore, human beings do not have free choice.

Obj. 5. The Philosopher says in the *Ethics*: "Each person seems to have an end in the way each person is constituted."[7] But it is not in our power to be any kind of thing; rather, this comes to us from nature. Therefore, it is natural to us that we pursue an end. Therefore, we do not by free choice pursue the end.

On the contrary, the Book of Sirach says: "God from the beginning constituted human beings and left them in the hands of their own counsel."[8] A gloss adds: "that is, in freedom of choice."[9]

I answer that human beings have free choice; otherwise, counsels, exhortations, commands, prohibitions, rewards, and punishments would be in vain. And for evidence of this, we should consider that some kinds of things act without judgment; for example, stones are moved downward, and all things lacking knowledge likewise act without judgment.

And other kinds of things, for example, irrational animals, act by reason of judgment but not free judgment. For example, sheep, when they see a wolf, judge by a natural but not free judgment that they should flee from the wolf, since they so judge by an instinct from nature, not by a comparison. And it is similar in the case of every judgment of irrational animals.

And human beings act by reason of judgment, since they by their cognitive power judge that they should flee from, or seek to gain, something. But because such judgments in the case of particular prospective actions are not by natural instinct but by some comparison by reason, so they act by free judgment, capable of being borne to contrary things. For reason regarding contingent matters leads to contrary things, as is evident in the syllogisms of logicians and the arguments of rhetoricians. But particular prospective actions are contingent things, and so judgments of reason about them are disposed toward different things and not determined to only one thing. And it is accordingly necessary that human beings have free choice, since they are rational.

Reply to Obj. 1. Sense appetites, although they obey reason, can nonetheless resist it in some things, by desiring contrary to what reason dictates, as I have said before.[10] Therefore, this is the good that human beings do not do when they will to do so, namely, "not to desire contrary to reason," as a gloss of Augustine says in the same place.[11]

Reply to Obj. 2. We should not so understand that saying of the Apostle as if human beings were not to will and act by free choice; rather, we should understand the saying to mean that free choice is not enough for willing and acting unless God should move and assist free choice.

Reply to Obj. 3. Free choice causes its own movement because human beings by free choice move themselves to act. But it does not of necessity belong to freedom that what is free be its own first cause, as neither is it required, for something to cause something else, that the former be the first cause of the latter. Therefore, God is the first cause that moves both natural and voluntary causes. And as God, by means of natural causes, by causing their movement, does not take away from their actions being from nature, so God, by causing the movement of voluntary causes, does not take away from their actions being voluntary but rather causes this characteristic in them, for he acts in each thing according to what is proper to it.

Reply to Obj. 4. We speak of "the path of human beings not being in their power" with respect to executing their choices, wherein they can be hindered, willy-nilly. But the choices themselves are in our power, although God's help is presupposed.

Reply to Obj. 5. Human beings have two kinds of properties: one kind from nature and the other kind something added. But we can understand the properties of human beings from nature either with respect to the intellectual part of the soul or with respect to the body and the powers connected to the body. Therefore, because human beings are a particular kind of thing by a natural property that we note by the intellectual part of the soul, they by nature desire their last end, namely, happiness. And this appetite is indeed natural and not subject to free will, as is evident from what I have said before.[12]

And on the part of the body and the powers connected to the body, human beings can be a particular kind of thing by a natural property insofar as human beings have such a combination or arrangement from any imprint of material causes. And such causes cannot make an imprint on the intellectual part of the soul, since the latter part is not the actuality of a material substance. Therefore, each person seems to have an end in the way each person is constituted by material properties, since such arrangements incline human beings to choose or reject particular things. But those inclinations are subject to the judgment of reason, which lower appetites obey, as I have said.[13] And so such inclinations are not prejudicial to freedom of choice.

And added properties are like characteristic dispositions and emotions, which incline individuals to one thing rather than another. But those inclinations are also subject to the judgment of reason. And such properties are also subject to reason insofar as it lies in our power to acquire them (whether by causing them or by disposing ourselves toward them) or to remove them from us. And so there is nothing inconsistent with freedom of choice.

Second Article

Is Free Choice a Power?

I proceed in this way to the second article: it seems that free choice is not a power.

Obj. 1. Free choice is simply free judgment. But judgment denotes an act, not a power. Therefore, free choice is not a power.

Obj. 2. Free choice is called "the faculty of the will and reason."[14] But faculty denotes the facility of a power, which facility indeed results from a characteristic disposition. Therefore, free choice is a characteristic disposition. (Bernard, too, says that free choice is "the soul's free characteristic disposition of itself."[15]) Therefore, free choice is not a power.

Obj. 3. Sin does not take away any natural power. But sin takes away free choice, for Augustine says that "human beings who exercise free choice wrongly lose both themselves and itself."[16] Therefore, free choice is not a power.

On the contrary, only a power, apparently, is the subject of a characteristic disposition. But free choice is the subject of grace, by the help of which free choice elects the good. Therefore, free choice is a power.

I answer that, although free choice in the strict meaning of the words denotes an act, yet we in common usage call the source of such an act (namely, the source whereby human beings judge freely) free choice. And both powers and characteristic dispositions are the sources of our acts; for example, we say that we know things both scientifically and by the power of the intellect. Therefore, free choice needs to be either a power or a characteristic disposition or a power with a characteristic disposition.

Moreover, two considerations clearly evidence that free choice is neither a characteristic disposition nor a power with a characteristic disposition. First, indeed, because free choice, if a characteristic disposition, needs to be a natural characteristic disposition, since it is natural to human beings that they have free choice. But we have no natural characteristic disposition for things subject to free choice. This is so because nature inclines us toward the things that are the objects of our natural characteristic dispositions (e.g., toward assenting to first principles), and the things toward which nature inclines us are not subject to free choice, as I have said about the appetite for happiness.[17] And so it is contrary to the proper nature of free choice that free choice be a natural characteristic disposition. And it is contrary to the naturalness of free choice that free choice be a characteristic disposition that is not from nature. And so we conclude that free choice is in no way a characteristic disposition.

Second, free choice is evidently neither a characteristic disposition nor a power with a characteristic disposition because we call characteristic dispositions things "by which we well or ill dispose ourselves toward actions or being acted upon," as the *Ethics* says.[18] For example, we by moderation dispose ourselves well toward desires, while we by lack of moderation dispose ourselves ill toward them; we by scientific discipline also dispose ourselves well toward activities of the intellect, when we know what is true, while we by the contrary characteristic disposition dispose ourselves ill toward such activities. But free choice is indifferently disposed toward choosing well or ill. And so free choice cannot be a characteristic disposition.

Therefore, we conclude that free choice is a power.

Reply to Obj. 1. We customarily signify a power by its act. And so we by the act of free judgment denote the power that is the source of that act. Otherwise, if free choice were to denote the act, free choice would not always abide in human beings.

Reply to Obj. 2. Faculty sometimes denotes a power ready to act. And then faculty is presupposed in the definition of free choice.

Moreover, Bernard does not understand characteristic dispositions as distinguished from powers but to signify dispositions whereby one is in some say disposed toward activities. And both powers and characteristic dispositions indeed bring this about, since powers dispose human beings to be capable of acting, and characteristic dispositions dispose them to be fit to act well or ill.

Reply to Obj. 3. We speak of human beings by sinning having lost free choice, not with regard to natural freedom, which is freedom from coercion, but with regard to freedom from fault and unhappiness. And

I shall speak about this later, in the treatment of morals in the second part of this work.[19]

Third Article

Is Free Choice an Appetitive Power?

I proceed in this way to the third article: it seems that free choice is a cognitive power, not an appetitive power.

Obj. 1. Damascene says that "free choice immediately accompanies the power of reason."[20] But the power of reason is a cognitive power. Therefore, free choice is a cognitive power.

Obj. 2. We call free choice a free judgment, as it were. But judging is the act of a cognitive power. Therefore, free choice is a cognitive power.

Obj. 3. Election chiefly belongs to free choice. But election seems to belong to knowledge, since election implies a comparison of one thing to another, and such belongs to a cognitive power. Therefore, free choice is a cognitive power.

On the contrary, the Philosopher says in the *Ethics* that election is "the desire of things in our power."[21] But desire is the act of an appetitive power. Therefore, election is also. But free choice is that by which we elect. Therefore, free choice is an appetitive power.

I answer that election is something that belongs to free choice, for we say that we have free choice because we can undertake one thing while rejecting another, and this is to elect. And so we need to consider the nature of free choice by considering election. But something from cognitive power and something from appetitive power work together to produce election. It is indeed required on the part of cognitive power that there be deliberation, by means of which we judge what is to be preferred to something else, and it is required on the part of appetitive power that such power, in desiring, accept what is judged by means of deliberation. And so Aristotle in book six of the *Ethics* leaves in doubt whether election belongs chiefly to appetitive power or cognitive power, for he says that election "is either the appetitive intellect or the intellectual appetite."[22] And he inclines in book three of the *Ethics* to the view that election is an intellectual appetite, calling election "a desire subject to deliberation."[23] And the reason why election is an appetitive appetite, is because means to an end are the proper object of election, and this object as such has the nature of the good that we call useful.

And so, since good as such is the object of appetite, it follows that election is chiefly the act of an appetitive power. And so free choice is an appetitive power.

Reply to Obj. 1. Appetitive powers accompany cognitive powers. And Damascene accordingly says that "free choice immediately accompanies the power of reason."

Reply to Obj. 2. Judgment, as it were, concludes and terminates deliberation. And deliberation is indeed first terminated by reason's judgment, and second by the appetite's acceptance. And so the Philosopher says in the *Ethics* that "judging by deliberating, we desire by deliberation."[24] And we in this way call election itself a judgment, and such judgment denotes free choice.

Reply to Obj. 3. The comparison implied in the term "election" belongs to the preceding deliberation, which belongs to reason. For the appetite, although it does not make comparisons, nonetheless has something like comparisons when it prefers one thing to another, since it is moved by a cognitive power that makes comparisons.

Notes

1. Rom. 7:15.
2. Rom. 9:16.
3. Aristotle, *Metaphysics* I, 2. 982b25–28.
4. Prov. 21:1.
5. Phil. 2:13.
6. Jer. 10:23.
7. *Ethics* III, 5. 1114a31–b1.
8. Sir. 15:14.
9. *Glossa ordinaria* (on Sir. 15:14). PL 113:1199. Cf. Rabanus Maurus, *In Ecclesiasticum* IV, 1. PL 109:865.
10. Q. 81, A. 3, *ad* 2.
11. Cf. Peter Lombard, *In Epistolam ad Romanos* 34, 35 (on 7:15–23). PL 191:1422–26.
12. Q. 82, AA. 1, 2.
13. Q. 81, A. 3.
14. Peter Lombard, *Sentences* II, dist. 24, no. 5. PL 192:702.
15. *Tractatus de gratia et libero arbitrio* 1, 2. PL 182:1002, 1004.
16. *Enchiridion* 30. PL 40:246.

17. Q. 82, AA. 1, 2.
18. Aristotle, *Ethics* II, 5. 1105b25–28.
19. I–II, QQ. 85, 109.
20. *De fide orthodoxa* II, 27. PG 94:960.
21. Ethics III, 3. 1113a9–12.
22. *Ethics* VI, 2. 1139b4–5.
23. *Ethics* III, 3. 1113a9–12.
24. Ibid.

ST I
Question 84
How the Soul, While United to the Body, Understands Material Things Inferior to Itself

[This question is divided into eight articles, all of which are included here.]

First Article

Does the Soul Know Material Substances Intellectually?

I proceed in this way to the first article: it seems that the soul does not know material substances intellectually.

Obj. 1. Augustine says in his *Soliloquiorum* that "the intellect cannot understand material substances, and only the senses can perceive material things."[1] And he says in his *Super Genesim* that the object of intellectual vision consists of things that are in the soul by their essence.[2] But material substances are not such. Therefore, the soul does not know material substances intellectually.

Obj. 2. The intellect is disposed toward sensibly perceptible things as the senses are disposed toward intelligible things. But the soul by means of the senses can in no way know immaterial things, which are intelligible things. Therefore, the soul by means of the intellect can in no way know material substances, which are sensibly perceptible things.

Obj. 3. Things necessary and always disposed in the same way constitute the object of the intellect. But every material substance can undergo change and is disposed in different ways. Therefore, the soul cannot know material substances intellectually.

On the contrary, the intellect has scientific knowledge. Therefore, if the intellect does not know material substances, it follows that the intellect has no scientific knowledge about material substances. And then the science of nature, of which changeable material substances are the object, will perish.

I answer, to clarify the question, that the first philosophers inquiring about the natures of things thought that there is nothing in the world besides material substances.   And because they perceived that all material substances can change, and supposed those things to be in continual flux, they judged that we can have no certitude about the reality of things. For we cannot know with certitude things in continual flux, since they perish before the mind judges about them. For example, Heraclitus said that "it is impossible to touch twice the water of a flowing stream," as the Philosopher relates in the *Metaphysics*.[3]

And Plato added to these philosophers. In order to be able to safeguard our having sure knowledge about reality intellectually, he held that there is, in addition to those material things, another type of beings, one that is separate from matter and motion.[4] And he called this type of beings "Forms" or "Ideas," by reason of the sharing in which he calls each of those individual and sensibly perceptible things either a human being or a horse or something of the sort. Therefore, he said that we relate sciences and definitions and whatever belongs to intellectual activity to the things that are immaterial and separate, and not to the things that are sensibly perceptible material substances. As a result, the soul understands the separate forms of the material substances but not the material substances.

But this explanation is clearly false for two reasons. First, indeed, because, since those forms are immaterial and unchangeable, knowledge of motion and matter (i.e., the object of natural science), and demonstration by causes that cause motion and are material, would be excluded from the sciences. And second, Plato's explanation is false because it seems laughable that, when we seek knowledge about things manifest to us, we adduce other, intermediate entities that cannot be the substances of those things, since the intermediate entities and the manifest things differ in their way of existing. And so, assuming that we know such separate substances, we would not thereby be able to judge about the sensibly perceived things.

Moreover, it seems that Plato deviated from the truth in this matter. For he, having judged that all knowledge is acquired through likenesses, believed that the form of a known object necessarily is in the knowing subject in the same way that the form is in the known object. And he considered that the form of something understood is in the intellect in a universal and immaterial and unchangeable way. And this is evidenced by the very activity of the intellect, which understands in a universal and a necessary way, since ways of acting are from the forms of efficient causes. And so he was of the opinion that the things understood would necessarily subsist in themselves in this way, namely, in an immaterial and unchangeable way.

But this is not necessary, since we observe even in sensibly perceived things themselves that forms are in different ways in one sensibly perceptible thing than in another; for example, when whiteness is more intensely in one thing, less intensely in another, and whiteness is accompanied by sweetness in one thing but not in another. And it is thus also that sensibly perceptible forms are in one way in things outside the soul, and in another way in the senses, which receive the forms of sensibly perceptible things apart from the things' matter (e.g., the color of gold apart from gold). And likewise, the intellect receives in its own way, an immaterial and unchangeable way, the forms of material substances, substances that are material and changeable, since things are received in recipients in the way of the recipients.

Therefore, we need to affirm that the soul intellectually knows material substances by a knowledge that is immaterial, universal, and necessary.

Reply to Obj. 1. We should understand the words of Augustine to refer to the means whereby the intellect knows, and not to the things that it knows. For the intellect knows material substances by understanding them by means of immaterial and intelligible forms, which by reason of their essence can be in the soul, and not by means of material substances or material and corporeal likenesses.

Reply to Obj. 2. As Augustine says in *The City of God*, we should not say that, as the senses know only material things, so the intellect knows only spiritual things, since the logical consequence would be that God and angels do not know material things.[5] And the reason for the difference between knowledge by the senses and knowledge by the intellect is because a lower power does not extend to things that belong to a higher power, while a higher power performs in a more excellent way things that belong to a lower power.

Reply to Obj. 3. Every change presupposes something constant, since substances remain constant when qualitative changes occur, and matter remains constant when changes of substantial form occur. Also, constant relationships belong to changeable things; for example, although Socrates is not always sitting, it is nonetheless inalterably true that he remains in one place while he is seated. And it is for this reason that nothing prevents us from having inalterable knowledge about changeable things.

Second Article

Does the Soul Know Material Things by Reason of Its Essence?

I proceed in this way to the second article: it seems that the soul knows material things by reason of its essence.

Obj. 1. Augustine says in his *De Trinitate* that the soul "blends and snatches images of material substances, images formed in itself of itself, since the soul contributes part of its substance to the things being formed."[6]   But the soul understands material substances by their likenesses. Therefore, the soul knows material things by reason of its essence, which the soul contributes to such likenesses being formed, and from which the soul forms those likenesses.

Obj. 2. The Philosopher says in the *De anima* that "the soul is in a certain way everything."[7]   Therefore, since like is known by like, it seems that the soul knows material things by reason of its very self.

Obj. 3. The soul is superior to material creatures. But inferior things exist in superior things in a more eminent way than they exist in themselves, as Denis says.[8] Therefore, all material creatures exist in a more excellent way in the very substance of the soul than they exist in themselves. Therefore, the soul can know material creatures by reason of its essence.

On the contrary, Augustine says in his *De Trinitate* that "the mind gathers knowledge of material things by means of the bodily senses."[9] But the bodily senses cannot know the soul itself. Therefore, the soul does not know material things by reason of its own substance.

I answer that ancient philosophers held that the soul knows material substances by reason of its essence, since it was implanted in the soul of every human being without exception that "like is known by like."[10] And they thought that the forms of known objects are in knowing subjects in the same way that the forms are in the things known. (Followers of Plato, however, held a contrary position. For Plato, since he noted that the intellectual soul is immaterial and knows in an immaterial way,[11] held that the forms of known things subsist in an immaterial way.) And the earlier philosophers of nature, since they attended to the fact that known things are corporeal and material, held that the known things need also to exist in a material way in the souls that know them. And so, in order to ascribe knowledge of everything to the soul, they held that the soul has a common nature with everything.

And since sources determine the nature of effects, they ascribed to the soul the nature of the source of everything. Consequently, those who asserted that the source of everything is fire held that the soul has the nature of fire. And other philosophers in a similar fashion held that the soul has the nature of air or water. And Empedocles, who posited four material elements and two causes of motion, likewise said that the soul is composed of them. And so, since the earlier philosophers posited things in the soul in a material way, they held that all knowledge of the soul is material, making no distinction between the intellect and the senses.

But I reject this opinion. First, indeed, because only potential effects exist in material sources, about which the earlier philosophers were speaking. But we do not know anything as potential but know things only as actual, as the *Metaphysics* makes clear.[12] And so we know potentiality itself only by actuality. Therefore, it would not be sufficient to ascribe the nature of things' sources to the soul in order that the soul would know all things, unless the natures and forms of individual effects (e.g., bones and flesh and the like) were to be in the soul, as Aristotle argues in the *De anima* against Empedocles.[13] Second, I reject the opinion of the earlier philosophers because there would be no reason why things that subsist in a material way outside the soul should lack knowledge, if it were necessary for known things to exist in a material way in knowing subjects; for example, if the soul by fire knows fire, even the fire that exists outside the soul should also know fire.

Therefore, we conclude that the material things that we know need to exist in the knower in an immaterial rather than a material way. And the reason why this is so is because acts of knowledge extend to things that exist outside the knower, for we know even things that exist outside of ourselves. But matter limits the forms of things to individual things. And so the nature of knowledge is evidently contrarily related to the nature of materiality. And so things that receive forms only in a material way, such as plants, are in no way cognitive, as the *De anima* says.[14] But the more immaterially something receives the forms of the things it knows, the more perfectly it knows. And so also the intellect, which abstracts forms both from matter and from the individuating conditions of matter, knows more perfectly than do the senses, which indeed receive the forms of known objects apart from matter but with the conditions of matter. And among the senses themselves, the sense of sight knows more than the other senses because it is less material, as I have said before.[15] And among intellects themselves, the more immaterial one is, the more perfect it is.

Therefore, it is clear from these considerations that, given an intellect that by its essence knows all things, its essence needs to possess all things in itself in an immaterial way. (Ancient philosophers similarly held that the soul's essence, in order to know all material things, is actually composed of the sources of all of them.) And it belongs to God that his essence comprise all things in an immaterial way, since effects pre-exist in their cause by reason of its power. Therefore, God alone understands all things by his essence, and neither the human soul nor even an angel does so by reason of its essence.

Reply to Obj. 1. Augustine is speaking there about the vision of imagination, which the images of material substances produce. When these images are being formed, the soul gives part of its substance as a subject lends itself to receive a form. And so the soul produces such images from its very self, not that the soul or any part of the soul be transformed to be this or that image, but as we speak about material substances becoming colored things as they receive the forms of color. And this understanding is evidenced by what follows. For he says that the soul "keeps in reserve something," namely, something not formed by such images, "that may freely judge about the form of such images," and he says that this thing is "the mind" or "the intellect."[16] And he says that the part of the soul that receives such images, namely, the power of imagination, is "common to us and beasts."[17]

Reply to Obj. 2. Aristotle did not hold that the soul is actually composed of all things, as the ancient philosophers of nature did, but he said that "the soul is everything in a certain way," inasmuch as the soul has potentiality for all things: by the senses, indeed, for sensibly perceptible things, and by the intellect for intelligible things.

Reply to Obj. 3. Every creature has a limited and fixed way of existing. And so the essence of a superior creature, although it has a likeness to an inferior creature inasmuch as they share a common genus, nonetheless is not completely like an inferior creature, since the superior creature is determined to a species beyond that of the inferior creature. But God's essence, as the source of all things without exception, is the perfect likeness of those things regarding everything we find in them.

Third Article

*Does the Soul Understand Every Kind of Thing
by Forms Implanted in It by Nature?*

I proceed in this way to the third article: it seems the soul understands every kind of thing by forms implanted in it by nature.

Obj. 1. Gregory says in his homily on the Ascension that "human beings, in common with angels, have understanding."[18] But angels understand every kind of thing by forms implanted by nature, and so the *Liber de causis* says that "every intelligent entity is replete with forms."[19] Therefore, the soul too has things' forms implanted by nature, by means of which forms the soul understands material things.

Obj. 2. The intellectual soul is more excellent than corporeal prime matter. But God created prime matter under the forms for which it has potentiality. Therefore, much more did God create intellectual souls under intelligible forms. And so the soul understands material things by forms implanted in it by nature.

Obj. 3. One can give true answers only about what one knows. But even an untutored person, a person without acquired knowledge, gives true answers about each of several things, provided only the person be questioned in an orderly way, as Plato relates in the *Meno* about such a person.[20] Therefore, persons have knowledge about things before they acquire knowledge. And such would be the case only if the soul were to possess forms implanted by nature. Therefore, the soul understands material things by forms implanted by nature.

On the contrary, the Philosopher, speaking about the intellect, says in the *De anima* that it is "like a writing tablet on which nothing is written."[21]

I answer that, since forms are sources of actions, things need to be related to the forms that are the sources of actions as the things are related to those actions. For example, if upward motion is due to lightness of weight, things borne upward only potentially need to be light only potentially, but things actually borne upward need to be actually light. And we observe that human beings, both as to the senses and to the intellect, sometimes know only potentially. And the actions of sensibly perceptible things on the senses bring human beings from such potentiality to actuality, so that they indeed perceive, and learning or discovery brings human beings from such potentiality to actuality, so that they understand. And so we need to affirm that the cognitive soul has potentiality both for the likenesses that are the sources of sense perception and for the likenesses that are the sources of understanding. And Aristotle for this reason held that the intellect, by means of which the soul understands, does not possess any forms implanted by nature but initially has potentiality for all such forms.

But things actually possessing forms sometimes cannot act according to the forms because of hindrances; for example, light things if they be prevented from being borne upward. Consequently, Plato held that the intellect of human beings is by nature replete with every intelligible form, but that union with the body impedes the intellect from being able to spring into action.[22]

But this dictum of Plato seems inappropriate. First, indeed, because it seems impossible that the soul, if it has natural knowledge of all things, should arrive at such a state of forgetfulness that it would not know that it has such knowledge, since human beings do not forget things they know by nature (e.g., that every whole is greater than any of its parts, and other such things). And the dictum seems especially inappropriate if we should hold that it is natural for the soul to be united to the body, as I have maintained before,[23] since it is inappropriate that what by nature belongs to something should totally prevent a natural activity of the thing. Second, the falsity of Plato's position is clearly evidenced by the fact that persons lacking a particular sense power lack knowledge of things perceived by that sense; for example, a person born blind cannot have knowledge of colors. And such would not be the case if the natures of all intelligible things were to be by nature implanted in the soul.

And so we need to say that the soul does not know material things by forms implanted by nature.

Reply to Obj. 1. Human beings are indeed one with the angels in understanding, but human beings fall short of the excellence of the angels' intellect, just as lower material substances, which, according to Gregory,[24] merely exist, fall short of the existence of higher material substances. For forms do not totally perfect the matter of lower material substances, and such matter has potentiality for forms that it does not possess, while forms totally perfect the matter of heavenly bodies, so that such matter has no potentiality for other forms, as I have maintained before.[25] And similarly, intelligible forms perfect the intellect of angels by reason of its nature, while the human intellect has potentiality for such forms.

Reply to Obj. 2. Prime matter has a substantial way of existing by reason of forms, and so it needed to be created under particular forms; otherwise, it would not be actual. Nonetheless, when it exists under one form, it has potentiality for other forms. But the intellect does not have a substantial way of existing by reason of intelligible forms, and so there is no comparison.

Reply to Obj. 3. Orderly questioning proceeds from universal, self-evident principles to particulars. And it is by such a process that knowledge is produced in the mind of the learner. And so, when the learner gives true answers about the things about which he is successively questioned, this is not because he knew those things before, but because he learned them then for the first time. For it does not matter at all whether the teacher proceeds from universal principles to conclusions by way of exposition or by way of interrogation, since, either way, what precedes, makes the mind of the listener certain about what follows.

Fourth Article

Do Intelligible Forms Flow into the Soul from Certain Separate Forms?

I proceed in this way to the fourth article: it seems that intelligible forms flow into the soul from certain separate forms.

Obj. 1. What is essentially such causes everything that is such by sharing; for example, we trace something on fire to fire as its cause. But the intellectual soul, as it actually understands, shares in intelligible things themselves, since the intellect actually understanding is in a certain way the thing actually understood. Therefore, the things that are as such, and by their essence actually understood, cause the intellectual soul actually to understand. But the things actually understood by their essence are forms that exist apart from matter. Therefore, certain separate forms cause the intelligible forms by which the soul understands.

Obj. 2. Intelligible things are related to the intellect as sensibly perceptible things are to the senses. But sensibly perceptible things actual outside the soul cause the forms of those things in the senses, the forms by which we sensibly perceive. Therefore, some actually intelligible things existing outside the soul cause the intelligible forms by which the intellect understands. But only forms separated from matter are such things. Therefore, the intelligible forms of our intellect issue from certain separate substances.

Obj. 3. Everything potential is brought to actuality by what is actual. Therefore, if our intellect, previously being potential, should afterwards actually understand, an intellect that is always actual needs to bring this about. But such an intellect is a separate intellect. Therefore, certain separate substances cause the intelligible forms by which we actually understand.

On the contrary, we would not, according to this view, need the senses in order to understand. And this is clearly false, especially since one who lacks one sense power can in no way have knowledge about the sensibly perceptible things belonging to that sense.

I answer that certain thinkers held that the intelligible forms of our intellect proceed from certain forms or separate substances. And they held this opinion in two ways. For Plato, as I have said,[26] held that the forms of sensibly perceptible things (e.g., the Form of Human Being, which he called human being as such, and the Form or Idea of Horse, which he called horse as such, and so forth) subsist as such apart from matter. Therefore, he held that both our souls and corporeal matter share in these separate forms, our souls, indeed, in order to know, and corporeal matter in order to be; for example, as corporeal matter is made this particular stone because the corporeal matter shares in the Idea of Stone, so our intellect is made to understand stone because the intellect shares in the Idea of Stone. And likenesses of the Ideas themselves in things sharing in the very Ideas cause the Ideas to be shared, as copies share in models. Therefore, as Plato held that the sensibly perceptible forms in corporeal matter flow from the Ideas as certain likenesses of them, so he held that the intelligible forms in our intellect are certain likenesses of the Ideas, likenesses issuing from them. And consequently, he related sciences and definitions to the Ideas, as I have said before.[27]

But it is contrary to the nature of sensibly perceptible things that their forms subsist apart from matter, as Aristotle demonstrated in many ways.[28] Therefore, Avicenna, setting aside Plato's position, held that the intelligible forms of all sensibly perceptible things indeed do not subsist apart from matter but pre-exist in an immaterial way in separate intellects.[29] And such forms are drawn from the first of these intellects to the second, and so in the case of the rest to the last separate intellect, which he called the active intellect, from which intelligible forms flow into our souls, and sensibly perceptible forms into corporeal matter, as he himself says.

And so Avicenna agreed with Plato in this respect, that the intelligible forms of our intellect flow from certain separate forms, but Avicenna locates those separate forms in an active intelligent entity, while Plato says that the separate forms subsist as such. The two also differ in that Avicenna holds that the intelligible forms do not abide in our intellect after the intellect ceases actively to understand; rather, the intellect needs repeatedly to direct itself [to the active intelligent entity] in order to receive the forms anew.[30] And so he does not hold that the soul's knowledge is implanted by nature, as does Plato, who holds that participations in the Ideas abide unchangeably in the soul.

But we cannot by this position ascribe a sufficient reason why our soul is united to the body. For we cannot say that intellectual souls are united to bodies because of the body, since forms do not exist because of matter, nor causes of motion because of moveable objects, but rather the converse. And the intellectual soul seems especially to need the body for the soul's characteristic activity, that is, understanding, since the intellectual soul, as to its existing, does not depend on the body. But if the soul were by its nature to be constituted fit to receive intelligible forms only by reason of the causal influence of certain separate sources, and were not to receive those forms from the senses, the soul would not need the body in order to understand. And so there would be no purpose to the soul being united to the body.

And if one should say that our soul, in order to understand, needs the senses, by means of which it is somehow awakened to consider the things whose intelligible forms it receives from the separate sources, this explanation does not suffice. The explanation would not suffice because such awakening seems necessary for the soul only insofar as the soul is in some kind of stupor (as the Platonists say) and forgetful, due to the union of the soul to the body, and so the senses would be of use to the intellectual soul only to take away the obstacle that comes to the soul as a result of its union with the body. Therefore, we still need to look for the reason why the soul is united to the body.

And if one should, following Avicenna,[31] say that the soul needs the senses because they arouse the soul to direct itself to the active intelligent entity from which it receives forms, even this explanation does not suffice. The explanation does not suffice because, if it is part of the soul's nature to understand by forms issuing from the active intelligent entity, it would follow that the soul by the inclination of its nature could sometimes direct itself to the active intelligent entity, or even that the soul, when aroused by a different sense power, would direct itself to the active intelligent entity in order to receive the forms of sensibly perceptible things that are the object of a sense power that a person lacks. And so a person born blind could have knowledge of colors, and this conclusion is clearly false.

And so we need to say that the intelligible forms by which our soul understands do not issue from separate forms.

Reply to Obj. 1. We trace the intelligible forms in which our intellect shares to a source by its essence intelligible, namely, God, as their first cause. But our intelligible forms come from that source by means of the forms of sensibly perceptible and material things, and we acquire knowledge by these forms, as Denis says.[32]

Reply to Obj. 2. Material things, by reason of the existing that they have outside the soul, can actually be sensibly perceptible without being actually intelligible. And so the cases with respect to the senses and the intellect are dissimilar.

Reply to Obj. 3. Our potential intellect is brought from potentiality to actuality by an actual being, that is, the active intellect, which is a power of our soul, as I have said.[33] And our potential intellect is not brought from potentiality to actuality by any separate intellect as a proximate cause, but perhaps by a separate intellect as a remote cause.

Fifth Article

Does the Intellectual Soul Know Material Things
in the Eternal Natures of Things?

I proceed in this way to the fifth article: it seems that the intellectual soul does not know material things in the eternal natures of things.

Obj. 1. We know better and antecedently that itself in which we know something. But the intellectual soul of human beings in the condition of our present life does not know the eternal natures of things, since the soul in that condition does not know God himself, in whom the eternal natures of things exist; rather, the soul "is united to him as to the unknown," as Denis says in his *De mysteria theologia.*[34] Therefore, the intellectual soul does not know all things in the eternal natures of things. *Obj. 2.* The Letter to the Romans says that "we see the invisible things" of God "through the things that he has made."[35] But we reckon the eternal natures of things among the invisible things of God. Therefore, we know the eternal natures of things through material things, and not the converse.

Obj. 3. The eternal natures of things are simply the [divine] ideas, for Augustine says in his *Octoginta trium quaestionum* that those "ideas are the stable natures of things that exist in the divine mind."[36] Therefore, if we should say that the intellectual soul knows all things in the eternal natures of things, we will revert to the opinion of Plato, who held that all knowledge is derived from the Ideas.

On the contrary, Augustine says in his *Confessions*: "If both of us perceive that what you say is true, and both of us perceive that what I say is true, where, I ask, do we perceive it? Neither I in you, nor you in me, of course, but both of us in that unchangeable truth that is above our minds."[37] But unchangeable truth is contained in the eternal natures of things. Therefore, the intellectual soul knows everything true in the eternal natures of things.

I answer as Augustine says in his *De doctrina Christiana*: "If those called philosophers have said anything by chance true and in accord with our faith, we should appropriate such from them as unjust possessors, for our use. For certain teachings of the pagans contain counterfeit and superstitious fabrications, which each of us, warding off association with the pagans, ought to avoid."[38] And so Augustine, who had been imbued with the teachings of the Platonists, adopted anything in their teachings that he found to be in accord with the faith, while he transformed into something better anything that he found to be adverse to our faith. And as I have said before,[39] Plato held that things' forms as such subsist apart from matter. And he called those forms Ideas and said that our intellect knows all things by sharing in the Ideas, so that, as corporeal matter is made stone by sharing in the Idea of Stone, so our intellect would know stone by sharing in the same Idea. But it seems foreign to faith that things' forms outside the things should subsist as such apart from matter, as the Platonists held when they said that "life as such" and "wisdom as such" are certain creative substances, as Denis says in his *De divinis nominibus*.[40] Therefore, in place of the Ideas that Plato posited, Augustine held in his *Octoginta trium quaestionum* that the natures of all creatures exist in the divine mind, and that all things are formed by these natures, and also that the human soul knows all things by them.[41]

Therefore, when we ask whether the human soul knows all things in the eternal natures of things, we need to reply that we say in two ways that something is known in something. In one way, as in a known object; for example, one sees in a mirror the things whose images are reflected in the mirror. And in this way, the soul in the condition of our present life cannot behold all things in the eternal natures of things, but the blessed, who behold God and all things in himself, do so.

We say in a second way that something is known in something as in a source of knowledge; for example, if we should say that we see in the sun the things that we see by the sun. And so we need to say that the human soul knows all things in the eternal natures of things, and it is by the soul's sharing in these natures that we know all things. For the very light of the intellect in us is but a shared likeness of the uncreated light, in which the eternal natures of things are contained. And so the Psalm says: "Many say, 'Who shows us what is good?'" to which question the Psalmist replies in these words: "The light of your countenance, O Lord, is imprinted upon us."[42] This is as if to say: the very imprint of the divine light in us points all things out to us.

Nevertheless, in order to have knowledge of material things, we need to receive intelligible forms from things, in addition to the intellectual light in us. Therefore, we do not have knowledge of material things only by sharing in the eternal natures of things, as the Platonists held that sharing in the Ideas of itself suffices to have knowledge. And so Augustine says in his *De Trinitate*: "Because philosophers convince us by the most certain proofs that the eternal natures of things cause everything temporal, could they thereby perceive in those very natures, or acquire from them: How many kinds of animals there are? What is the origin of each? Did not the philosophers seek all these things by investigating times and places?"[43]

And that Augustine would not have so understood that we know all things "in the eternal natures" of things or "in unchangeable truth" as if we behold the eternal natures themselves, is evidenced by the fact that he himself says in his *Octoginta trium quaestionum* that "rational souls that have been holy and pure," such as the souls of the blessed, and "not each and every one is alleged to be suitable for that vision," namely, of the eternal natures.[44]

Reply to the Objections. And the foregoing makes clear the answers to the objections.

Sixth Article

Do We Obtain Intellectual Knowledge from Sensibly Perceptible Things?

I proceed in this way to the sixth article: it seems that we do not obtain intellectual knowledge from sensibly perceptible things.

Obj. 1. Augustine says in his *Octoginta trium quaestionum* that "we should not expect genuine truth from the bodily senses."[45] And he proves this in two ways. In one way, because "everything touched by the bodily senses is continually altered, and we cannot perceive what does not abide." In the second way, because "we still experience images of everything perceived by the body, even when the thing is not present to the external senses, as in the course of sleep or anger, but we are not able to distinguish whether we perceive the sensibly perceptible things themselves or their counterfeit images. And we cannot perceive anything that we do not distinguish from something counterfeit." And so he concludes that we should not expect truth from the senses. But intellectual knowledge understands truth. Therefore, we should not expect intellectual knowledge from the senses.

Obj. 2. Augustine says in his *Super Genesim*: "We ought not to think that the body has any effect on the spirit, as if the spirit, like matter, should be subject to the body's causal action, for causes are in every way more excellent than the things respecting which they produce effects."[46] And so he concludes that "the body does not cause bodily images to be in the spirit, but the spirit itself causes those images to be in itself." Therefore, intellectual knowledge is not derived from sensibly perceptible things.

Obj. 3. Effects do not surpass the power of their causes. But intellectual knowledge surpasses sensibly perceptible things, for we understand some things that the senses cannot perceive. Therefore, intellectual knowledge is not derived from sensibly perceptible things.

On the contrary, the Philosopher shows in the *Metaphysics*[47] and at the end of the *Posterior Analytics*[48] that our knowledge originates from the senses.

I answer that there have been three opinions of philosophers on this question. For example, Democritus held that "the only cause of any knowledge of ours is when images come from the material substances about which we are thinking, and enter our souls," as Augustine says in his letter to Dioscorus.[49] And Aristotle likewise says in his *De somno et vigilia* that Democritus held that knowledge is caused "by images and effluences."[50] And the reason for this position was that both Democritus himself and the other ancient philosophers of nature did not hold the intellect to differ from the senses, as Aristotle relates in the *De anima.*[51] And so, because sensibly perceptible things affect the senses, the ancient philosophers of nature thought that only alterations by sensibly perceptible things cause all our knowledge. And Democritus indeed claimed that the effluences of images cause those alterations.

But Plato on the contrary held that the intellect differs from the senses, and that the intellect is indeed an immaterial power that does not utilize a bodily organ in its activity. And because something material cannot affect something immaterial, he held that intellectual knowledge is not caused by alteration of the senses by sensibly perceptible things but by sharing in separate intelligible forms, as I have said.[52] He also held the senses to be intrinsically active powers. And so neither do sensibly perceptible things affect the senses themselves, since the senses are immaterial powers. But sensibly perceptible things affect the sense organs, and the soul is somehow aroused by this alteration to produce in itself the forms of sensibly perceptible things. And Augustine seems to touch on this opinion in his *Super Genesim*, where he says that "the body does not sensibly perceive, but the soul does through the body, which the soul employs like a messenger to form within itself what is reported from without."[53] Therefore, in the opinion of Plato, neither intellectual knowledge, nor even sense knowledge totally, comes from sensibly perceptible things; rather, sensibly perceptible things arouse the sensory soul to perceive sensibly, and the senses similarly arouse the intellectual soul to understand.

And Aristotle took a middle course. For he held with Plato that the intellect differs from the senses.[54] But he held the senses do not have their characteristic activities without the body participating, so that sense perception is not the activity of the soul alone but the activity of the composite. And he held likewise about every activity of the sensory part of the soul. Therefore, because it is not incongruous that sensibly perceptible things outside the soul cause things in the composite, Aristotle agreed with Democritus that the impressions of sensibly perceptible things on the senses cause the activities of the sensory part of the soul, not by way of effluences from those things, as Democritus held, but by some kind of causal action. (For Democritus also held that an influx of atoms causes every action, as the *De generatione et corruptione* makes clear.[55])

And Aristotle held that the intellect engages in its activity without the participation of the body.[56] Moreover, nothing material can make an imprint on something immaterial. And so, according to Aristotle, impressions made by sensibly perceptible things do not alone suffice to cause intellectual activity, but something more excellent is required, since "what acts, is more distinguished than what is acted upon," as he himself says.[57] But this does not mean that our intellectual knowledge is caused in us only by impressions made by some higher things, as Plato held; rather, the higher and more excellent efficient cause that we call the active intellect, about which I have already spoken before,[58] by a process of abstraction makes the images received by the senses actually intelligible.

Accordingly, therefore, the senses cause intellectual activity regarding the sense images. But because sense images do not suffice to affect the potential intellect, and the active intellect needs to make the sense images actually intelligible, we cannot say that sense knowledge is the entire and complete cause of intellectual knowledge, but sense knowledge is rather, in some sense, the cause's matter.

Reply to Obj. 1. By those words, Augustine gives us to understand that we should not expect truth entirely from the senses. For we need the light of the active intellect, by which we know unchangeably the truth in changeable things, and distinguish those very things from their likenesses.

Reply to Obj. 2. Augustine is not there speaking about knowledge by the intellect but about knowledge by the power of imagination. And because according to the opinion of Plato, the power of imagination has activity that belongs to the soul alone, Augustine, to show that the soul itself imprints the likenesses of material substances on the power of imagination, and that material substances do not, used the same argument that Aristotle used to show that the active intellect is something distinct, namely, the argument that "what acts, is more distinguished than what is acted upon."[59] And according to the opinion of Plato, it is beyond doubt necessary to hold that there is in the power of imagination not only a passive power but also an active power. But if we, following the opinion of Aristotle,[60] should hold that the activity of the power of imagination belongs to the composite, there is no resulting difficulty. This is so because sensibly perceptible material substances are more excellent than the sense organs of animals in that the former substances are related to the latter organs as actual beings to potential beings, as, for example, something actually colored is related to an eye's pupil, which is potentially colored.

Still, although the causal motion of sensibly perceptible things produces the first alteration in the power of imagination, since "imagining is a movement caused by the senses," as the *De anima* says,[61] we could nonetheless say that human beings have an activity of the soul that by division and composition forms diverse images of things, even images not received by the senses. And we can understand the words of Augustine accordingly.

Reply to Obj. 3. Sense knowledge is not the whole cause of intellectual knowledge. And so it is not extraordinary that intellectual knowledge surpasses sense knowledge.

Seventh Article

Can the Intellect Without Recourse to Sense Images Actually Understand by Means of Intelligible Forms in Its Possession?

I proceed in this way to the seventh article: it seems that the intellect without recourse to sense images can actually understand by means of intellectual forms in its possession.

Obj. 1. The intellectual form that the intellect receives, actualizes the intellect. But the intellect actually understanding is its very act of understanding. Therefore, intelligible forms suffice for the intellect actually to understand without having recourse to sense images.

Obj. 2. The power of imagination depends on the external senses more than the intellect depends on the power of imagination. But the power of imagination can actually imagine when sensibly perceptible things are absent. Therefore, much more can the intellect actually understand without recourse to sense images.

Obj. 3. No sense images belong to immaterial things, since the power of imagination does not transcend time and space. Therefore, if our intellect could not actually understand anything without recourse to sense images, it would follow that it could not understand anything immaterial. And this conclusion is clearly false, since we understand truth itself, and God and angels.

On the contrary, the Philosopher says in the *De anima* that "the soul understands nothing without a sense image."[62]

I answer that our intellect in the condition of our present life, in which condition the intellect is united to a body with a capacity to be acted upon, cannot actually understand anything without having recourse to sense images. And there are two indications to evidence this. First, indeed, because injury to a bodily organ would in no way impede the activity of the intellect, since the intellect does not use a bodily organ, if the intellect's activity were not to need the act of a power that uses a bodily organ. But the external senses and the power of imagination and other powers belonging to the sensory part of the soul use bodily organs. And so it is clear that, for the intellect actually to understand, not only by acquiring knowledge anew but also by using knowledge already acquired, we need acts of the power of imagination and other powers. For example, we perceive that human beings are prevented from actually understanding even things of which they previously acquired knowledge, if injury to a bodily organ prevents acts of the power of imagination, as in the case of those afflicted with a brain disease, and likewise if injury to a bodily organ prevents acts of the power of memory, as in the case of those afflicted by drowsiness.

Second, our intellect in the condition of our present life cannot actually understand without having recourse to sense images because all of us can experience in ourselves that we, when we try to understand something, form certain sense images for ourselves to serve as examples, in which we see, as it were, what we are striving to understand. And so it is also the case that, when we wish to cause others to understand something, we propose to them examples, by means of which they can form sense images for themselves in order to understand.

And the reason why our intellect in the condition of our present life cannot actually understand without having recourse to sense images is because the power to know is proportioned to the knowable object. And so the proper objects of the angelic intellect, which is completely separate from a body, are intelligible substances separate from material substances, and the angelic intellect knows material things by such intelligible things. But the proper objects of the human intellect, which is united to a body, are essences or natures existing in corporeal matter, and the human intellect by means of such natures of visible things also rises to some kind of knowledge of invisible things. Moreover, it belongs to the essence of such natures of visible things that they exist in individual things, and there is no such existence apart from corporeal matter; for example, it belongs to the essence of the nature of stone to exist in particular stones, and it belongs to the essence of the nature of horse to exist in particular horses, and so forth. And so we can completely and truly know the nature of stones or the nature of any material thing only insofar as we know that nature as it exists in a particular stone or material thing. But we know particular things by our senses and our power of imagination. And so, in order for the intellect actually to understand its proper objects, it needs to have recourse to sense images to spy out the universal natures existing in particular things.

But if the proper objects of our intellect were to be separate forms, or if the natures of sensibly perceptible things were not to subsist in particular things, as the Platonists say, our intellect would not always need to have recourse to sense images when it understands.

Reply to Obj. 1. Forms preserved in the potential intellect exist in it, when it is not actually understanding, by way of a characteristic disposition, as I have said before.[63] And so the preservation of forms, by itself, does not suffice for us actually to understand; rather, we need to use them as befits the things of which they are the forms, that is, the natures existing in particular things.

Reply to Obj. 2. Even sense images themselves are likenesses of particular things, and so the power of imagination, unlike the intellect, does not need any other likenesses of particular things.

Reply to Obj. 3. We know immaterial things, of which we have no sense images, in relation to sensibly perceptible material substances, of which we do have sense images. For example, we understand truth by considering the things about which we spy out the truth, and we know God as their cause, and by what surpasses them, and by eliminating their defects, as Denis says[64]; also, we can in the condition of our present life know other immaterial substances only by eliminating defects from, and in some relation to, material substances. And so, when we understand something about such immaterial substances, we need to have recourse to sense images, although we have no sense images of the immaterial substances themselves.

Eighth Article

Does Restraint of the Senses Prevent the Intellect's Judgment?

I proceed in this way to the eighth article: it seems that restraint of the senses does not prevent the intellect's judgment.

Obj. 1. Superior things do not depend on inferior things. But the intellect's judgment is superior to the senses. Therefore, restraint of the senses does not prevent the intellect's judgment.

Obj. 2. Syllogizing is an act of the intellect. But the senses are restrained in sleep, as the *De somno et vigilia* says,[65] and yet it sometimes happens that sleepers syllogize. Therefore, restraint of the senses does not prevent the intellect's judgment.

On the contrary, we do not impute as sin morally impermissible things that happen in the course of sleep, as Augustine says in his *Super Genesim.*[66] But this would not be the case if human beings in the course of sleep were to have the free use of reason and the intellect. Therefore, restraint of the senses prevents the use of reason.

I answer that the proper objects proportioned to our intellect are the natures of sensibly perceptible things, as I have said.[67] And we cannot give perfect judgments about things unless we happen to know everything that pertains to those things, and this is especially the case if we happen not to know the term and end of our judgments. For the Philosopher says in the *De coelo* that, "as the end of practical science is action, so the end of natural science is what the senses chiefly perceive"[68]; for example, a blacksmith seeks knowledge about knives only because of his activity, that he produce these particular knives, and likewise natural scientists seek to know the nature of stone and the nature of horse only in order to know the natures of things perceived by the senses. And it is obvious that a blacksmith could not form perfect judgments about knives if he were not to know his activity, and likewise natural scientists cannot form perfect judgments about the things of nature if they be ignorant of sensibly perceptible things. But we know everything that we understand in our present condition, in relation to sensibly perceptible things of nature. And so our intellect cannot form perfect judgments when the senses, by which we know sensibly perceptible things, are restrained.

Reply to Obj. 1. Although the intellect is superior to the senses, it nonetheless in some way receives from them, and its first and foremost objects are based on sensibly perceptible things. And so restraint of the senses necessarily prevents the intellect's judgment.

Reply to Obj. 2. The senses are restrained in sleepers because of certain exhalations and released vapors, as the *De somno et vigilia* says.[69] And so the senses happen to be restrained to a greater or lesser extent as such exhalations are disposed. For example, after heavy exhalation of vapors, both the senses and the power of imagination are restrained, so that no sense images are discernible, as especially happens when one falls asleep after much food and drink. And if there has been a bit milder exhalation of vapors, sense images are discernible but distorted and unrelated, as happens in the case of those with a fever. And if the exhalation of vapors is still more settled, related sense images are discernible, as is most accustomed to happen at the end of a period of sleep, and in human beings who are temperate and have a strong imagination. And if the exhalation of vapors has been slight, not only does the power of imagination remain free, but also the common sense itself is partially freed, so that human beings in the course of sleep sometimes judge that the things perceived by them are dreams, discerning, as it were, between things and the likenesses of things. But the common sense nonetheless remains partially restrained, and so, although it distinguishes some likenesses from things, it is nonetheless always deceived in particulars.

Therefore, as the senses and the power of imagination are freed in the course of sleep, the intellect's power of judging is also freed, but not totally. And so those who syllogize in their sleep, when they awaken, always recognize that they have made some mistake.

Notes

1. *Soliloquiorum* II, 4. PL 32:888.
2. *Super Genesim ad litteram* XII, 24. PL 34:474.
3. *Metaphysics* III, 5. 1010a7–15.
4. *Phaedo* 49. 100B–-102A.
5. *The City of God* XXII, 29. PL 41:800.
6. *De Trinitate* X, 5. PL 42:977.
7. *De anima* III, 8. 431b20–28.
8. *De coelesti hierarchia* 12. PG 3:293.
9. *De Trinitate* IX, 3. PL 42:963.
10. Cf. Aristotle, *De anima* I, 2, 5. 404b11–18, 409b18–410a13.

11. Cf. *Phaedo* 27-28. 79C–80B.

12. Aristotle, *Metaphysics* VIII, 9. 1051a21–33.

13. *De anima* I, 5. 409b18–410a13.

14. Aristotle, *De anima* II, 12. 424a28–b3.

15. Q. 78, A. 3.

16. See n. 6, supra.

17. Ibid.

18. *Homiliarum in Evangelia* II, *homilia* 29. PL 76:1214.

19. *Liber de causis*, prop. 10.

20. *Meno* 15 et seq. 81C et seq.

21. *De anima* III, 4. 429b29–430a2.

22. *Phaedo* 18 et seq. 72E et seq. *Meno*, loc. cit. *Phaedrus* 30.
249D–250C.

23. Q. 76, A. 1.

24. See n. 18, supra.

25. Q. 66, A. 2.

26. Q. 84, A. 1.

27. Ibid.

28. *Metaphysics* VI, 14–15. 1039a24–b19.

29. *De anima*, part 5, chap. 5. *Metaphysics*, tract. 8, chap. 6, and tract. 8,
chaps. 4–5.

30. Cf. *De anima*, part 5, chap. 6.

31. Cf. *De anima*, part 5, chap. 5.

32. *De divinis nominibus* 7. PG 3:868.

33. Q. 79, A. 4.

34. *De mystica theologia* 1. PG 3:1001.

35. Rom. 1:20.

36. *Octoginta trium quaestionum*, Q. 46. PL 40:30.

37. *Confessions* XII, 25. PL 32:840.

38. *De doctrina Christiana* II, 40. PL 34:63.

39. Q. 84, A. 4.

40. *De divinis nominibus* 11. PG 3:953.

41. See n. 36, supra.

42. Ps. 4:6.

43. *De Trinitate* IV, 16. PL 42:902.

44. See n. 36, supra.

45. *Octoginta trium quaestionum*, Q. 9. PL 40:13.

46. *Super Genesim ad litteram* XII, 16. PL 34:467.

47. *Metaphysics* I, 1. 980a28–b25, 980b28–981a2.

48. *Posterior Analytics* II, 19. 100a3–14.

49. *Epistola* 118, 4. PL 33:445.

50. *De divinatione per somnia* 2. 463. Both this work and the work miscited by St. Thomas in the text belong to the *Parva naturalia*.

51. *De anima* III, 3. 427a17–29.

52. Q. 84, AA. 4, 5.

53. *Super Genesim ad litteram* XII, 24. PL 34:475.

54. *De anima* III, 3. 427b6–14.

55. Aristotle, *De generatione et corruptione* I, 8. 324b25–325a2.

56. *De anima* III, 4. 429a18–27.

57. *De anima* III, 5. 430a17–19.

58. Q. 79, AA. 3, 4.

59. See n. 57, supra.

60. *De anima* I, 1. 403a5–10.

61. *De anima* III, 3. 428b10–17.

62. *De anima* III, 7. 431a14–17.

63. Q. 79, A. 6.

64. *De divinis nominibus* 1. PG 3:593, 597.

65. *De somno et vigilia* 1. 454.

66. *Super Genesim ad litteram* XII, 15. PL 34:466.

67. Q. 84, A. 7.

68. *De coelo* III, 7. 306a16–17.

69. *De somno et vigilia* 3. 457.

ST I
Question 85
On the Ways and Order of Understanding

[This question is divided into eight articles, seven of which are included here.]

First Article

Does Our Intellect Understand Corporeal and Material Things by Abstracting from Sense Images?

I proceed in this way to the first article: it seems that our intellect does not understand corporeal and material things by abstracting from sense images.

Obj. 1. Every intellect that understands a thing otherwise than the thing is, errs. But the forms of material things are not taken away from individual things, whose likenesses are sense images. Therefore, if we should understand material things by taking forms away from sense images of the things, our intellect will err.

Obj. 2. Material things are things of nature, and matter is included in the definition of such things. But we cannot understand anything apart from what is included in its definition. Therefore, we cannot understand things apart from matter. But matter is the source of individuation. Therefore, we cannot understand material things by abstracting universals from individual things, that is, by abstracting intelligible forms from sense images.

Obj. 3. The *De anima* says that sense images are related to the intellectual soul as colors are to sight.[1] But vision is not produced by abstracting certain forms from colors; rather, vision is produced by colors imprinting themselves on the power of sight. Therefore, neither does understanding happen because anything is abstracted from sense images; rather understanding happens because sense images imprint themselves on the intellect.

Obj. 4. As the *De anima* says, the intellectual soul has two powers, namely, the potential intellect and the active intellect.[2] But it does not belong to the potential intellect to abstract intelligible forms from sense images; rather, it belongs to the potential intellect to receive such forms after they have been abstracted. And neither also does it seem to belong to the active intellect to abstract intelligible forms from sense images, since the active intellect is related to sense images as light is to colors, and light acts on colors rather than abstracts anything from them. Therefore, in no way do we understand by abstracting from sense images.

Obj. 5. The Philosopher says in the *De anima* that "the intellect understands the forms in sense images."[3] Therefore, the intellect does not understand forms by abstracting them.

On the contrary, the *De anima* says that "things are objects of the intellect insofar as they can be separated from matter."[4] Therefore, we necessarily understand material things insofar as they are abstracted from matter and from the material likenesses of things, that is, sense images.

I answer that objects of knowledge are proportioned to cognitive powers, as I have said before.[5] And there are three grades of cognitive powers. For example, one kind of cognitive power, namely, that of the senses, is the actuality of bodily organs. And so the object of every sense power is a form as it exists in corporeal matter. And because such matter is the source of individuation, every power of the sensory part of the soul consequently knows only individual things.

And there is another kind of cognitive power, such as the angelic intellect, that is neither the actuality of a bodily organ nor in any way joined to corporeal matter. And so the object of such a cognitive power is a form subsisting apart from matter. For while angels do know material things, they nonetheless know them only in immaterial things, namely, either themselves or God.

But the human intellect is disposed in a middle way, for the human intellect is not the actuality of any bodily organ but still a power of the soul, that is, the form of a body, as is clear from what I have said before.[6] And so its proper object is to know forms that indeed exist individually in corporeal matter, but not to know such forms as they exist in such matter. But to know what exists in individual matter, in a way other than it exists in such matter, is to abstract a form from individual matter, which sense images represent. And so we need to say that our intellect understands material things by abstracting from sense images, and that we come by means of material things so considered to some kind of knowledge of immaterial things, just as, conversely, angels know material things by means of immaterial things.

And Plato, attending only to the immateriality of the human intellect and not to the fact that the human intellect is united to a body, held that the objects of the intellect are separate ideas, and that we understand by sharing in abstract ideas rather, indeed, than by abstracting forms from sense images, as I have said before.[7]

Reply to Obj. 1. There are two ways of taking things away. In one way, we take away by way of composition and division, as, for example, when we understand that something is not in something else or is separate from it. In the second way, we take away by way of unqualified and absolute consideration, as, for example, when we understand one thing without considering anything about anything else. Therefore, for the intellect in the first way of taking away to take away things that are not really taken away, has some falsity. But for the intellect in the second way of taking away to take away things that are not really taken away, has no falsity, as is clearly evident in the case of sensibly perceptible things. For example, if we should understand or declare that there is no color in a colored material substance, or that the color is separate from the material substance, there will be falsity in the opinion or statement. But if we should consider color and its properties without considering anything about a colored apple, or if we should also express in words what we so understand, there will be no falsity in the opinion or statement. For apple does not belong to the nature of color, and so nothing prevents us from understanding color without understanding anything about an apple.

I say in like manner that we can consider things that belong to the nature of every kind of material things, for example, the species of stone or human being or horse, apart from the individual sources of material things, which sources do not belong to the nature of species. And this is to take the universal away from the particular, or intelligible forms from sense images, that is, to consider the nature of species without considering the individual sources that sense images represent.

Therefore, when we say that the intellect that understands a thing otherwise than the thing is, errs, that statement is true if the word "otherwise" refers to the thing understood. For the intellect errs when it understands a thing to be otherwise than the thing is. And so the intellect would err if it were to take the form stone away from matter in such a way as to understand that the form does not exist in matter, as Plato held.

But the proposition that the intellect that understands a thing otherwise than it is, errs, is false if we should understand the word "otherwise" to refer to the one who understands. For it is not false to say that the way of the one who understands, in understanding, differs from the way of things in existing; it is true because things understood exist in an immaterial way, in the way of the intellect, in the one who understands, and not in a material way, in the way of material things.

Reply to Obj. 2. Certain thinkers held that the species of things of nature consist only of forms, and that matter is not part of the species.[8] But if we followed this opinion, we would not posit matter in the definitions of things of nature. And so we need to say otherwise, that there are two kinds of matter, namely, common matter and designated or individual matter; indeed, common matter such as flesh and bones, and individual matter such as this particular flesh and these particular bones. Therefore, the intellect abstracts the forms of things of nature from individual sensibly perceptible matter but not from common sensibly perceptible matter. For example, the intellect abstracts the form of human being from this particular flesh and these particular bones, which do not belong to the nature of the human species but are parts of the individual human being, as the *Metaphysics* says,[9] and so we can consider the form of human being apart from this particular flesh and these particular bones. But the intellect cannot abstract the form of human being from flesh and bones.

And our intellect can abstract mathematical forms from both individual sensibly perceptible matter and from common sensibly perceptible matter, but only from individual intelligible matter and not from common intelligible matter. For we call sensibly perceptible matter corporeal insofar as the matter is the subject of sensibly perceptible properties, namely, hot and cold, hard and soft, and such like. And we call intelligible matter a substance insofar as the matter is the subject of extension. And a substance evidently has extension before it has sensibly perceptible properties. And so we can consider such quantities as numbers and dimensions and shapes, which are limitations of extension, apart from sensibly perceptible properties, and this is to abstract quantities from sensibly perceptible matter. But we cannot consider quantities without understanding the substance that is the subject of extension, which would be to abstract quantities from common intelligible matter. Still, we can consider quantities apart from this or that particular substance, which is to abstract quantities from individual intelligible matter.

And there are some things, such as being, one, potentiality and actuality, and the like, that we can abstract even from common intelligible matter, and such things can also exist apart from any matter, as is evident in the case of immaterial substances.

And because Plato did not consider what I have said about the two ways of taking things away,[10] he held that everything we said the intellect abstracts, is abstract in reality.

Reply to Obj. 3. Colors, as existing in corporeal matter, have the same way of existing that the power of sight has, and so they can imprint their likenesses on the power of sight. But sense images, since they are the likenesses of individual things and in bodily organs, do not have the same way of existing that the human intellect has, as is clear from what I have said.[11] And so sense images cannot by their own power imprint themselves on the potential intellect. But the power of the active intellect, by its recourse to sense images, produces likenesses in the potential intellect. And these likenesses, only regarding the nature of species, indeed represent the things of which we have sense images. And it is in this way that we say that we abstract intelligible forms from sense images, not that the numerically identical forms previously present in sense images later come to be in the potential intellect, as material substances are taken from one place and transported to another.

Reply to Obj. 4. Not only does the active intellect illumine sense images, but also the power of the active intellect abstracts intelligible forms from them. The active intellect indeed illumines the images, since, as the union of the sensory part of the soul to the intellectual part makes the sensory part more powerful, so the power of the active intellect renders sense images apt for the intelligible imports to be abstracted from them. And the active intellect abstracts intelligible forms from sense images, since we can by the power of the active intellect take into our contemplation the natures of species apart from individual conditions. And in the likenesses of these natures, the potential intellect receives forms.

Reply to Obj. 5. Our intellect both abstracts intelligible forms from sense images, in that it considers things' natures as universal, and yet understands those natures in sense images, since it cannot, without recourse to sense images, understand even the things whose forms it abstracts, as I have said before.[12]

Second Article

Are the Intelligible Forms Abstracted from Sense Images
Related to Our Intellect as the Things It Understands?

I proceed in this way to the second article: it seems that the intelligible forms abstracted from sense images are related to our intellect as the things it understands.

Obj. 1. Things actually understood are in the one who understands, since things actually understood are the very intellect actually understanding. But nothing about things understood except their intelligible forms are in the intellect actually understanding. Therefore, such forms are the very things actually understood.

Obj. 2. Things actually understood need to be in something; otherwise, they would be nothing. But they are not in things outside the soul, since, things outside the soul being material, nothing in them can be actually understood. We conclude, therefore, that what is actually understood is in the intellect. And so there are in the intellect only the aforementioned intelligible forms.

Obj. 3. The Philosopher says in the *De interpretatione* that "words signify the things that belong to the soul's potentialities being acted upon."[13] But words signify things understood, since we by words signify what we understand. Therefore, the soul's very potentialities being acted upon, namely, the intelligible forms, are the things we actually understand.

On the contrary, intelligible forms are related to the intellect as sensibly perceptible forms are related to the senses. But sensibly perceptible forms are not what the senses perceive, but are rather the means by which the senses perceive. Therefore, intelligible forms are not what the intellect actually understands, but the means by which the intellect understands.

I answer that some thinkers held that our cognitive powers know only their own potentialities being acted upon; for example, that the senses perceive only their organs' potentialities being acted upon. And the intellect accordingly understands only its potentiality being acted upon, that is, the intelligible forms that it receives. And according to this view, such forms are the very things that the intellect understands.

But two considerations show this opinion to be clearly false. First, indeed, because the things that we understand, and the things that are the objects of science, are the same. Therefore, if the forms in the soul were to be the only things we understand, it would logically follow that only the intelligible forms within the soul and not things outside the soul would be the objects of every science; for example, according to the Platonists, the objects of every science are the Ideas, and they held that the Ideas are the things we actually understand.

Second, the opinion is false because its consequence would be the error of the ancient philosophers who said that "Everything that seems to be true, is true,"[14] and so that contradictory propositions would be true at the same time. For, if a power knows only its own potentiality being acted upon, it judges only about that. And so things seem to be as cognitive powers are affected. Therefore, the judgments of cognitive powers will always be about the things that they are judging, namely, their own potentialities being acted upon, as such, and so every judgment will be true. For example, if the sense of taste perceives only its own potentiality being acted upon, a person with a healthy sense of taste will judge truly when the person judges honey to be sweet, and a person with a diseased sense of taste will likewise judge truly when the person judges honey to be bitter, since each judges as the person's sense of taste is affected. And so it follows that every opinion and every perception whatsoever will be equally true.

And so we need to say that intelligible forms are related to the intellect as the means by which the intellect understands. And the following argument makes this evident. For, although there are two kinds of action, one that remains in the efficient cause (for example, acts of seeing and understanding), and the other one that passes into something external (for example, acts of heating and cutting), as the *Metaphysics* says,[15] some form produces each kind of action. And as the forms that produce actions extending to external things are likenesses of the objects of the actions (for example, the heat of what produces heat, is the likeness of what becomes hot), the forms that produce actions that remain in efficient causes are likewise likenesses of the objects of those actions. And so the likenesses of visible things are the means by which the power of sight sees, and the likenesses of things understood, that is, the intelligible forms, are the forms by which the intellect understands.

But because the intellect is reflexively conscious of its very self, it by that reflex consciousness understands both its acts of understanding and the forms whereby it understands. And so intelligible forms are secondarily things that it understands, although the things of which the intelligible forms are likenesses are the things it understands first.

And this is also made clear by the opinion of the ancient philosophers, who held that "like things are known by like things." For they held that the soul would know the earth outside itself by means of the earth inside itself, and so forth.[16] Therefore, if, instead of the earth, we understand the form of the earth, following the teaching of Aristotle (who says that "the form of stone, not any stone, is in the soul"[17],) it would logically follow that the soul knows things outside the soul by means of intelligible forms.

Reply to Obj. 1. Things understood are in those who understand, by the things' likenesses. And this is the way in which we say that things actually understood are the intellect actually understanding, since the likenesses of things understood are the form of the intellect, just as the likenesses of sensibly perceptible things are the forms of the senses actually perceiving. And so it does not follow that abstracted intelligible forms are what we understand, but it follows that the forms are likenesses of what we understand.

Reply to Obj. 2. By the words "things actually understood" we imply two things, namely, the things understood and the fact that we understand the things themselves. And we likewise understand two things by the expression "abstract universals," namely, the very natures of the things and the abstract character or universality of those natures. Therefore, the very natures that either being understood or being abstract or the import of universality befalls, exist only in singular things, but the very fact that the natures are understood or abstract, or the import of universality, exists in the intellect. And we can consider this by something similar in the senses. For example, the sense of sight sees the color of an apple without smelling its odor. Therefore, if one should ask where is the color that is perceived apart from the smell, it is evident that the perceived color exists only in the apple, but that the sense of sight happens to perceive the color without perceiving the smell because the sense of sight has likenesses of color, not of smell. Similarly, the human nature that we understand, exists only in this or that particular human being. But that humanity is known apart from individual conditions (i.e., that it is abstract) and so with an import of universality, happens to belong to humanity as it is perceived by the intellect, which has the likenesses of specific natures and not of individual sources.

Reply to Obj. 3. We find two kinds of activity in the sensory part of the soul. One kind is by alteration alone, and sensibly perceptible things affecting the senses bring about such activities of the external senses in this way. The other kind consists of producing forms, as the power of imagination forms for itself images of absent things or even of things never seen. And both of these activities are united in the intellect. For we indeed first consider the potential intellect's potentiality being acted upon as intelligible forms actualize the potential intellect. And indeed when so actualized by intelligible forms, the intellect secondly forms either definitions or divisions or compositions, and we signify such by words. And so the natures signified by terms are definitions, and propositions signify the intellect's compositions and divisions. Therefore, words do not signify intelligible forms themselves; rather, words signify the things that the intellect forms for itself in order to judge about external things.

Third Article

Are More Universal Things the First Things We Know Intellectually?

I proceed in this way to the third article: it seems that more universal things are not the first things we know intellectually.

Obj. 1. Things prior and more knowable in the order of nature are subsequent and less knowable in our knowledge. But universals are prior in the order of nature, since "those things are prior that are not convertible with corollaries of subsisting."[18] Therefore, universals are subsequent in our intellect's knowledge.

Obj. 2. Composite things are, in our knowledge, prior to simple things. But universals are simpler than composite things. Therefore, in our knowledge, we know universals subsequently.

Obj. 3. The Philosopher says in the *Physics* that things defined fall within our cognizance before parts of their definitions do.[19] But more universal things are parts of the definitions of less universal things; for example, animal is part of the definition of human being. Therefore, in our knowledge, we know universals subsequently.

Obj. 4. We arrive at causes and sources through effects. But universals are certain sources of knowledge. Therefore, in our knowledge, we know universals subsequently.

On the contrary, the *Physics* says that "we ought to arrive at particulars from universals."[20]

I answer that we ought to consider two things concerning the knowledge of our intellect. First, indeed, that our intellectual knowledge originates in some way from sense knowledge. And because the objects of the senses are individual things, while the objects of the intellect are universals, knowledge of individual things, in our knowledge, is necessarily prior to knowledge of universals.

Second, we need to consider that our intellect goes from potentiality to actuality. And everything going from potentiality to actuality comes first to an incomplete actuality in between potentiality and actuality before coming to complete actuality. Moreover, the complete actuality of the intellect that the intellect attains is full knowledge, knowledge whereby the intellect knows things in a distinct and determined way. But the intellect's incomplete actuality consists of incomplete knowledge, knowledge whereby the intellect knows things in an indistinct way and a way subject to some confusion, for we in one respect actually know the things so known, and in another respect potentially know them. And so the Philosopher says in the *Physics* that "the things first evident to us and certain are rather confused, but we later know them by distinguishing their sources and elements in a distinct way."[21] And it is evident that to know something containing several things, without having specific knowledge of each of the latter, is to know something in a way subject to some confusion. And we can in this way know both a universal whole, which contains parts potentially, and also an integrated whole, since we can know every whole in a somewhat confused way, without knowing the parts distinctly. And to know distinctly parts contained in a universal whole is to know things less general. For example, to know animal in an indistinct way is to know animal as such, while to know animal in a distinct way is to know animal as rational or irrational, that is, to know a human being or a lion. Therefore, our intellect may know animal before it may know human being, and the reasoning is the same whenever we should relate something more universal to something less universal.

And because the senses, just like the intellect, go from potentiality to actuality, the same order of knowledge is evident in the senses. For we by the senses discern things more general before we discern things less general, regarding both place and time. Regarding place, indeed, as, for example, when we perceive that something seen at a distance is a material substance before we perceive that it is an animal, and we perceive that it is an animal before we perceive that it is a human being, and we perceive that it is a human being before we perceive that it is Socrates or Plato.   And regarding time, since children initially distinguish human beings from other things before they distinguish one human being from another. And so "children initially call all adult males fathers, and subsequently distinguish each one," as the *Physics* says.[22]

And the reason for this is evident; it is evident because one who knows something indistinctly still has potentiality to know sources of distinction; for example, one who knows a genus has potentiality to know specific differences. And so it is clear that indistinct knowledge is in between potentiality and actuality.

And so we need to say that, in our knowledge, knowledge of individual things is prior to knowledge of universals, since sense knowledge is prior to intellectual knowledge. But regarding both the senses and the intellect, more general knowledge is prior to less general knowledge.

Reply to Obj. 1. We can consider universals in two ways. In one way, as we consider universal natures along with an import of universality. And since the import of universality, namely, that one and the same thing have a relationship to many things, is the product of the intellect's abstracting, universals so considered are necessarily subsequent. And so *De anima* says that "animal as universal is either nothing or something subsequent."[23] (But, according to Plato, who held universals to be subsistent, universals so considered would be prior to particulars, which, according to him, exist only by sharing in the subsistent universals that he called Ideas.[24])

In the second way, we can consider universals with respect to the natures themselves (to wit, the nature of being animal or the nature of being human) as found in particular things. And then we need to say that there are two kinds of orders of nature. One is by way of coming to be and of time, and in this way, things that are imperfect and potential are prior. And in this way, the more general is by the order of nature first, and this is clearly evident in the coming to be of human being and animal, since "the animal comes to be before the human being does," as the *De generatione animalium* says.[25] The second kind of order of nature is the order of perfection, or of what nature strives for; for example, actuality is by nature unqualifiedly prior to potentiality, and the perfect is by nature unqualifiedly prior to the imperfect. And in this way, the less general is by nature prior to the more general; for example, human being is by nature prior to animal, since nature's striving does not stand still at the coming to be of animal, but nature strives to cause human being to come to be.

Reply to Obj. 2. We relate more general universals to less general universals as wholes and as parts. As a whole, indeed, insofar as the greater universal potentially contains both the less universal and other things; for example, animal potentially contains both human being and horse. And as a part, insofar as the less general universal contains in its essence both the more general universal and other things; for example, human being contains in its essence both animal and rational. Therefore, we know animal considered in itself before we know human being, but we know human being before we know that animal is part of the essence of human being.

Reply to Obj. 3. We can know a part in two ways. In one way, absolutely, as the part is in itself, and so nothing prevents us from knowing parts before we know the whole; for example, from knowing stones before we know a house. In the second way, we can know parts insofar as they belong to a particular whole, and then we necessarily know the whole before we know the parts; for example, we know a house with some confusion before we distinguish the house's individual parts. Therefore, we need to say that we know the things that define, considered absolutely, before we know the things to be defined; otherwise, the things that define would not make known the things to be defined. But we later know the things that define as parts of definitions; for example, we know human being with some confusion before we know how to distinguish everything that belongs to the essence of human being.

Reply to Obj. 4. Universals, as understood with an import of universality, are indeed in some way sources of knowing, insofar as the import of universality results from our way of understanding, that is, by abstraction. But not every source of knowing needs to be a source of existing, as Plato held, since we sometimes know causes by their effects, and substances by their accidents. And so, according to the opinion of Aristotle, universals so understood are not sources of existing, or substances, as the *Metaphysics* makes clear.[26]

And if we should consider the very natures of genera and species as those natures exist in individual things, then those natures somehow have the aspect of a formal source with respect to individual things, since things are individual by reason of matter, and we take in the nature of species from forms. And we relate a generic nature to a specific nature rather as a material source, since we take in a generic nature from what is material in a thing, but we take in a specific nature from what is formal in it; for example, we take in the nature of animal from sense powers but the nature of human being from intellectual power. And so the ultimate aim of nature is to produce species, not individuals or genera, since forms are the goals of coming to be, while matter exists because of forms. Moreover, it is not necessary that, in our knowledge, knowledge of every cause or source be subsequent to knowledge of effects, since we sometimes know unknown effects by means of their sensibly perceptible causes, and sometimes the converse.

Fourth Article

Can We Understand Many Things at the Same Time?

I proceed in this way to the fourth article: it seems that we can understand many things at the same time.

Obj. 1. The intellect transcends time. But things prior and subsequent belong to time. Therefore, the intellect understands different things at the same time, not successively.

Obj. 2. Nothing prevents different noncontrary forms from being actually present in the same thing at the same time; for example, odor and color are actually present in apples at the same time. But different intelligible forms are not contrary. Therefore, nothing prevents one and the same intellect from being simultaneously actualized by different intelligible forms. And so the intellect can understand many things at the same time.

Obj. 3. The intellect understands something whole, for instance, a human being or a house, at the same time. But every whole contains numerous parts. Therefore, the intellect understands many things at the same time.

Obj. 4. We cannot know the distinction of one thing from another unless we know both things at the same time, as the *De anima* says,[27] and the reasoning is the same about any other relation. But our intellect knows the distinction of one thing from another, and the relation of one thing to another. Therefore, the intellect knows many things at the same time.

On the contrary, the *Topics* says that "to understand is only one thing, but to know is many things."[28]

I answer that the intellect can indeed understand many things as one, but not many things as many, and I say "as one" or "as many" to mean by one or several intelligible forms. For the manner of every action results from the form that is the source of the action. Therefore, the intellect can understand at the same time whatever it can understand under one form, and so God perceives everything at once, since he perceives everything by one thing, that is, his essence. But the intellect does not understand at the same time whatever it understands by different forms. And the reason for this is because several forms of the same genus but of different species cannot at the same time perfect the same subject; for example, different colors cannot at the same time color, nor can different shapes at the same time shape, the same material substance as such. And all intelligible forms belong to the same genus, since they perfect the same intellectual power, although the things of which they are the forms, belong to different genera. Therefore, different intelligible forms cannot at the same time perfect the same intellect to understand different things actually.

Reply to Obj. 1. The intellect transcends the time that is the measure of the motion of material things. But the very plurality of intelligible forms causes a certain succession of acts of understanding, and by such succession, one act succeeds another. And Augustine, when he says in his *Super Genesim* that "God moves spiritual creatures through time," calls such succession time.[29]

Reply to Obj. 2. Not only is it impossible for contrary forms to exist at the same time in the same subject, but neither can any forms of the same genus, even if they be not contrary, as the cited examples of color and shape make clear.[30]

Reply to Obj. 3. We can understand parts in two ways. In one way, with some confusion, as parts of a whole, and then we know them by the one form of the whole. In the second way, with distinct knowledge, as we know each part by its own form, and then we do not understand them at the same time.

Reply to Obj. 4. When the intellect understands the distinction of one thing from another, or the relation of one thing to another, it knows each of the things distinguished or related under the aspect of the very relation or distinction, just as I have said that it knows parts under the aspect of the whole.[31]

Fifth Article

Does Our Intellect Understand by Composing and Dividing?

I proceed in this way to the fifth article: it seems that our intellect does not understand by composing and dividing.

Obj. 1. We only compose and divide many things. But the intellect cannot at the same time understand many things. Therefore, the intellect cannot understand by composing and dividing.

Obj. 2. Past, present, or future time is attached to every composition and division. But the intellect abstracts from time, just as it does from other particular conditions. Therefore, the intellect does not understand by composing and dividing.

Obj. 3. The intellect understands by being made like things. But the intellect's compositions and divisions consist of nothing in things, since we find in things only what predicates and subjects signify, and these are one and the same if the compositions are true; for example, human being is truly what is animal. Therefore, the intellect does not compose and divide anything in things.

On the contrary, words signify the intellect's concepts, as the Philosopher says in the *De Interpretatione.*[32] But words compose and divide, as affirmative and negative propositions demonstrate. Therefore, the intellect composes and divides.

I answer that the human intellect needs to understand by composing and dividing. For the human intellect, since it goes from potentiality to actuality, bears some resemblance to things that can come to be, things that do not possess their perfection immediately but acquire it in successive stages. And similarly, the human intellect does not in its first understanding immediately acquire complete knowledge of things; rather, it understands something about those very things, for example, their essences, which are the first and proper object of the intellect. And then the intellect understands the properties and accidents and dispositions that accompany the things' essences. And the intellect accordingly needs to compose one understood thing with, or divide one understood thing from, another, and to advance from one composition or division to another, and this is to reason.

But the intellects of angels and God are constituted as things that cannot pass away,[33] things that possess their whole perfection immediately from the beginning. And so the intellects of angels and

God perfectly possess complete knowledge of things immediately. And so their intellects, in knowing the essences of things, immediately know about the things whatever we can know by composing and dividing and reasoning.

And so the human intellect knows by composing and dividing, as well as by reasoning. And the intellects of God and angels indeed know composition and division and reasoning, not by composing and dividing and reasoning, but by understanding pure essences.

Reply to Obj. 1. Distinctions or relations cause the intellect's compositions and divisions. And so the intellect knows as many things by composing and dividing as it knows by distinguishing and relating things.

Reply to Obj. 2. The intellect both abstracts from sense images and yet actually understands only by having recourse to sense images, as I have said before.[34] And insofar as the intellect has recourse to sense images, time is attached to its composition and divisions.

Reply to Obj. 3. The intellect receives the likenesses of things in the way of the intellect and not in the way of the things. And so something on the part of things indeed corresponds to the intellect's composition and division, but it is not disposed in things in the same way that it is disposed in the intellect. For the proper object of the intellect is the essence of a material thing, which thing falls within the power of the senses and the power of imagination. And we find two kinds of composition in material things. First, indeed, the composition of form and matter, and to this composition there corresponds the composition of the intellect whereby the intellect predicates universal wholes of their parts. For we from common matter take in genera, and from forms the differences that complete species, and from individual matter particular things. And the second composition in material things is one of accidents and their subjects, and to this real composition there corresponds the composition of the intellect whereby the intellect predicates accidents of subjects, as, for example, when we say that a human being is white.

Nevertheless, the intellect's compositions differ from the compositions in things, since the components in things are different things, while the intellect's compositions signify the identity of the components. For example, the intellect does not compose a subject and a predicate so as to say that a human being is whiteness, but the intellect says that a human being is white, that is, that a human being is something possessing whiteness. And being a human being and possessing whiteness are identical in the subject. And cases of the composition of form and matter are similar. For example, animal signifies something that has a sensory nature, and rational signifies something that has an intellectual nature, and human being signifies something that has both, and Socrates signifies something that has all of these along with individual matter. And in this aspect of identify, the intellect by predication composes one thing with another.

Sixth Article

Can the Intellect Be False?

I proceed in this way to the sixth article: it seems that the intellect can be false.

Obj. 1. The Philosopher says in the *Metaphysics* that "truth and falsity are in the mind."[35] But the mind and the intellect are the same thing, as I have said before.[36] Therefore, there is falsity in the intellect.

Obj. 2. Opinion and reasoning belong to the intellect. But we find falsity in both opinions and reasoning. Therefore, there can be falsity in the intellect.

Obj. 3. There is sin in the intellectual part of the soul. But falsity accompanies sin, since "they err who do evil," as the Book of Proverbs says.[37] Therefore, there can be falsity in the intellect.

On the contrary, Augustine says in his *Octoginta trium quaestionum* that "all those in error do not understand the things in which they err."[38] And the Philosopher says in the *De anima* that "the intellect is always correct."[39]

I answer that the Philosopher in the *De anima* compares the intellect to the senses in this respect.[40] For the senses are not deceived about their proper objects (for example, the sense of sight about color), except perhaps by accident, by hindrances related to sense organs (for example, when the sense of taste of persons with a fever judges sweet things to be bitter, since the persons' tongues are replete with harmful juices). And the senses are deceived about things that can be perceived by more than one sense, as when the senses discern about size or shape (for example, when the sense [of sight] judges that the sun is a foot in diameter, although the sun is larger than the earth). And much more are the senses deceived about sensibly perceptible things by the things' accidental characteristics (for example, when the sense [of sight], because of likeness of color, determines that vinegar is honey). And the reason for this lies in what is evident, since every power as such is intrinsically ordered to its proper object. And such things are always disposed in the same way. And so, as long as the power remains, its judgment about its proper object does not fail.

Now, the essences of things are the proper object of the intellect. And so, properly speaking, the intellect cannot err regarding the essences of things. But the intellect can err regarding the things that accompany the essences or quiddities of things when the intellect relates one thing to another, whether by composing or by dividing, or also by reasoning. And this is also the reason why the intellect cannot err about those propositions immediately known when the essences of their terms are known, as happens in the case of first principles. And there also arises from such principles, by way of scientific certitude, unerring truth about conclusions.

But the intellect may by accident be deceived about what something is, in things composed by the intellect. This does not happen regarding sense organs, since the intellect is not a power that utilizes sense organs; rather, it happens regarding intervening compositions that concern definitions, either when the definition of one thing is false about something else (e.g., the definition of circle is false about triangle) or when a definition in itself is false, one involving a composition of contradictory things (e.g., if one should understand "winged rational animal" as the definition of some thing). And so we cannot be deceived in the case of simple things, in the definition of which no composition can intervene; rather, in such cases, we fail to attain any knowledge of them at all, as the *Metaphysics* says.[41]

Reply to the Objs. With respect to the first objection, the Philosopher says that there is falsity in the mind by reason of the intellect's composing and dividing. And we need to respond in like manner to the second objection regarding opinion and reasoning, and to the third objection regarding the error of sinners, which consists in the inclination of the mind toward desirable things. But the intellect is never deceived in its absolute consideration of the essences of things, and of the things it knows through those essences. And the authorities cited to the contrary are speaking in this way.

Seventh Article

*Can One Person Understand the Very Same Thing
Better than Another Person Can?*

I proceed in this way to the seventh article: it seems that one person cannot understand the very same thing better than another person can.

Obj. 1. Augustine says in his *Octoginta trium quaestionum*: "Whoever understands something otherwise than it is, does not understand it. Therefore, we undoubtedly have perfect understanding, and there cannot be any understanding more excellent than such understanding. And so it is beyond doubt that we do not go through endless steps to understand each thing, and that one person cannot understand anything better than another person does."[42]

Obj. 2. The intellect, when it understands, is true. But truth, since it is a certain equation of the intellect and things, does not admit of more or less, for we do not properly say that anything is more or less equal. Therefore, neither do we say that anything is more or less understood.

Obj. 3. The intellect is what most belongs to the human form. But different forms cause different species. Therefore, if one human being understands more than another, it seems that they would not belong to the same species.

On the contrary, we find by experience that some persons understand more deeply than others do; for example, those who are able to trace conclusions to first principles and first causes understand more deeply than those who are able only to trace conclusions to proximate causes.

I answer that we can understand in two ways that some understand the very same thing better than others do. In one way, we can understand that the word "better" modifies the act of understanding with respect to the thing understood. And then one person cannot understand the same thing more than another can, since one would err and not understand if one were to understand the thing otherwise than it is, whether better or worse than it is, as Augustine proves.[43] In the second way, we can understand the word "better" to modify the act of understanding with respect to those who understand. And then one person can understand the same thing better than another, since one person has greater power of understanding, just as, in the case of bodily sight, those with more powerful and more accurate vision see things better than others do.

And regarding the intellect, there may be greater power of understanding in two ways. In one way, indeed, there may be greater power regarding the very intellect that is more perfect. For it is evident that the better disposed the material substance, the more excellent the soul allotted to it, and this is clearly evident in things of different species. And the reason for this is because actualities and forms are received in matter according to the capacity of the matter. And so also in the case of human beings, some, because they have better disposed bodies, are allotted souls with a greater power of understanding, and so the *De anima* says that "we perceive that those with supple flesh are mentally well fit."[44] In the second way, there may be greater power of understanding regarding the lower powers that the intellect needs for its activity. For those whose power of imagination and cogitative power and power of memory are better disposed, are better disposed to understand.

Reply to Obj. 1. The response is clear from what I have said.

Reply to Obj. 2. The response is likewise clear from what I have said, since the truth of the intellect consists in the fact that the intellect understands things to be exactly as they are.

Reply to Obj. 3. The difference of forms that comes only from the different arrangement of matter results only in a difference in number, not a difference in species, since different individuals have different forms, forms differentiated by matter.

Notes

1. Aristotle, *De anima* III, 7. 431a14–17.
2. Aristotle, De anima III, 5. 430a10–17.
3. *De anima* III, 7. 431b2–9.
4. Aristotle, *De anima* III, 4. 429b18–22.
5. Q. 84, A. 7.
6. Q. 76, A. 1.
7. Q. 84, A. 1.
8. See Q. 75, A. 4.
9. Aristotle, *Metaphysics* VI, 10. 1035b33–1036a13.
10. In the response to the first objection.

11. In the body of the article.

12. Q. 84, A. 7.

13. *De interpretatione* I, 1. 16a3–4.

14. Cf. Aristotle, *Metaphysics* III, 5. 1009a6–16.

15. Aristotle, *Metaphysics* VIII, 8. 1050a23–b2.

16. Cf. Aristotle, *De anima* I, 2, 5. 404b11–15, 410a27–b2.

17. *De anima* III, 8. 431b28–432a3.

18. Aristotle, *Categories* 12. 14a29–35.

19. *Physics* I, 1. 184a26–b12.

20. Aristotle, *Physics* I, 1. 184a16–24.

21. *Physics* I, 1. 184b16–24.

22. *Physics* I, 1. 184b12–14.

23. Aristotle, *De anima* I, 1. 402a10–b8.

24. Cf. Q. 84, A. 1.

25. Aristotle, *De generatione animalium* II, 3. 736b2–4.

26. Aristotle, *Metaphysics* VI, 13. 1038b8–16.

27. Aristotle, *De anima* III, 2. 426b23–29.

28. Aristotle, *Topics* II, 10. 114b34–35.

29. *Super Genesim ad litteram* VIII, 20, 22. PL 34:388, 389.

30. In the body of the article.

31. In the response to the third objection.

32. *De interpretatione* I, 1. 16a3–4.

33. I.e., the heavenly bodies, which Aristotle and St. Thomas considered substances incapable of substantial change.

34. Q. 85, A. 7, and Q. 85, A. 1.

35. *Metaphysics* V, 4. 1027b25–29.

36. Q. 79, citations of Augustine in A. 1, Obj. 1, and in A. 8, *On the contrary.*

37. Prov. 14:22.

38. *Octoginta trium quaestionum*, Q. 32. PL 40:22.

39. *De anima* III, 10. 433a26–31.

40. *De anima* III, 6. 430b26–31.

41. Aristotle, *Metaphysics* VIII, 10. 1051b23–33.

42. See n. 38, supra.

43. Ibid.

44. Aristotle, *De anima* II, 9. 421a16–26.

ST I

Question 86

What Our Intellect Knows in the Case of Material Things

[This question is divided into four articles, all of which are included here.]

First Article

Does Our Intellect Know Individual Things?

I proceed in this way to the first article: it seems that our intellect knows individual things.

Obj. 1. Those who know compositions know the terms of the compositions. But our intellect knows this composition, Socrates is a human being, since it belongs to the intellect to form such propositions. Therefore, our intellect knows the individual thing that is Socrates.

Obj. 2. The practical intellect governs our actions. But individual things are the objects of our actions. Therefore, the practical intellect knows individual things.

Obj. 3. Our intellect understands its very self. But the intellect itself is something individual; otherwise, the intellect would have no acts, since acts belong to individual things. Therefore, our intellect knows individual things.

Obj. 4. A higher power can do whatever lower powers can. But the senses know individual things. Therefore, much more does the intellect know individual things.

On the contrary, the Philosopher says in the *Physics* that "the power of reason knows universals, while sense powers know individual things."[1]

I answer that our intellect cannot directly and primarily know what is individual in material things. And the reason for this is because the source of individuality in material things is individual matter, while our intellect understands by abstracting intelligible forms from individual matter, as I have said before.[2] But what is abstracted from individual matter is something universal. And so the intellect directly knows only universals.

The intellect can, however, know individual things indirectly and reflexively, as it were. This is because, as I have said before,[3] even after the intellect has abstracted intelligible forms, it can by means of them actually understand only when it has recourse to the sense images in which it understands the intelligible forms, as the *De anima* says.[4] Therefore, the intellect directly understands universals themselves by intelligible forms, and indirectly understands the individual things of which there are sense images.

Reply to Obj. 1. And the intellect in the latter way forms the proposition, Socrates is a human being. And so the response to the first objection is clear.

Reply to Obj. 2. The choice of something to be done is, as it were, the conclusion of a syllogism by the practical intellect, as the *Ethics* says.[5] But the practical intellect cannot directly draw conclusions about individual things from universal propositions except by means of understanding singular propositions. And so the universal principles of the practical intellect do not cause conclusions except by means of individual perceptions by the sensory part of the soul, as the *De anima* says.[6]

Reply to Obj. 3. Individual things as such are compatible with intelligibility, but individual things as material are not, since we do not understand except in an immaterial way. And so, if there be an individual immaterial thing like the intellect, it is compatible with intelligibility.

Reply to Obj. 4. A higher power can do what lower powers can, but it does so in a more excellent way. And so the intellect knows in an immaterial and abstract way, which is to know the universal, what the senses know in a material and concrete way, which is to know individual things directly.

Second Article

Can Our Intellect Know Unlimited Things?

I proceed in this way to the second article: it seems that our intellect can know unlimited things.

Obj. 1. God transcends all unlimited things. But our intellect can know

God, as I have said before.[7] Therefore, much more can our intellect know every other unlimited thing.

Obj. 2. Our intellect is by nature constituted to know genera and species. But there are unlimited species of certain genera, such as the species of number, proportion, and shape. Therefore, our intellect can know unlimited things.

Obj. 3. If one material substance were not to prevent another material substance from existing in the very same place, nothing would prevent an unlimited number of material substances being in one place. But one intelligible form does not prevent another intelligible form from existing at the same time in the same intellect, since the intellect may know many things habitually. Therefore, nothing prevents our intellect from having habitual knowledge of an unlimited number of things.

Obj. 4. The intellect, since it is not a power of corporeal matter, as I have said before,[8] seems to be an unlimited power. But an unlimited power is power over an unlimited number of things. Therefore, our intellect can know an unlimited number of things.

On the contrary, the *Physics* says that "we do not know the unlimited as such."[9]

I answer that, since powers are proportioned to their objects, the intellect needs to be related to the unlimited in the same way that its object, which is the essence of something material, is related to the unlimited. And we do not find in material things anything actually unlimited; rather, we find in material things only things potentially unlimited, as one thing comes after another thing, as the *Physics* says.[10] And so we find in our intellect something potentially infinite, namely, in the intellect's understanding one thing after another, since our intellect never understands so many things that it could not understand more things.

And our intellect cannot actually or habitually know unlimited things. Not actually, indeed, since our intellect can at the same time actually know only what it knows by one form. And nothing unlimited has only one form; otherwise, the unlimited would have the nature of something whole and complete. And so our intellect can know something unlimited only by understanding one part of it after another, as the *Physics* makes clear from the definition of unlimited, for the unlimited is that "of which there is always something further to take, however much we take."[11] And so we could actually know something unlimited only if we were to count all of its parts, and that is impossible.

And by the same reasoning, we cannot understand unlimited things habitually. For our habitual knowledge is the product of actual consideration, since understanding makes us knowledgeable, as the *Ethics* says.[12] And so we would only be able to have habitual knowledge of unlimited things as distinct knowledge if we were to have considered all of the unlimited things, by counting them as we know them successively, and this is impossible. And so our intellect cannot know unlimited things either actually or habitually, but only potentially, as I have said.

Reply to Obj. 1. We call God unlimited because he is a form that is not limited by any matter, as I have said before,[13] but we call something unlimited in the case of material things by reason of their lacking the limit of form. And because we know form as such and do not know matter apart from form, we consequently do not know any material thing that is unlimited, as such. And the formal thing that is unlimited, that is, God, is knowable as such, but unknown relative to ourselves because of the deficiency of our intellect, which in the condition of our present life has a disposition from nature to know material things. And so we in our present condition can know God only by means of the material things he has caused. But in our future condition, our glory will take away the deficiency of our intellect, and then we shall be able to behold God in his essence, although not comprehensively.

Reply to Obj. 2. Our intellect is by nature constituted to know species by abstracting from sense images. And so our intellect cannot know either actually or habitually the forms of numbers and shapes that one has not imagined, except perhaps in general and in the case of universal principles, which is to know potentially and confusedly.

Reply to Obj. 3. If two or more material substances were to be in one place, it would not be necessary for them to occupy that place successively, so that the material substances located there be counted by their very successive occupation of the place. But intelligible forms come into our intellect successively, since we do not actually understand many things at the same time. And so it is necessary that there be a definite and not an unlimited number of forms in our intellect.

Reply to Obj. 4. Our intellect knows the unlimited in the same way that the intellect is unlimited in power. For the intellect's power is unlimited, insofar as corporeal matter does not limit the intellect. And the intellect knows universals, which are abstracted from individual matter, and the intellect is consequently not limited to anything individual, but, as regards itself, extends to an unlimited number of individual things.

Third Article

Does Our Intellect Know Contingent Things?

I proceed in this way to the third article: it seems that the intellect does not know contingent things.

Obj. 1. The objects of the intellect and wisdom and science are necessary things, not contingent things, as the *Ethics* says.[14]

Obj. 2. "Time measures things that at times exist and at other times do not exist," as the *Physics* says.[15] But the intellect abstracts from time as well as other conditions of matter. Therefore, since it is characteristic of contingent things at times to exist and at other times not to exist, it seems that the intellect does not know contingent things.

On the contrary, there is every kind of science in the intellect. But certain sciences have contingent things as their object. For example, there are moral sciences, which have human acts subject to free choice as their object, and there are also natural sciences, which have contingent things as their object with respect to the part of the sciences that treats of things that come to be and pass away. Therefore, the intellect knows contingent things.

I answer that we can consider contingent things in two ways: in one way, as contingent; in the other way, as we find some necessity in contingent things. For example, the very fact that Socrates is running is indeed in itself contingent, but the relationship of running to motion is necessary, for it is necessary that Socrates be in motion if he is running.

Moreover, matter causes things to be contingent, since contingent things can exist or not exist, and potentiality belongs to matter. But necessity results from the nature of form, since the things resulting from form are necessarily present in things. And matter is the source of individuation, while we understand universal natures by abstracting forms from particular matter. And I have said before that universals are intrinsically and directly the object of the intellect,[16] and individual things are the objects of the senses. And individual things are also indirectly in some way the object of the intellect, as I have said before.[17] Therefore, the senses indeed directly know contingent things as such, while the intellect knows such things indirectly, and the intellect knows the universal and necessary natures of contingent things.

And so, if we look to the universal natures of knowable things, necessary things are the object of every science. But if we look to the knowable things themselves, then necessary things are the objects of certain sciences, and contingent things the objects of other sciences.

Reply to the Objs. And this explanation makes clear the response to the objections.

Fourth Article

Does Our Intellect Know Future Things?

I proceed in this way to the fourth article: it seems that our intellect knows future things.

Obj. 1. Our intellect knows by means of intelligible forms, which abstract from "here" and "now," and so are impartially disposed toward every point of time. But our intellect can know present things. Therefore, our intellect can know future things.

Obj. 2. Human beings, when drawn away from their senses, can know some future things, as is evident in the case of those asleep and those in a frenzy. But human being are more intellectually active when they are drawn away from their senses. Therefore, the intellect, as regards itself, knows future things.

Obj. 3. The intellectual knowledge of human beings is more effective than any knowledge belonging to irrational animals. But some animals know some kinds of future things; for example, crows, when they crow repeatedly, signal that rain is imminent. Therefore, much more can the human intellect know future things.

On the contrary, the Book of Ecclesiastes says: "Great is the affliction of human beings, who do not know things of the past, and who cannot by any communication know things of the future."[18]

I answer that we need to make the same distinction about knowledge of future things that we made about knowledge of contingent things.[19] For future things themselves, as they fall within time, are individual things, things that the human intellect can know only reflexively, as I have said before.[20] But aspects of future things can be universal and knowable by the intellect, and there can also be sciences about future things.

Nonetheless, as we generally speak about knowledge of future things, we need to note that we can know future things in two ways: in one way, in themselves; in the other way, in their causes. Only God can know future things indeed in themselves, and they are even present things to him when they are future things in relation to the course of history, since his eternal vision is borne at once over the whole course of time, as I have said before when I treated of God's knowledge.[21]

But we too can know future things as they exist in their causes. And we know future things with scientific certitude if they indeed exist in their causes as causes from which they necessarily result; for example, astronomers predict future eclipses. And if future things exist in their causes in such a way that they result from the causes in a majority of cases, then we can know them by an inference either more or less certain, as the causes are either more or less inclined to produce such effects.

Reply to Obj. 1. That argument is valid about the knowledge that arises from the universal natures of causes, and we can know future things from such natures by the relation of effects to causes.

Reply to Obj. 2. As Augustine says in his *Confessions*, the soul has a certain power of prophecy, so that the soul can by its nature know future things.[22] And so the soul comes to share in knowledge of future things when it is drawn away from the bodily senses and in some way has recourse to itself.

And this opinion would indeed be reasonable if we were to hold, as the Platonists held,[23] that the soul receives its knowledge of things by sharing in the Ideas, since the soul would by its nature then know the universal causes of all effects, although the body would impede it. And so the soul knows future things when it is drawn away from the bodily senses.

But because such a way of knowing is not inborn to our intellect, but rather it is inborn to our intellect to receive its knowledge from the senses, so, when the soul is drawn away from the senses, it is not by the soul's nature but rather by impressions from some higher immaterial and material causes that the intellect knows future things. Indeed the intellect knows future things by impressions from higher immaterial causes, as, for example, when God's power through the ministry of the angels illumines the human intellect and disposes sense images for human beings to know some future things. Or even when the activity of devils causes some excitement in the imagination to signal beforehand some future things that the devils know, as I have said before.[24] And the human soul is by nature more constituted to receive such impressions from immaterial causes when it is drawn away from the senses, since this condition makes the human soul approximate immaterial substances more closely, and makes the human soul freer from external disturbances.

And the intellect may also know future things by impressions from higher material causes. For it is evident that higher material substances impress themselves on lower material substances. And so, since sense powers are the actualities of bodily organs, impressions from heavenly bodies consequently in some way affect the imagination. And so, since heavenly bodies cause many future things,[25] some signs of certain future things are causes in the imagination. And these signs are more perceived at night and by those asleep than they are during the day and by those awake because, as the *De somno et vigilia* says: "Things communicated during the day are weaker than those communicated at night, since night air is calmer as a result of there being less noise at night. And the things communicated affect the bodily senses because of sleep, since those asleep perceive slight internal movements more than those awake do. And such movements cause the sense images by which one foresees future things."[26]

Reply to Obj. 3. Irrational animals possess nothing beyond the power of imagination to dispose their sense images (as human beings have the power of reason), and so the imagination of irrational animals is entirely the product of impressions from heavenly bodies. And so we can better discern certain future things, such as rain and the like, from the movements of irrational animals than we can from the movements of human beings, who move themselves by the deliberation of reason. And so the Philosopher says in the *De somno et vigilia* that "some of the stupidest people foresee things best, since their understanding is not burdened by cares and is almost barren and empty of all things and is drawn to be moved by causes that move it.[27]

Notes

1. *Physics* I, 5. 189a5.
2. Q. 85, A. 1.
3. Q. 85, A. 7.
4. Aristotle, *De anima* III, 7. 431b2–9.
5. Aristotle, *Ethics* VII, 3. 1147a24–31.
6. Aristotle, *De anima* III, 11. 434a16–21.
7. Q. 12, A. 1.

8. Q. 76, A. 1.
9. Aristotle, *Physics* I, 4. 186b7.
10. Aristotle, *Physics* III, 5. 206a18–29.
11. Aristotle, *Physics* III, 6. 207a7.
12. Aristotle, *Ethics* II, 1. 1103a26–b2.
13. Q. 7, A. 1.
14. Aristotle, *Ethics* VI, 6. 1140b31–1141a8.
15. Aristotle, *Physics* IV, 12. 221b29.
16. Q. 86, A. 1.
17. Ibid.
18. Eccl. 8:6–7.
19. Cf. Q. 86, A. 3.
20. Q. 86, A. 1.
21. Q. 14, A. 13.
22. Actually, *Super Genesim ad litteram* XII, 13. PL 34:464.
23. Plato, *Republic* VI, 19. 508.
24. Q. 57, A. 3.
25. Cf. Q. 115.
26. Actually, Aristotle, *De divinatione per somnia* 2. 464a12.
27. Actually, Aristotle, *De divinatione per somnia* 2. 464a18.

ST I

Question 87

How the Intellectual Soul Knows Itself
and the Things Existing in Itself

[This question is divided into four articles, all of which are included here.]

First Article

Does the Intellectual Soul Know Itself by Means of Its Essence?

I proceed in this way to the first article: it seems that the intellectual soul knows itself by means of its essence.

Obj. 1. Augustine says in his *De Trinitate* that "the mind knows itself by means of itself, since it is immaterial."[1]

Obj. 2. Both angels and human souls belong to the genus of intellectual substance. But angels understand themselves by means of their essences. Therefore, human souls also do.

Obj. 3. "In immaterial things, the intellect and what is understood, are identical," as the *De anima* says.[2] But the human mind is immaterial, since it is not the actuality of a material substance, as I have said before.[3] Therefore, in the human mind, the intellect and what is understood, are identical. Therefore, the human mind understands itself by means of its essence.

On the contrary, the *De anima* says that "the intellect understands itself just as it understands other things."[4] But the intellect understands other things by means of their likenesses, not by means of their essences. Therefore, neither does it understand itself by means of its essence.

I answer that everything is knowable insofar as it is actual, and unknowable insofar as it is potential, as the *Metaphysics* says,[5] for thus are things beings and true and, as actual, fall within our knowledge. And this is indeed clearly evident in the case of sensibly perceptible things, since the power of sight perceives only things actually colored, not things potentially colored. And it is likewise evident that the intellect, insofar as it knows material things, knows only what is actual, and so it knows prime matter only in relationship to form, as the *Physics* says.[6] And so also in the case of immaterial substances, each is disposed to be intelligible by means of its essence insofar as it is disposed to be actual by means of its essence.

Therefore, God's essence, which is pure and complete actuality, is by its very self absolutely and completely intelligible. And so God by means of his essence understands both himself and everything.

And the essences of angels are indeed in the genus of intelligible things as actualities, but not as pure or complete actualities. And so their essences do not complete their understanding, for, although angels understand themselves by means of their essences, they nonetheless cannot know everything by means of their essences; rather, they know things other than themselves by means of the likenesses of those things.

But the human intellect is in the genus of intelligible things as a purely potential reality, just as prime matter is in the genus of sensibly perceptible things as a purely potential reality. And it is for this reason that we call the human intellect potential. Therefore, the human intellect, considered in its essence, is disposed as potentially understanding. And so it by itself has the power to understand, and not the power to be understood except as it becomes actual. For even the Platonists (since, in their view, the intellect understands only by sharing in the intelligible, and what shares is inferior to what is shared) held that the rank of intelligible beings is superior to the rank of intellects.

Therefore, if the human intellect were to become actual by sharing in separate intelligible forms, as the Platonists held,[7] the human intellect would understand itself by such sharing in immaterial things. But it is inborn to our intellect, in the condition of our present life, to have material and sensibly perceptible things as its object, as I have said before.[8] Consequently, our intellect understands itself thus, as it is actualized by the forms that the light of the active intellect abstracts from sensibly perceptible things, and the active intellect actualizes intelligible things themselves and the potential intellect by means of those intelligible things. Therefore, our intellect knows itself by means of its acts, not by means of its essence.

And our intellect does so in two ways. In one way, in particular, as Socrates or Plato perceives that he has an intellectual soul by reason of the fact that he perceives that he is understanding. In the second way, in general, as we consider the nature of the human mind by considering the intellect's activity. (But it is true that the judgment and efficacy of the knowledge by which we know the nature of the soul, belongs to us because the light of our intellect derives from divine truth, which contains the natures of all things, as I have said before.[9] And so also Augustine says in his *De Trinitate*: "We consider the unassailable truth whereby we define as perfectly as we can, not what kind of thing the mind of every human being is, but what kind of thing the mind of every human being ought to be by reason of the eternal natures of things."[10])

And there is a difference between these two kinds of knowledge. For the mind's very presence, which is the source of acts whereby the mind perceives itself, suffices to have the first kind of knowledge about the mind. And so we say that the mind knows itself by its own presence. But the mind's presence does not suffice to have the second kind of knowledge about the mind; rather, a painstaking and discriminating inquiry is required. And so, too, many do not know the nature of the soul, and many have also erred about the nature of the soul. And consequently, Augustine in his *De Trinitate* says about such an inquiry by the mind: "The mind should not seek to discern itself as if it were absent, but it should seek to discern itself as present,"[11] that is, to know its difference from other things, which is to know its essence and nature.

Reply to Obj. 1. The mind knows itself by means of itself, since it at length arrives at knowledge of its very self, granted that it does so by means of its own activity, since the mind, because it loves itself, knows itself, as Augustine alternately says in the same place. For we can say that something is self-evident in two ways: either because we come to knowledge of it through nothing else, as, for example, we say that first principles are self-evident, or because things are knowable incidentally, as, for example, colors are intrinsically visible, but substances incidentally such.

Reply to Obj. 2. Angels' essences are constituted as actualities in the genus of intelligible things, and so their essences are disposed to be both intellects and the things angels' intellects understand. And so angels know their essences by their very selves. But not so the human intellect, which is either entirely potential with respect to intelligible things, as the potential intellect, or is the actuality of intelligible things abstracted from sense images, as the active intellect.

Reply to Obj. 3. That saying of the Philosopher is without exception true in the case of every intellect. For as the senses actually perceiving are the perceptible things, by reason of the perceptible things' likenesses that are the forms of the senses actually perceiving, so the intellect actually understanding is the thing actually understood, by reason of the understood thing's likeness that is the form of the intellect actually understanding. And so the human intellect, which becomes actual by reason of the form of the thing understood, is understood by reason of the same form, as its own form. And to say that "the intellect and what is understood, are identical in immaterial things" is the same as if we were to say that "the intellect and what is understood are identical in things actually understood." For we actually understand things by reason of the fact that they are immaterial. But there is a difference in this immateriality, since the essences of some kinds of things are immaterial, such as the separate substances that we call angels, each of which is both understood and understanding, while there are other kinds of things whose essences are not without matter, and only the likenesses abstracted from such things exist apart from matter. And so too the Commentator says in his commentary on the *De anima* that the cited proposition is only true about separate substances,[12] since something not true in the case of other things is in some way true in their case, as I have said.[13]

Second Article

*Does Our Intellect Know the Characteristic Dispositions
of the Soul by Their Essences?*

I proceed in this way to the second article: it seems that our intellect knows the characteristic dispositions of the soul by their essences.
Obj. 1. Augustine says in his *De Trinitate*: "We do not perceive faith in the heart in which it exists, in the same way that we perceive the souls of other human beings by reason of their bodily movements, but we know such faith most certainly, and our consciousness so proclaims."[14]
And the argument is the same about other characteristic dispositions of the soul. Therefore, we know the soul's characteristic dispositions by their very selves and not by the soul's acts.
Obj. 2. We know material things, which exist outside the soul, by reason of the fact that their likenesses are present in the soul, and so we say that we know material things by their likenesses. But the soul's characteristic dispositions are present in the soul by their essences. Therefore, we know the soul's characteristic dispositions by their essences.

Obj. 3. "The cause of anything being such is such even more."[15] But the soul's characteristic dispositions and intelligible forms cause the soul to know other things.   Therefore, still more does the soul know its characteristic dispositions and intelligible forms in themselves.

On the contrary, characteristic dispositions, just like powers, are the sources of acts. But "acts and actions are conceptually prior to powers," as the *De anima* says.[16]   Therefore, by the same reasoning, acts and actions are prior to characteristic dispositions.   And so we know characteristic dispositions by their acts, just as we know powers by their acts.

I answer that characteristic dispositions are in some way in between pure potentiality and pure actuality.   And I have already said that we know nothing except insofar as it is actual.[17]   Therefore, insofar as characteristic dispositions fall short of complete actuality, they fall short of being knowable in themselves but need to be known by means of their acts.   Such is the case either when we perceive that we have characteristic dispositions by the fact that we perceive that we produce the acts belonging to such dispositions, or when we inquire into the natures and essences of characteristic dispositions by considering the dispositions' acts.   And the very presence of a characteristic disposition indeed produces the first way of knowing that disposition, since the very fact of its presence causes the acts, in which we immediately perceive it. And keen inquiry produces the second way of knowing a characteristic disposition, as I have said before about the mind.[18]

Reply to Obj. 1.   Although we do not know faith by external bodily movements, yet even the person in whom faith exists perceives it by interior acts of the heart.[19]   For persons know that they have faith only by reason of the fact that they perceive that they believe.

Reply to Obj. 2.   Characteristic dispositions are not present in our intellect as objects of the intellect, since the object of our intellect in the condition of our present life consists of the natures of material things, as I have said before.[20]   Rather, characteristic dispositions are present in our intellect as the means by which the intellect understands.

Reply to Obj. 3.   The statement "The cause of anything being such is such even more" is true if understood about things that belong to the same order (e.g., to the same kind of cause).   For instance, if we should say that health is for the sake of life, it logically follows that life is more desirable than health.   But the statement is not true if we should understand it to be about things of different orders.   For instance, if we should say that health is the result of medicine, then it does not logically follow that medicine is more desirable than health, since health belongs to the order of final causes, and medicine belongs to the order of efficient causes. Therefore, if we should understand two things, both of which intrinsically belong to the order of objects of knowledge, we shall have more knowledge of the one by reason of which we know the other; for example, we have more knowledge of principles than of conclusions. But characteristic dispositions as such do not belong to the order of objects of knowledge, nor do we know some things because of characteristic dispositions as known objects; rather, we know some things because of the characteristic dispositions or forms by means of which we as knowers know. And so the argument is not valid.

Third Article

Does the Intellect Know Its Own Acts?

I proceed in this way to the third article: it seems that the intellect does not know its own acts.

Obj. 1. Strictly speaking, the things we know are the things that are the objects of cognitive powers. But cognitive acts are different from the objects of cognitive powers. Therefore, the intellect does not know its own acts.

Obj. 2. It is by acts that we know everything that we know. Therefore, if the intellect knows its act, it knows its act by an act, and, again, it knows the latter act by another act. Therefore, there will be an infinite regress, and this seems impossible.

Obj. 3. As the senses are ordered to their acts, so also is the intellect ordered to its acts. But the proper senses do not perceive their acts; rather, perceiving acts of the senses belongs to the common sense, as the *De anima* says.[21] Therefore, neither does the intellect understand its acts.

On the contrary, Augustine says in his *De Trinitate*: "I understand that I understand."[22]

I answer that everything is known as it is actual, as I have already said.[23] And the ultimate perfection of the intellect is its action, since the action of the intellect is not like action that extends to something else, which action is the perfection of the thing produced (for example, the action of building is the perfection of the thing built), but the action of the intellect abides in the knower as the knower's perfection and actuality, as the *Metaphysics* says.[24] Therefore, such action, namely, the intellect's very act of understanding, is the first thing that is understood about the intellect.

But different kinds of intellects are disposed in this respect in different ways. For example, there is one kind of intellect, namely, the divine intellect, that is its very act of understanding. And so in the case of God, that he understands that he understands, and that he understands his essence, are identical, since his essence is his understanding.

And there is another kind of intellect, namely, the angelic intellect, that is not identical with its act of understanding, as I have said before,[25] and yet the first object of its act of understanding is the angelic essence. And so, although there is in the case of angels a conceptual distinction between their understanding that they understand, and their understanding their essence, they nonetheless understand both at once and by the same act, since understanding their essence is the characteristic perfection of their essence, and things are understood with their perfection at once and by the same act.

And there is still another kind of intellect, namely, the human intellect, which is not identical with its acts of understanding, nor is its essence itself the first object of its understanding; rather, the first object of the human intellect's understanding is something external, namely, the nature of a material thing. And so what the human intellect primarily knows is such an object. And the human intellect secondarily knows the very acts by which it knows such objects, and knows the intellect itself, whose perfection is the very act of understanding, by such acts. And so the Philosopher says that the human intellect knows its objects before its acts, and its acts before its powers.[26]

Reply to Obj. 1. The object of the intellect is something universal, namely, being and the true, and the very act of understanding is also included in this object. And so the intellect can understand its acts. But not primarily, since the first object of our intellect in our present condition is the being and the true considered in material things, and not every being and everything true, as I have said.[27] And the intellect comes to knowledge of all other things by reason of material things.

Reply to Obj. 2. The very act of human understanding is not the actuality and perfection of the material nature understood, so that we could by the same act understand the nature of a material thing and the very act of understanding, as, for example, we by the same act understand things with their perfection. And so there is one act by which the intellect understands stone, and another act by which the intellect understands that it understands stone, and so forth. Nor is it improper that the intellect have unlimited potentiality, as I have said before.[28]

Reply to Obj. 3. The proper senses perceive by reason of the fact that sensibly perceptible external objects affect material bodily organs. And it is impossible that anything material affect itself; rather, one material thing affects another. And so the common sense perceives the acts of the proper senses. But the intellect does not understand by the material alteration of a bodily organ, and so there is no comparison between the senses and the intellect.

Fourth Article

Does the Intellect Understand Acts of the Will?

I proceed in this way to the fourth article: it seems that the intellect does not understand acts of the will.

Obj. 1. The intellect knows only things in some way present in the intellect. But acts of the will are not present in the intellect, since the intellect and the will are different powers. Therefore, the intellect does not know acts of the will.

Obj. 2. Objects specify acts. But the object of the will is different from the object of the intellect. Therefore, acts of the will are also specifically different from the object of the intellect. Therefore, the intellect does not know acts of the will.

Obj. 3. Augustine in his *Confessions* ascribes to the soul's desires that they are known "neither by their images, like material substances, nor by their presence, like skills, but by certain ideas."[29] But it does not seem that there can be in the soul other ideas of things than either the essences of known things or their likenesses. Therefore, it seems impossible for the intellect to know the soul's desires, which are acts of the will.

On the contrary, Augustine says in his *De Trinitate*: "I understand that I will."[30]

I answer that, as I have said before,[31] acts of the will are simply inclinations that result from understood forms, just as natural appetites are inclinations that result from the forms of nature. And the inclination of each kind of thing is in the things themselves by their way of existing.

And so things of nature have natural inclinations by way of nature, and sentient things have inclinations called sense appetites by way of sense perception, and similarly, intelligent things, as sources and proper subjects, have intellectual inclinations, which are acts of the will, by way of intellectual knowledge. And so the Philosopher too uses this way of speaking in the *De anima*, saying that "the will is in the power of reason."[32] Consequently, intelligent things understand what is in them by way of intellectual knowledge. And so the intellect understands acts of the will both insofar as persons perceive that they are willing, and insofar as persons know the nature of such acts. And consequently, the intellect understands the nature of the acts' source, which is a characteristic disposition or the power.

Reply to Obj. 1. That argument would be valid if the will and intellect, as different powers, were thereby also to be different in their subject, for what is in the will would then not be present in the intellect. But as matters stand, since both are rooted in one and the same substance of the soul, and since one is in some way the source of the other, it follows that what is in the will is also in some way in the intellect.

Reply to Obj. 2. The good and the true, which are the objects of the will and the intellect, are indeed conceptually different, but one of them includes the other, as I have said before,[33] for the true is one kind of good, and the good is one kind of true. And so things of the will fall within the power of the intellect, and things of the intellect fall within the power of the will.

Reply to Obj. 3. The soul's desires are not in the intellect only by their likenesses, like material substances, or by their presence as in a subject, like skills, but the soul's desires are in the intellect as effects are in causes that have ideas of their effects. And so Augustine is saying that the soul's desires are in the power of memory by certain ideas.

Notes

1. *De Trinitate* IX, 3. PL 42:963.

2. Aristotle, *De anima* III, 4. 430a3.

3. Q. 76, a. 1, *ad* 4.

4. Aristotle, *De anima* III, 4. 430a2.

5. Aristotle, *Metaphysics* VIII, 9. 1051a21–33.

6. Aristotle, *Physics* I, 7. 191a7–15.

7. Plato, *Republic* VI, 19. 508.

8. Q. 84, A. 7.

9. Q. 84, A. 5.

10. *De Trinitate* IX, 6. PL 42:966.

11. *De Trinitate* X, 9. PL 42:980.

12. Averroës, *In libros De anima* III, comm. 15.

13. In the response to the second objection.

14. *De Trinitate* XIII, 1. PL 42:1014.

15. Aristotle, *Posterior Analytics* I, 2. 72a29–32.

16. Aristotle, *De anima* II, 4. 415a18.

17. Q. 87, A. 1.

18. Ibid.

19. Cf. Q. 112, A. 5.

20. Q. 85, A. 7; Q. 85, A. 8; Q. 86, A. 2.

21. Aristotle, *De anima* III, 2. 425b12–427a16.

22. *De Trinitate* X, 11. PL 42:983.

23. Q. 87, AA. 1, 2.

24. Aristotle, *Metaphysics* VIII, 8. 1050a23–b2.

25. Q. 79, A. 1.

26. *De anima* II, 4. 415a16–22.

27. Q. 84, A. 7.

28. Q. 86, A. 2.

29. *Confessions* X, 17. PL 32:790.

30. *De Trinitate* X, 11. PL 42:983.

31. Q. 59, A. 1.

32. *De anima* III, 9. 432b5.

33. Q. 16, A. 4, *ad* 1; Q. 82, A. 4, *ad* 1.

ST I

Question 88

How the Soul Knows Things Superior to Itself

[This question is divided into three articles, all of which are included here.]

First Article

Can the Human Soul in the Condition of Our Present Life Understand Immaterial Substances Precisely as Such?

I proceed in this way to the first article: it seems that the human soul in the condition of our present life can understand immaterial substances precisely as such.

Obj. 1. Augustine says in his *De Trinitate*: "As the mind itself acquires knowledge of material things by means of the bodily senses, so it acquires knowledge of immaterial things by means of its very self."[1] But immaterial things are immaterial substances. Therefore, the mind understands immaterial substances.

Obj. 2. Like knows like. But the human mind is more like immaterial things, since the mind itself is immaterial, as is clear from what I have said before.[2] Therefore, since our mind understands material things, much more does it understand immaterial things.

Obj. 3. The fact that we do not sensibly perceive in the highest degree things that are in themselves most sensibly perceptible, derives from the fact that the superior qualities of sensibly perceptible things weaken senses. But the superior qualities of intelligible things do not weaken the intellect, as the *De anima* says.[3] Therefore, things that are in themselves most intelligible are also most intelligible to us. But since material things are intelligible only because we make them actually intelligible, by abstracting from matter, it is evident that substances by their nature immaterial are as such more intelligible. Therefore, we understand such substances much more than we understand material things.

Obj. 4. The Commentator says in his commentary on the *Metaphysics* that if we are unable to understand abstract substances, "nature would then have acted purposelessly, since it produced things by nature intelligible in themselves that no intellect understands."[4] But nothing in nature is purposeless or in vain. Therefore, we can understand immaterial substances.

Obj. 5. As the senses are ordered to sensibly perceptible things, so the intellect is ordered to intelligible things. But our power of sight can see every kind of material substance, whether the material substance be in the heavens and incapable of passing away, or here below and capable of passing away. Therefore, our intellect can understand every kind of intelligible substance, even superior and immaterial intelligible substances.

On the contrary, the Book of Wisdom says: "Who will search out the things in heaven?"[5] But the Gospel of Matthew says that immaterial substances abide in heaven: "Their angels abide in heaven," etc.[6] Therefore, we cannot know immaterial substances by human inquiry.

I answer that, according to the opinion of Plato, immaterial substances are not only known by us but are the first things that we understand. For Plato held that subsistent immaterial forms, which he called Ideas, are the proper object of our intellect,[7] and so we understand them first and intrinsically. Nonetheless, the soul's knowledge is connected to material things as the powers of imagination and the senses are intermingled with the power of the intellect. And so the more the intellect has been purified, the more it perceives the intelligible truth of immaterial things.

But in the opinion of Aristotle,[8] which we find by experience to be more true than Plato's, our intellect in the condition of our present life is by nature ordered to the essences of material things, and so our intellect understands only by recourse to sense images, as is clear from what I have said before.[9] And so we evidently cannot understand first and intrinsically, in the way of knowing experienced by us, immaterial substances, which do not fall within the power of the senses and imagination.

And yet Averroës in his commentary on the *De anima* holds that human beings in this life can finally arrive at understanding of separate substances by the connection or union of a separate substance with us that he called the active intellect.[10] And the latter separate substance, because it is such, by its nature indeed understands separate substances. And so, since it has been perfectly united to us, in order that we might thus be able to understand perfectly by means of it, we as well understand separate substances, just as we now understand material things by means of the potential intellect united to us.

And he held that the active intellect is united to us as follows. For, inasmuch as we understand by means of the active intellect and the intelligible things we contemplate (as is evident when we understand conclusions by means of understood principles), we need to relate the active intellect to the understood things we contemplate, either as a chief efficient cause to an instrumental cause, or as a form to matter. For he in these two ways ascribes our intellect's action to two sources: to the chief efficient cause and its instrument (as we ascribe the action of sawing to a workman and his saw), and to the form and to the subject in which the form inheres (as we ascribe the action of heating to heat and fire). But either way, the active intellect will be related to intelligible contemplated things as perfections are related to perfectible things, and as actualities are related to potentialities. And subjects receive perfect things and perfections at the same time; for example, the eye's pupil receives actually visible things and light at the same time. Therefore, the potential intellect receives understood contemplated things and the active intellect at the same time. And the more numerous the understood contemplated things we receive, the closer we come to the active intellect being perfectly united to us. Consequently, when we shall know every kind of understood contemplated thing, the active intellect will be perfectly united to us, and we shall be able to know every kind of material and immaterial thing by means of it. And he holds that the final happiness of human beings consists in this.[11]

Nor does it matter, as pertains to the proposed explanation, whether the potential intellect in the final state of happiness understands separate substances by means of the active intellect (as he himself thought), or (as he attributes to Alexander[12]) the potential intellect never understands separate substances (since he held that the potential intellect can pass away), but human beings understand separate substances by means of the active intellect.

But the foregoing opinion cannot be true. First, indeed, because, if the active intellect is a separate substance, we could not formally understand by means of that very substance. It is impossible because the means by which an efficient cause formally causes is the cause's form and actuality, for every efficient cause causes inasmuch as it is actual. This is like what I also said before about the potential intellect.[13]

Second, Averroës's opinion cannot be true because the active intellect, if it is a separate substance, would not in the aforementioned way be united to us substantially; rather, only its light would be united to us, as we partake of the theoretical things that we understand, and there would be no union with respect to other activities of the active intellect, with the consequence that we could not understand immaterial substances by means of it. For example, when we see colors that the sun illumines, the sun is not substantially united to us; rather, only the sun's light is united to us, in order that we may see the colors.

Third, Averroës's opinion cannot be true because, supposing that the active intellect would in the aforementioned way be substantially united to us, still, the Averroists maintain that the active intellect is entirely united to us by the totality of understood contemplated things rather than by one or two intelligible things. But the totality of understood contemplated things falls short of the power of the active intellect, since understanding separate substances exceeds understanding all kinds of material things. And so the active intellect would evidently not be so united to us that we could understand separate substances by means of it even if we were to understand every kind of material thing.

Fourth, Averroës's opinion cannot be true because it rarely happens that anyone in this world knows every kind of material thing, and so none or few would arrive at happiness. And this is contrary to the Philosopher, who says in the *Ethics* that happiness "is a universal good that can come to all who are virtuous."[14] It is also contrary to reason that members of a species would in rather few cases achieve the end of the species.

Fifth, Averroës's opinion cannot be true because the Philosopher says expressly in the *Ethics* that happiness is "activity according to perfect virtue."[15] And after enumerating many virtues, Aristotle concludes in the tenth book that the ultimate happiness of human beings, which consists in knowledge of the most intelligible things, is achieved in the virtue of wisdom,[16] which he held in the sixth book to be the chief theoretical science.[17] And so Aristotle clearly situated the final happiness of human beings in the knowledge of separate substances that can be obtained by theoretical sciences, and not by the connection with the active intellect concocted by certain thinkers.

Sixth, Averroës's opinion cannot be true because I have shown before that the active intellect is not a separate substance but a power of the soul that by its activity extends to the same things that the potential intellect by its receptivity reaches.[18] This is so because, as the *De anima* says, the potential intellect is the intellect "in which all things become intelligible," the active intellect the intellect "which makes all things intelligible."[19] Every intellect, therefore, in the condition of our present life, extends only to material things, which the active intellect makes actually intelligible, and which the potential intellect receives. And so we in the condition of our present life cannot understand immaterial substances, whether by means of the potential intellect or by means of the active intellect.

Reply to Obj. 1. We can on the authority of Augustine hold that our mind can of itself know what it is possible for it to understand regarding knowledge of immaterial things. And this is so true that philosophers likewise say that theoretical knowledge about the soul is a source for knowing separate substances. For our soul arrives at possessing some knowledge about immaterial substances, the knowledge that it happens to have, by reason of the fact that our soul knows itself—not that the soul, by knowing itself, knows immaterial substances in an absolute and perfect way.

Reply to Obj. 2. Likeness of nature is not a sufficient explanation of knowledge; otherwise, we would need to say what Empedocles said, that the nature of everything should belong to the soul in order that the soul might know everything.[20] But knowing requires that knowers possess likenesses of known things, certain forms of the very things, as it were. And nature constitutes our potential intellect, in the condition of our present life, to be actualized by the likenesses of material things that we abstract from sense images. And so our potential intellect knows material things rather than immaterial substances.

Reply to Obj. 3. There needs to be proportion between cognitive objects and cognitive powers, as there needs to be proportion between active things and passive things, and proportion between perfections and perfectible things. And so the reason why the senses do not grasp superior sensible qualities is not only because such qualities weaken sense organs, but also because such qualities are not proportionate to sense powers. And immaterial substances are in the latter way disproportionate to our intellect in its present state, and so our intellect cannot understand them.

Reply to Obj. 4. That argument of the Commentator is deficient in many ways. First, indeed, because it does not logically follow that no intellect would understand separate substances if we do not understand them, since they understand themselves and one another.

Second, the argument is deficient because it is not the end of separate substances that they be understood by us. And we say that things that do not achieve the ends for which they exist are purposeless and in vain. And so it does not logically follow that immaterial substances are in vain even if we were in no way to understand them.

Reply to Obj. 5. The senses know celestial and earthly material substances in the same way, namely, by alterations of sense organs by sensibly perceptible things. But we do not in the same way understand immaterial substances, which we cannot understand in that way, since they have no sense images.

Second Article

Can Our Intellect by Its Knowledge of Material Things
Come to Understand Immaterial Substances?

I proceed in this way to the second article: it seems that our intellect by its knowledge of material things can come to understand immaterial substances.

Obj. 1. Denis says in his *Coelestia hierarchia* that "it is impossible for the human mind to be raised up to that immaterial contemplation of the heavenly hierarchies unless the human mind as such employs material guidance."[21] Therefore, we conclude that material things can guide us to understand immaterial substances.

Obj. 2. The intellect has scientific knowledge. But immaterial substances are the objects of sciences and definitions, for Damascene defines angel,[22] and both theological and philosophical disciplines deal with some examples of angels. Therefore, we can understand immaterial substances.

Obj. 3. The human soul belongs to the genus of immaterial substances. But we can understand the human soul itself by its own activity, activity whereby it understands material things. Therefore, we can also understand other immaterial substances by their effects in material things.

On the contrary, Denis says in his *De divinis nominibus* that "we cannot understand intelligible things by sensible things, nor simple things by composite things, nor immaterial things by material things."[23]

I answer that Averroës relates in his commentary on the *De anima* that a certain thinker by the name of Avemplace held that we can by true philosophical principles come to understand immaterial substances through our understanding of material substances.[24] For, since nature constitutes our intellect to abstract the essences of material things from matter, our intellect could by further abstractions abstract from things material in such essences, if there still be such. And since this process does not go on endlessly, our intellect would at length be able to come to understand essences that are altogether immaterial. And this is to understand immaterial substances.

And one would in effect say this if immaterial substances were to be the forms and types of such material things, as the Platonists held.[25] But if we do not hold this but hold that immaterial substances are altogether of a different nature than the essences of material things, our intellect will never arrive at anything like an immaterial substance, howsoever much the intellect abstracts the essences of material things from matter. And so we cannot perfectly understand immaterial substances by means of material substances.

Reply to Obj. 1. We can rise from material things to some sort of knowledge of immaterial things but not to perfect knowledge, since there is no adequate comparison between material and immaterial things. Rather, any likenesses that we take from material things in order to understand immaterial things are very unlike the latter, as Denis says in his *De coelestia hierarchia.*[26]

Reply to Obj. 2. Sciences treat of higher things by way of removing things; for example, Aristotle obtained knowledge in this way about heavenly bodies by negating the properties of lower material substances.[27] And much less, therefore, can we know immaterial substances in such a way as to understand their essences. And sciences deal with examples concerning immaterial substances by way of removing things, and by certain relationships to material things.

Reply to Obj. 3. The human soul understands itself by reason of its understanding, that is, by reason of its characteristic activity, which perfectly manifests its power and nature. But we cannot know perfectly the power and nature of immaterial substances by such activity, or by anything else that we find in material things, since material things are not commensurate with the powers of immaterial substances.

Reply to Obj. 4. Created immaterial substances indeed do not belong to the same natural genus to which material substances belong, since immaterial substances do not have the same natural potentiality and

matter that material substances have.   Nonetheless, immaterial
substances belong to the same logical genus that material substances do,
since immaterial as well as material substances belong to the category of
substance, inasmuch as the essences of immaterial substances are not
identical with their existing. But God and material things belong to no
natural or logical genus, since God in no way belongs to any genus, as
I have said before.[28] And so we can affirmatively know things about
angels by their likeness to material things regarding common aspects
(although not regarding their specific natures) but nothing in any way
about God.

Third Article

Is God the First Thing that the Human Mind Knows?

I proceed in this way to the third article: it seems that God is the first
thing that the human mind knows.
Obj. 1. The thing in which we know everything else, and the thing in
which we judge about other things, is the thing that the intellect first
knows, as light is the thing that the eye first knows, and first principles
are the thing that the intellect first knows. But we know everything in
the light of the first truth, and we judge about everything by that light, as
Augustine says in his *De Trinitate*[29] and his *De vera religione*.[30]
Therefore, God is the thing we first know.
Obj. 2. "What causes something to be such, is still more so."[31] But God
causes all our knowledge, for he himself is "the true light that enlightens
every human being that comes into this world," as the Gospel of John
says.[32] Therefore, God is the thing that we know first and foremost.
Obj. 3. What we know first in an image is the model whereby we form
the image. But our minds have an image of God, as Augustine says.[33]
Therefore, the thing that we first know in our minds is God.
     On the contrary, the Gospel of John says: "No one has ever seen
God."[34]
     I answer that the human intellect, since it cannot in the condition of
our present life understand created immaterial substances, as I have
said,[35] much less can it understand the essence of the uncreated
substance. And so we need to say unqualifiedly that God is not the first
thing that we know; rather, we need to say that we arrive at knowledge
of God through creatures, as the Apostle says: "We see clearly the

invisible things of God when we understand them by means of the things that he has made."[36] And the first things that we understand in the condition of our present life are the essences of material things, and such essences are the object of our intellect, as I have said before in many places.[37]

Reply to Obj. 1. We understand and judge everything in the light of the first truth insofar as the very light of our intellect, whether by nature or by grace, is nothing but an imprint of the first truth, as I have said before.[38] And so, since the very light of our intellect is not related to our intellect as the thing the intellect understands, but as the means whereby the intellect understands, much less is God the thing that our intellect first understands.

Reply to Obj. 2. We need to understand the saying "What causes something to be such, is still more so" to refer to things that belong to the same order, as I have said before.[39] But we know things other than God because of God, not because he is the first thing known, but because he is the first cause of our power to know.

Reply to Obj. 3. If our souls were to have a perfect image of God, as the Son is the perfect image of the Father, our minds would at once understand God. But our souls have an imperfect image of God, and so the argument does not hold.

Notes

1. *De Trinitate* IX, 3. PL 42:963.

2. Q. 76, A. 1.

3. Aristotle, *De anima* III, 4. 429a29–b5.

4. Averroës, *In libros Metaphysicorum* II (Ia in the Bekker notation), comm. 1.

5. Wis. 9:16.

6. Mt. 18:10.

7. *Phaedo* 49. 100B–102A. *Timaeus* 5 and 18. 27C–D and 51–52C.

8. *De anima* III, 7. 431a14–17, b2–9.

9. Q. 84, A. 7.

10. *In libros De anima* III, in the digression of comm. 36.

11. Cf. *De animae beatitudine* 4.

12. See n. 10, supra.

13. Q. 76, A. 1.

14. *Ethics* I, 8. 1099b18–20.

15. *Ethics* I, 10. 1101a14–21.

16. *Ethics* X, 8. 1178b24–32.

17. *Ethics* VI, 7. 1141b2–3.

18. Q. 79, A. 4.

19. Aristotle, *De anima* III, 5. 430a10–17.

20. Cf. Aristotle, *De anima* I, 2. 404a11–15.

21. *De coelestia hierarchia* 1. PG 3:121.

22. *De fide orthodoxa* II, 3. PG 94:865.

23. *De divinis nominibus* 1. PG 3:588.

24. See n. 10, supra.

25. See n. 7, supra, and Q. 84, AA. 1 and 4.

26. *De coelestia hierarchia* 2. PG 3:137.

27. *De coelo et mundo* I, 3. 269b18–270b25.

28. Q. 3, A. 5.

29. *De Trinitate* XII, 2. PL 42:999.

30. *De vera religione* 31. PL 34:147–48.

31. Aristotle, *Posterior Analytics* I, 2. 72a29–32.

32. Jn. 1:9.

33. *De Trinitate* XII, 4 and 7. PL 42:1000, 1003, 1004–1005.

34. Jn. 1:18.

35. Q. 88, A. 1.

36. Rom. 1:20.

37. Q. 84, A. 7. Q. 85, A. 8. Q. 87, A. 2, *ad* 2.

38. Q. 12, A. 2, *ad* 3. Q. 84, A. 5.

39. Q. 87, A. 2, *ad* 3.

Question 90

On the First Production of Human Beings Regarding the Soul

[This question is divided into four articles, all of which are included here.]

First Article

Is the Soul Made, or Is It Part of God's Substance?

I proceed in this way to the first article: it seems that the soul is not made but is part of God's substance.

Obj. 1. The Book of Genesis says: "God produced human beings out of the dust of the earth and breathed the breath of life into their faces, and human beings were made into living souls."[1] But one who breathes emits something from self. Therefore, the soul whereby human beings live is part of God's substance.

Obj. 2. The soul is a pure form, as I have maintained before.[2] But forms are actualities. Therefore, the soul is pure actuality, and this belongs to God alone. Therefore, the soul is part of God's substance.

Obj. 3. Things that exist and in no way differ, are the same. But God and mind exist and in no way differ, since they would have to differ in particular ways and thus be composite. Therefore, God and the human mind are the same.

On the contrary, Augustine in his work *De origine animae* enumerates certain things, and he says that they are "very much and clearly wrong, and contrary to the Catholic faith."[3] And the chief of these is that some people say that "God made souls out of himself, not out of nothing."[4]

I answer that to say that the soul is part of God's substance involves an evident impossibility. For, as is clear from what I have said,[5] the human soul sometimes has potential understanding, and acquires knowledge somehow from things, and has different powers. And all such things are foreign to the nature of God, who is pure actuality, and receives nothing from anything else, and has no different parts, as I have proved before.[6]

And this error seems to have derived from two positions taken by ancient philosophers. For the first philosophers who undertook to consider the natures of things were unable to go beyond their imagination and held that only material substances exist. And so they said that God is some sort of material substance, and they judged that that substance is the source of other material substances. And because they held that the soul partakes of the nature of the material substance that they said is the soul's source, as the *De anima* says,[7] it logically followed that the soul would be part of God's nature. And following the same position, Manicheans, who thought that God is some sort of material light, likewise held that the soul, as some sort of part of that light, is united to the body.

And then there was an advance to the point where some philosophers grasped that something immaterial exists as the form of material substances but not separate from them. And so also Varro said that "God is a soul that governs the world by moving things and by design," as Augustine relates in *The City of God*.[8] Therefore, some philosophers held the souls of human beings to be parts of that one soul, just as human beings are parts of the one world; only by the differences between material substances were the intellects of those philosophers able to reach the differences between grades of immaterial substances.

But all of these things are impossible, as I have proved before.[9] And so it is clearly false that the soul is part of God's substance.

Reply to Obj. 1. We should not understand breathing in a material sense; rather, to say that God breathes, is the same as to say that he causes breathing. And also, human beings, when they breathe in the material sense, do not emit anything of their substance but something of an extraneous nature.

Reply to Obj. 2. The soul, although essentially a pure form, is nonetheless not its own existing but a being by sharing, as is clear from what I have said before.[10] And so, unlike God, the soul is not pure actuality.

Reply to Obj. 3. Taken in the strict sense, things that differ, differ by something, and so we look for differences where there are harmonies. And so, since things that differ, differ in something and agree in something, they need to be somehow composite. And accordingly, although everything that differs is something diverse, yet not everything diverse is something that differs, as the *Metaphysics* says.[11] For simple things are diverse in themselves, and they do not differ by reason of component things that differ. For example, human beings and asses differ by the specific difference of having or not having reason, and we cannot say about them that they are further differentiated by other differences.

Second Article

Does Creation Bring the Soul into Existence?

I proceed in this way to the second article: it seems that creation does not bring the soul into existence.

Obj. 1. Things that contain something material are made out of matter. But the soul contains something material, since it is not pure actuality. Therefore, the soul is made out of matter. Therefore, the soul is not created.

Obj. 2. Every actuality of some matter seems to be drawn out of the potentiality of that matter. For every actuality pre-exists potentiality in matter, since matter has potentiality for actuality. But the soul is the actuality of corporeal matter, as the definition of matter indicates.[12] Therefore, the soul is drawn out of the potentiality of matter.

Obj. 3. The soul is one kind of form. Therefore, if creation produces the soul, like reasoning leads to the conclusion that creation produces every other form. And then no form will spring into existence by coming-to-be. And this conclusion is improper.

On the contrary, the Book of Genesis says: "God created human beings according to his own image."[13] But human beings, regarding their souls, exist according to God's image. Therefore, the soul comes into existence by creation.

I answer that only creation can produce a rational soul, and this is not true about other forms. And the reason for this is that things need to be made in ways that are proper to their existing, since being made is the way to existing. And we say in the strict sense that things that themselves have existing, things subsistent in their existing, as it were, exist, and so we properly and truly call only substances beings. On the other hand, accidents do not have existing, although something exists by reason of them, and that is why we call them beings. For example, we call whiteness a being because things are white by reason of it. And this is why the *Metaphysics* says that accidents "belong to beings rather than are beings."[14]   And the reasoning is the same about all other nonsubsistent forms. And so, in the strict sense, being made is not a property of any nonsubsistent form; rather, we say that such forms are made because composite subsistent things are made.

But the rational soul is a subsistent form, as I have maintained before.[15] And so, in the strict sense, existing and being made belong to it. And because the rational soul cannot be made out of pre-existing underlying matter, whether corporeal matter (since the soul would then have a corporeal nature) or spiritual matter (since spiritual substances would then be transformed into one another), we need to say that only creation can make the human soul.

Reply to Obj. 1. In the case of the soul, its noncomposite essence itself serves as the material element, and the soul's formal element is its shared existing, and this shared existing necessarily exists along with the soul's essence, since existing intrinsically results from form.

And the argument would be the same if we were to suppose that the soul is composed of some sort of spiritual matter, as some people say.[16] This is so because spiritual matter, like the matter of heavenly bodies, has no potentiality for another form; otherwise, the soul could pass away. And so in no way can the soul be made out of underlying matter.

Reply to Obj. 2. For actuality to be drawn out of the potentiality of matter is for something previously potential to become something actual, and is nothing else. But the rational soul does not have its existing as an existence dependent on corporeal matter, and has subsistent existing, and surpasses the potentiality of corporeal matter, as I have said before.[17] Therefore, the rational soul is not drawn out of the potentiality of matter.

Reply to Obj. 3. There is no comparison between the rational soul and other forms, as I have said.[18]

Third Article

Does God Directly Produce the Rational Soul?

I proceed in this way to the third article: it seems that God does not directly produce the rational soul but does so by means of the angels.

Obj. 1. Immaterial things have an arrangement superior to that of material things. But higher material substances produce lower material substances, as Denis says in his *De divinis nominibus*.[19] Therefore, higher spirits, that is, angels, likewise produce lower spirits, that is, rational souls.

Obj. 2. The end of things corresponds to their beginning, since God is beginning and end of things. Therefore, the springing of things from their source corresponds to their being brought to their end. But "the most excellent things bring about the lowest things," as Denis says.[20] Therefore, the most excellent things, namely, the angels, also bring the lowest things, namely, souls, into existence.

Obj. 3. "Something that can produce something like itself is perfect," as the *Meteorology* says.[21] But immaterial substances are much more perfect than material substances are. Therefore, since material substances produce things specifically like themselves, much more could angels produce things by nature specifically inferior to themselves, namely, rational souls.

On the contrary, the Book of Genesis says that God himself "breathed the breath of life into the face of human beings."[22]

I answer that certain thinkers held that angels, when they act under the power of God, produce rational souls.[23] But this is altogether impossible and foreign to our faith. For I have shown that only creation can produce the rational soul.[24] And only God can create, since only the first efficient cause can cause without the existence of something being presupposed. This is so because second efficient causes always presuppose something that exists from the first efficient cause, as I have maintained before.[25] And anything that produces an effect out of something whose existence is presupposed causes by effecting a change. And so God alone causes by creating, while every other efficient cause causes only by effecting a change. And because no transformation of any matter can produce a rational soul, so only God acting directly can produce a rational soul.

Replies to the Objections. And the foregoing makes clear the responses to the objections. For the fact that material substances cause either things like themselves or lesser things, and the fact that higher things bring about lower things, all such effects come about by some change.

Fourth Article

Was the Human Soul Produced Before the Body?

I proceed in this way to the fourth article: it seems that the human soul was produced before the body.

Obj. 1. The action of creating things preceded the action of differentiating and adorning them, as I have maintained before.[26] But creation brought the soul into existence, while the body was produced at the end of adorning things. Therefore, the human soul was produced before the body.

Obj. 2. The rational soul has more in common with the angels than with irrational animals. But angels were created before material substances, or with corporeal matter immediately from the beginning, while the human body was produced on the sixth day, when irrational animals as well were produced. Therefore, the human soul was created before the body.

Obj. 3. Ends are proportioned to beginnings. But the soul abides at the end after the body passes away. Therefore, the soul was also created at the beginning before the body was produced.

On the contrary, a special actuality is produced in a special potentiality. Therefore, since the soul is the special actuality of the body, the soul is produced in the body.

I answer that Origen held that both the soul of the first human being and the souls of all human beings, along with the angels, were created before the bodies of human beings were created.[27] For he believed that all spiritual substances, both human souls and angels, are equal in the status of their nature and differ only in their merit. Consequently, some spiritual substances, that is, the souls of human beings and those of heavenly bodies, are united to bodies, while other spiritual substances abide in their simplicity in different grades. And we have already spoken about this opinion before,[28] and so we do not need now to add anything.

And Augustine, for a different reason, says in his *Super Genesim* that the soul of the first human being was created along with the angels before its body was created.[29] He said this because he supposes that the body of the first human being was not actually produced in the works of the first six days but produced only regarding its causal sources. And we cannot say this about the soul, since the soul was not produced out of any pre-existing corporeal or spiritual matter, nor could any created power produce the soul. And so apparently the soul itself was created along with the angels in the works of the six days, when everything was made, and the soul's own will afterwards induced the soul to manage the body. But he does not say this by way of assertion, as his words show. For he says: "We may believe, if no authority of Scripture or consideration of truth dictates to the contrary, that a human being was made on the sixth day in such a way that the causal source of the human body be indeed created in the worldly elements, but that the soul itself was already created."[30]

And this could, of course, be allowed by those who hold that the soul intrinsically constitutes a complete species and nature, and that the soul is not united to the body as the body's form but only as the body's manager.[31] But this is altogether impossible if the soul is united to the body as the body's form and is by nature part of human nature. For God evidently instituted the first things in their complete natural condition, as the species of each thing required. And the soul, since it is part of human nature, has its natural completion only insofar as it is united to the body. And so it would not have been proper for the soul to be created without a body.

Therefore, if we support the opinion of Augustine about the works of the six days,[32] we could say that the human soul preceded the body in the work of the six days by a certain generic likeness, insofar as the soul has an intellectual nature in common with the angels. But the soul itself was created at the same time as the body. And according to other saints, both the soul and the body of the first human being were produced in the works of the six days.[33]

Reply to Obj. 1. If the nature of the soul were to include the whole species, so that the species as such would be created, the argument of this objection would prove that the soul as such was created at the beginning of creation. But because the soul is by its nature the form of the body, the soul needed to be created in a body, not separately.

Reply to Obj. 2. And the answer to the second objection is similar. For the soul, if it as such were to contain the species, would have more in common with angels. But the soul, since it is the form of the body, belongs to the genus of animal as the formal source of its species.

Reply to Obj. 3. It happens by reason of a deficiency of the body, to wit, death, that the soul survives the body. And at the beginning of the soul's creation, this deficiency indeed did not need to be.

Notes

1. Gen. 2:7.
2. Q. 75, A. 1.

3. *De origine animae* III, 15. PL 44:522.

4. Ibid.

5. Q. 77, A. 2. Q. 79, A. 2. Q. 84, A. 6.

6. Q. 3, AA. 1, 7. Q. 9, A. 1.

7. Aristotle, *De anima* I, 2. 405b10–30.

8. *The City of God* IV, 31. PL 41:138.

9. Q. 3, AA. 1, 8. Q. 50, A. 2, *ad* 4. Q. 75, A. 1.

10. Q. 75, A. 5, *ad* 4.

11. Aristotle, *Metaphysics* IX, 3. 1054b23–32.

12. Cf. Aristotle, *De anima* II, 1. 412a15–22.

13. Gen. 1:27.

14. Aristotle, *Metaphysics* VI, 1. 1028a15–20.

15. Q. 75, A. 2.

16. Cf. Bonaventure, *In libros Sententiarum* II, dist. 17, A. 1, Q. 2.

17. Q. 75, A. 2.

18. In the body of the article.

19. *De divinis nominibus* 4. PG 3:700.

20. *Ecclesiae historia* 5. PG 3:504.

21. Aristotle, *Meteorology* IV, 3. 380a11–15.

22. Gen. 2:7.

23. The Seleucians, a Gnostic sect. Cf. Augustine, *De haeresibus* 59. PL 42:41.

24. Q. 90, A. 2.

25. Q. 65, A. 3.

26. Q. 66, A. 1. Q. 70, A. 1.

27. *Peri Archon* I, 6; II, 9. PG 11:165, 225.

28. Q. 47, A. 2.

29. *Super Genesim ad litteram* VII, 24–28. PL 34:368–72.

30. Ibid., chap. 24. PL 34:368.

31. Plato, *Alcibiades* 25. 129E–130.

32. Cf. Q. 74, A. 2.

33. Cf. ibid. Basil, *In hexaemeron, homilia* 2. PG 29:29 et seq. Ambrose, *In hexaemeron* I, 7–8. PL 14:135 et seq. John Chrysostom, *In Genesim, homilia* 2. PG 53:31.

ST I

Question 91

On the Production of the Body of the First Human Being

[This question is divided into four articles, the second of which is included here.]

Second Article

Did God Directly Produce the Human Body?

I proceed in this way to the first article: it seems that God did not directly produce the human body.

Obj. 1. Augustine says in his *De Trinitate* that God ordered material things by means of angelic creatures.[1] But the human body was produced out of corporeal matter, as I have said.[2] Therefore, the human body needed to be produced by means of the angels and not directly by God.

Obj. 2. God does not need to produce directly what a created power can make. But the created power of heavenly bodies can produce a human body, since the active power of heavenly bodies even causes some animals to be generated from the decomposition of organic matter. And Albumazar says that human beings are generated only in temperate climes, not in places where heat or cold is too abundant.[3] Therefore, God did not need to produce the human body directly.

Obj. 3. Nothing comes to be out of corporeal matter except by some transformation of matter. But the movement of heavenly bodies, the first movement, causes every material transformation. Therefore, since the human body is produced out of corporeal matter, it seems that heavenly bodies had an active part in the human body's production.

Obj. 4. Augustine says in his *Super Genesim* that the human being, regarding the body, was made during the works of the six days as regards causal sources that God incorporated in material creatures,[4] and that the actual human body was produced later. But some material power can produce what pre-exists in material creatures as regards causal sources. Therefore, some created power produced the human body, and God did not do so directly.

On the contrary, the Book of Sirach says: "God created human beings out of the earth."[5]

I answer that no created power could cause the first production of the human body; rather, God did so directly. Some thinkers indeed held that the forms in corporeal matter are derived from certain immaterial forms.[6] But the Philosopher in the *Metaphysics* attacks this opinion because it intrinsically belongs to composites, not to forms, to be made,[7] as I have explained before.[8] And because efficient causes need to be like their effects, pure forms, which exist apart from matter, are unfit to produce forms that exist in matter, forms that come to be only because composites come to be. And so forms that exist in matter need to cause the forms that exist in matter, as composites cause composites to come to be. And although God is altogether immaterial, he is nonetheless the only one who can by his power produce matter by creating it. And so it belongs to himself alone to produce matter by creating it. And so it belongs to himself alone to produce forms in matter without the help of any antecedent material form. And it is for this reason that angels can transform material substances only by using certain causal elements, as Augustine says in his *De Trinitate*.[9]

Therefore, since no human body had yet been produced whose power might produce something specifically similar by way of generation, it was necessary that God directly produce the first human body.

Reply to Obj. 1. Although angels perform a ministry for God in things that he does regarding material substances, God nonetheless accomplishes something in material creatures that angels can in no way accomplish; for example, he raises the dead and gives sight to the blind. And he by such power also produced the body of the first human being out of the dust of the earth.

But it could be the case that angels might have performed a ministry in the production of the body of the first human being, just as they will perform a ministry at the last resurrection by gathering up the dust.

Reply to Obj. 2. Perfect animals, which semen generates, cannot be generated only by the power of heavenly bodies, as Avicenna imagined.[10] This is so even though the power of heavenly bodies assists in the natural generation of perfect animals, for the Philosopher says in the

Physics that "human beings and the sun beget human beings out of matter."[11] And it is for this reason that a temperate clime is required for the generation of human beings and other perfect animals.

But the power of heavenly bodies suffices to cause the generation of some imperfect animals from matter so disposed, for more things are evidently required for the production of perfect things than for the production of imperfect things.

Reply to Obj. 3. The movement of the heavens causes natural transformations but not those that arise outside the order of nature and by divine power alone, such as that the dead be raised to life, that the blind be made to see. And the production of a human being out of the dust of the earth is like those cases.

Reply to Obj. 4. We say in two ways that something pre-exists as regards causal sources in creatures. In one way, by active and passive potentiality such that both something can be made out of pre-existing matter, and that a pre-existing creature can make it. In the second way, by passive potentiality alone, namely, such that God can produce something out of pre-existing matter. And it is in the latter way, according to Augustine, that the human body pre-existed in the works produced by causal sources.

Notes

1. *De Trinitate* III, 4. PL 42:873.
2. Q. 91, A. 1.
3. In an introductory book on the art of astronomy.
4. *Super Genesim ad litteram* VII, 24. PL 34:368.
5. Sir. 17:1.
6. Cf. Q. 65, A. 4. Plato, *Phaedo* 49. 100B–101E. *Timaeus* 18. 50B–E. Avicenna, *Metaphysics*, tract. 9, chap. 5.
7. *Metaphysics* VI, 8. 1033b8–19. Ibid. VI, 9. 1034b7–16.
8. Q. 45, A. 8. Q. 65, A. 4. Q. 90, A. 2.
9. *De Trinitate* III, 8-9. PL 42:875–78.
10. *De anima*, part 4, chap.5, and part 4, chap. 7. *De animalibus* XV, 1. Cf. Q. 71, A. 1, *ad* 1.
11. *Physics* II, 2. 194b13.

ST I

Question 118

On the Transmission of Human Beings by Human Beings, Regarding the Soul

[This question is divided into three articles, two of which are included here.]

Second Article

Does Semen Produce the Intellectual Soul?

I proceed in this way to the first article: it seems that semen produces the intellectual soul.

Obj. 1. The Book of Genesis says: "Sixty six was the number of all the souls that came out of Jacob's thigh."[1] But something comes out of a human thigh only because semen produces it. Therefore, semen produces the intellectual soul.

Obj. 2. The intellectual, sensory, and nutritive souls in human beings are substantially one and the same soul, as I have shown before.[2] But as in the case of other animals, semen produces the sensory soul in human beings. And so also the Philosopher says in the *De generatione animalium* that the animal and the human being are not produced at the same time; rather, the animal with a sensory soul is produced first.[3] Therefore, semen also produces the intellectual soul.

Obj. 3. When activity results in form and matter, there is one and the same efficient cause of both; otherwise, nothing unconditionally one would arise out of the form and the matter. But the intellectual soul is the form of the body, and the power of semen produces the body. Therefore, the power of semen also produces the intellectual soul.

Obj. 4. Human beings beget things specifically like themselves. But the rational soul is a constitutive part of the human species. Therefore, the rational soul comes from the begetter.

Obj. 5. It is improper to say that God cooperates with sinners. But if God were to create rational souls, he would sometimes cooperate with adulterers, whose unlawful intercourse sometimes produces offspring.

Therefore, God does not create rational souls.

On the contrary, the work *De ecclesiasticis dognatibus* says that "intercourse does not produce rational souls."[4]

I answer that the active powers in matter cannot expand their activity to produce immaterial effects. And it is evident that the source of intellection in human beings is a source that transcends matter, since that source has an activity in which the body does not share. And so the power in semen cannot produce the source of intellection.

And similarly, the power in semen cannot produce the source of intellection because such power causes by the power of the soul of the begetter, as the soul of the begetter actualizes the body and makes use of the body itself in the soul's activity. But the body does not share in the activity of the intellect. And so the power of intellection, as intellection, cannot extend to the semen. And so the Philosopher says in the *De generatione animalium*: "We conclude that only the intellect comes from something outside the body."[5]

And similarly, the intellectual soul, since it has activity that does not depend on the body, is subsistent, as I have maintained before,[6] and so its existing and its coming into existence belong to it. And since the intellectual soul is an immaterial substance, begetting cannot produce it; rather, only creating by God can produce it. Therefore, to maintain that the begetter produces the intellectual soul, is the same as to maintain that the intellectual soul is not subsistent and so passes away with the body. And so it is heretical to assert that the soul is transmitted with the semen.

Reply to Obj. 1. The cited authority by synecdoche posits the part for the whole, that is, the soul for the whole human being.

Reply to Obj. 2. Some thinkers have said that the vital activities evident in embryos do not come from their souls but from their mothers' souls[7] or from the productive power in semen.[8] But both of these opinions are false, for vital activities (e.g., sense perception, nutrition, and growth) cannot come from an external source. And so we need to say that a soul pre-exists in the embryo: initially, indeed, the nutritive soul, and subsequently the sensory soul, and finally the intellectual soul.

Therefore, some thinkers say that a second soul, the sensory soul, is added to the vegetative soul that was first present, and also that a third soul, the intellectual soul, is added to the sensory soul.[9] And so human beings have three souls, and one of these has potentiality for the others. And I have disproved this opinion before.[10]

And so other thinkers say that the same soul, which was at first only vegetative, later comes by the power in semen to be also sensory, and finally comes to be intellectual, not indeed by the efficient power of the semen but by the power of a higher efficient cause, namely, the power of God, who illumines the soul from without.[11] And this is why the Philosopher says that the intellect comes from something external.[12]

But this opinion cannot be the case. First, indeed, because no substantial form takes in more or less; rather, the addition of a greater perfection produces a different species; for example, the addition of a unit produces a different species of number. Nor is it possible for a form numerically one and the same to belong to different species.

Second, the cited opinion cannot be the case because the generation of animals would thereby be successive movement, going gradually from the imperfect to the perfect, as happens in the case of alterations.

Third, the cited opinion cannot be the case because the generation of animal and human being would thereby not be generation without qualification, since the subject undergoing generation would be an actual being. For example, if there is a vegetable soul in the matter of an offspring, and that soul later comes gradually to be perfect, the addition of a subsequent perfection will always be without the loss of the previous perfection. And this is contrary to the nature of generation without qualification.

Fourth, the cited opinion cannot be the case because what God's action causes either is or is not something subsistent. If what God's action causes, is something subsistent, then it needs to be something essentially different from the pre-existing form, which was not subsistent, and so we are back to the opinion of those who hold that there are several souls in the body. If what God's action causes, is not something subsistent but some perfection of the pre-existing soul, then it necessarily follows that the intellectual soul passes away when the body does, and this is impossible.

And there is another way of speaking about the matter, the one by those who hold that there is only one intellect in all human beings.[13] And I have disproved this position before.[14]

And so we should say that both in the case of human beings and in the case of other animals, the previous form passes away whenever a more perfect form comes, since the coming-to-be of one thing is always the passing away of another. But this happens in such a way that the subsequent form possesses whatever the prior form had, and still more. And so both human beings and other animals arrive at their ultimate substantial form by the coming-to-be and the passing away of a number of forms. And this is empirically evident in the case of animals that are generated out of the decomposition of organic matter. Therefore, we need to say that God creates the intellectual soul at the end of the process of human generation, a soul that is both sensory and nutritive, at which time the pre-existing forms pass away.

Reply to Obj. 3. The argument of this objection is valid in the case of different efficient causes that are not ordered to one another. But if there be many efficient causes ordered to one another, nothing prevents the power of a higher efficient cause resulting in the ultimate form, and the powers of lower efficient causes resulting only in some disposition of the matter. For example, in the generation of animals, the power of semen disposes the matter, and the power of the soul bestows the form. And what I have set forth before makes evident that the whole of material nature causes as the instrument of immaterial power and especially of God.[15] And so nothing prevents material substances being produced by material powers, and the intellectual soul coming only from God.

Reply to Obj. 4. Human beings beget things like themselves inasmuch as the power of the semen of human beings disposes matter to receive such forms.

Reply to Obj. 5. Whatever in the acts of adulterers belongs to nature is good, and God cooperates with it. But whatever belongs to a disordered will is evil, and God does not cooperate with that.

Third Article

Were Human Souls Created Together at the Beginning of the World?

I proceed in this way to the third article: it seems that human souls were created together at the beginning of the world.

Obj. 1. The Book of Genesis says: "God rested from all the work that he had accomplished."[16] But such would not be the case if God were to create new souls every day. Therefore, all souls were created at once.

Obj. 2. Spiritual substances most of all belong to the perfection of the universe. Therefore, if souls were to be created along with their bodies, countless spiritual substances would be daily added to the perfection of the universe, and so the universe at the beginning would be imperfect. But this is contrary to what the Book of Genesis says, that "God completed all his work."[17]

Obj. 3. The end of things corresponds to their beginning. But the intellectual soul abides after the body has been destroyed. Therefore, the intellectual soul began to exist before the body did.

On the contrary, the work *De ecclesiasticis dogmatibus* says that "the soul is created along with the body."[18]

I answer that certain thinkers held that intellectual souls have the same condition as spiritual substances that are not united to bodies, and that intellectual souls are by accident united to bodies.[19] And so they held that the souls of human beings were created along with the angels at the beginning.

But this opinion is false. First, indeed, it is false regarding its foundation. For if it were accidental to the human soul to be united to the body, it would logically follow that human beings, who are constituted by such a union, would be accidental beings, or that the human soul would be the human being. And the latter conclusion is false, as I have shown before.[20] Moreover, the very fact that human beings and angels have different ways of understanding shows that the human soul has a different nature than the angels have, as I have shown before.[21] For human beings understand by receiving images from the senses and having recourse to the sense images, as I have shown before.[22] And so the human soul needs to be united to the body, which it needs for the activities of its sensory part. And we cannot say this about the angels.

Second, falsity is apparent in the position itself. For if it is natural for the human soul to be united to the body, it is contrary to nature for it to be without a body, and the soul existing apart from the body lacks the perfection of its nature. And it was unfitting that God should begin his work with incomplete things and things at variance with nature. For example, God did not make human beings without hands or feet, and hands and feet are natural parts of human beings. Therefore, much less did he make the souls without bodies.

And if one should say that it is unnatural for souls to be united to bodies, we need to seek the reason why souls are so united. And we need to say that either the soul's will or some other cause causes the union. If the soul's will is the cause, such willing seems incongruous. First, indeed, such willing seems incongruous because it would be unreasonable if the soul were to will to be united to a body and not to need the body. (For if the soul were to need the body, it would be natural for the soul to be united to a body, since "nature is not deficient in necessary things."[23]) Second, such willing seems incongruous because there would be no reason why the will of a soul created at the beginning of the world would, after the passage of so much time, consent at the present moment to be united to a body. For spiritual substances, as things beyond the orbits of the heavens, transcend time. Third, such willing seems incongruous because it would seem to be by chance that a particular soul would be united to a particular body, since, for this to take place, there would be required a concursus of two wills, namely, the will of the soul coming to the body and the will of the human being begetting the body.

And if the soul's union with the body exceeds the soul's power to will it, or exceeds the soul's nature, the union needs to result from a cause coercing the soul, and then the union will be a punishment and a hardship for the soul. And this accords with the error of Origen, who held that souls are united to bodies as punishment for sin.

And so, since all these things are incongruous, we should acknowledge without reservation that souls are not created before their bodies are, but souls are created at the time when they are infused into bodies.

Reply to Obj. 1. The Book of Genesis says that God rested on the seventh day, not indeed from all work (since the Gospel of John says: "My Father works even to this moment"[24]), but from establishing new genera and species of things that did not in some way pre-exist in this sense by a specific likeness in the first works, in the course of which Adam's soul was created.

Reply to Obj. 2. Something can be added every day to the perfection of the universe as to the number of individuals but not as to the number of species.

Reply to Obj. 3. The fact that the soul abides apart from the body happens by reason of the passing away of the body, and the passing away of the body is the result of sin. And so it was unfitting that the works of God should begin in this way, since, as it is written in the Book of Wisdom: "God did not bring about death," but "the wicked by their hands and their words brought about" death.[25]

Notes

1. Gen. 46:26.
2. Q. 76, A. 3.

3. *De generatione animalium* II, 3. 736b2–4.

4. Gennadius, *De ecclesiasticis dogmatibus* 14. PL 58:984.

5. *De generatione animalium* II, 3. 736b27.

6. Q. 75, A. 2.

7. Cf. Aristotle, *De generatione animalium* II, 1. 733b32.

8. Cf. Avicenna, *De anima*, part 15, chap. 2.

9. Cf. Q. 76, A. 3.

10. Q. 76, A. 3.

11. Cf. Albert the Great, *De animalibus* XVI, tract. 1, chap. 11.

12. See n. 5, supra.

13. Cf. Averroës, *In De anima* III, comm. 5, digression, part 5.

14. Q. 76, A. 2.

15. Q. 105, A. 5. Q. 110, A. 1.

16. Gen. 2:2.

17. Ibid.

18. Gennadius, *De ecclesiasticis dogmatibus* 14 and 18. PL 58:984, 985.

19. Origen, *Peri Archon* I, 6 and 8. PG 11:166, 178. II, 9. PG 11:229.

20. Q. 75, A. 4.

21. Q. 55, A. 2. Q. 85, A. 1.

22. Q. 84, AA. 6, 7. Q. 85, A. 1.

23. Aristotle, *De anima* III, 9. 432b19–26.

24. Jn. 5:17.

25. Wis. 1:13, 16.

GLOSSARY

Accident: *An attribute that inheres in another and cannot subsist in itself.* What does not inhere in another, but subsists in itself, is a substance. John, for example, is a substance, while his height is an accident; the latter cannot exist apart from the former. *See* Actuality, Property, Substance.

Action: *Activity.* There are two basic kinds of action. Immanent action, the activity of living things, perfects the being that acts. Plants have the immanent activities of nutrition, growth, and reproduction. Animals have the additional immanent activities of sense perception and sense appetites. Human beings have the additional immanent activities of understanding and willing. God alone has perfectly immanent activity, that is, understanding and willing apart from any accompanying transient effect. Transient action produces an effect in something other than the cause that acts. In other words, transient action is efficient causality. Action in the strict sense refers to transient action. *See* Cause.

Actuality: *The perfection of a being.* Existence is the primary actuality of every being. A specific (substantial) form actualizes finite beings and distinguishes one kind of being from another. Particular (accidental) characteristics further actualize finite beings. Joan, for example, is perfected and actualized by her act of existence, her human form, and her particular attributes (her knowledge, her virtue, her physical attributes). *See* Accident, Form, Matter, Potentiality, Substance.

Appetite: *The active tendency of finite beings to actualize their capacities.* Inanimate material beings have natural appetites. Plants have additional vegetative appetites (for nourishment, growth, and reproduction). Animals have additional sense appetites (concupiscible, irascible). Human beings have an additional intellectual appetite (the will). *See* Concupiscible, Irascible, Will.

Cause: *A being that influences the being or coming-to-be of something else.* In common parlance, the term refers primarily to an efficient cause, that is, the cause that by its activity produces an effect; a builder and those who work under him, for example, are the efficient causes of the house they build. Efficient causes can be univocal or nonunivocal. An efficient cause is univocal when it and its effect belong to the same species; human beings, for example, are univocal efficient causes of the bodies of the human beings they beget. An efficient cause is nonunivocal when it and its effect do not belong to the same species; God, for example, is the nonunivocal efficient cause of the things he creates, since he belongs to no species and so shares no species or genus with any creature.

But there are other causes than efficient causes. A final cause is the end for the sake of which an efficient cause acts; a builder, for example, builds a house to make money (subjective purpose) and to provide a shelter for someone (objective purpose). An exemplary cause is the idea or model of a desired effect in the mind of an intellectual efficient cause that preconceives the effect; a builder, for example, conceives the form of the house that he intends to build.

Efficient, final, and exemplary causes are extrinsic to the effects they cause. In addition, form, which makes an effect to be what it is, and matter, which receives a form, are correlative intrinsic causes; a house, for example, is composed of bricks and wood (matter), which are given a structure or shape (form). *See* Form, Matter, Source.

Coming to Be: *See* Generation and Corruption.

Concupiscible: *Type of sensible appetite whose object is the pleasant.* Love and hate, desire and aversion, joy and sorrow are examples of movements of the concupiscible appetite. *See* Appetite, Irascible.

Efficient Cause: *See* Cause.

Essence: *What makes something to be what it substantially is.* The human essence, for example, makes human beings to be what they are as substances, namely, rational animals. When the essence of a being is considered as the ultimate source of the being's activities and development, it is called the being's nature; human nature, for example, is the ultimate source of the human activities (activities of reason and activities according to reason) whereby human beings develop themselves. *See* Accident, Form, Property, Substance.

Exemplary Cause: *See* Cause.

Final Cause: *See* Cause.

Form: *The cause that intrinsically makes a being to be substantially or accidentally what it is.* The human form, for example, makes John to be what he is as a substance, and other forms make him to be what he is accidentally (tall, thin, red-headed). *See* Accident, Substance.

Formal Cause: *See* Cause.

Generation and Corruption: *The coming-to-be and passing away of a material substance.* In a substantial change, matter (prime) gains a particular form (substantial), and so a new material substance comes to be (generation). The same matter also loses a substantial form, and so the previous material substance as such ceases to exist (corruption). *See* Form, Matter.

Genus: *See* Species.

Habit: *The characteristic disposition or inclination to act in a certain way.* Habits may belong to the body, the intellect, or the will, be innate or acquired, be natural or supernatural, be good or bad. For example, logical argumentation is a habit of the intellect; moderation is a habit of the will; timidity may be an innate habit; cleanliness is an acquired habit; courage is a natural habit; faith is a supernatural habit; generosity is a good habit; stinginess is a bad habit.

Intellect: *The faculty of understanding.* St. Thomas, following Aristotle, holds that there is an active power of the intellect that moves the passive or potential power of the intellect to apprehend the essences of material things, form judgments, and reason discursively.

Irascible: *Type of sensible appetite whose object is that which is useful for the individual or the species but which is difficult to achieve.* The object does not appear as something pleasant, and can be achieved only by overcoming opposition. Hope and despair, fear and anger are examples of movements of the irascible appetite. *See* Appetite, Concupiscible.

Material Cause: *See* Cause.

Matter: *The cause or "stuff" out of which and with which something material is produced.* The material causes of a house, for example, are its bricks, mortar, wood. Prime matter individualizes and so limits a specific substantial form, and it provides the subject and capacity for material things to change from one substance into another. Although prime matter is no-thing, it is a source or cause in everything material. It can receive any communicable substantial form and so has limitless capacity for any such form. *See* Cause, Form, Potentiality.

Motion: *Movement.* Motion literally and primarily refers to locomotion, that is, change of position. But the term can refer more broadly to any change or transition from one state or condition to another. According to St. Thomas, it is a self-evident first principle of understanding that whatever undergoes motion does so as a result of causal action by something else.

Nature: *See* Essence.

Nonunivocal Cause: *See* Cause.

Passing Away: *See* Generation and Corruption.

Potentiality: *The capacity to be or become something.* The potentiality of a being limits its actuality; frogs, for example, can swim, but they cannot fly. Finite beings can change accidentally; John, for example, can go bald. Finite material things can also change from one substance into another; grass, for example, when consumed by a cow, becomes part of the cow. Potentiality in the active sense is the same as power. *See* Accident, Actuality, Matter, Power.

Power: *The active capacity to perform a certain type of activity.* For example, the power of sight. *See* Potentiality.

Property: *A quality or characteristic that necessarily belongs to a substance; a proper accident.* Joan's ability to use language, for example, unlike the color of her hair, is a characteristic proper to her as a human being. *See* Accident, Substance.

Science (Aristotelian): *Knowledge about things through their causes.* Science consists of understanding the efficient, final, material, and formal causes of things. Physical, psychological, and social sciences study the secondary causes of material and human things, while philosophy (metaphysics) studies the first causes of being as such. For Aristotle, philosophy is the highest science, but for St. Thomas, theology, the study of God in the light of Christian revelation, is the highest science. *See* Cause.

Senses: *Faculties of perception through bodily organs.* The external senses (sight, hearing, smell, taste, touch) have proper objects, that is, objects that each sense alone perceives, and common objects, that is, objects related to quantity that more than one sense can perceive. The internal senses (the common or unifying sense, imagination, memory, and the cogitative sense) derive from data provided by the external senses.

Soul: *The substantial form of a living material thing.* The soul is the ultimate intrinsic source whereby living material things differ from nonliving material things. There are three kinds of souls: the vegetative soul capable of nutrition, growth, and reproduction; the sensory soul capable of sense perception; the rational soul capable of intellection. The only soul in human beings is the rational soul, which also has the powers of vegetative and sensory souls. The rational soul is intrinsically independent of matter for its existence and activity. *See* Form, Substance.

Source: *That from which something else proceeds.* The essence of a frog, specifically its form, for example, is an ontological source or cause, that is, the source or cause from which the frog's activity proceeds. The premisses of arguments are logical sources or principles, that is, the sources or principles from which conclusions logically proceed. *See* Cause.

Species: *The substantial identity of material things insofar as that identity is common to many things.* The species concept (e.g., human being) is composed of a genus concept (e.g., animal), which indicates the essence of certain material things in an incompletely determined way, and of a specific difference distinguishing things of the same genus (e.g., rational). The species concept, or definition, thus expresses the whole substance or essence of a particular kind of material thing.

Specific Difference: *See* Species.

Subject: *That in which something else inheres.* In the strict sense, subjects are substances underlying accidents. In a broader sense, prime matter can be called the subject of substantial form, the soul the subject of powers, and powers the subjects of virtues. See Accident, Form, Matter, Substance.

Substance: *What exists in itself and not in another.* Finite individual substances "stand under" (Latin: *substare*) accidents and persist through accidental changes. Human beings, for example, are composed of substance (body-soul) and accidents (size, shape, color, etc.). *See* Accident, Property, Subject.

Synderesis: *The habit of first moral principles.* Human beings have an innate disposition to understand the first principles of human action. Human beings are disposed by nature to recognize that they should seek the good proper to their nature, and that the human good includes preserving one's life in reasonable ways, mating and educating offspring in reasonable ways, and living cooperatively with others in an organized society. *See* Habit.

Will: *The intellectual appetite, the intellectual faculty of desire.* The will necessarily wills the ultimate human perfection, happiness, but freely wills particular goods, since the latter are only partially good.

SELECT BIBLIOGRAPHY

On Aristotle's philosophical system, see:

Grene, Marjorie. *A Portrait of Aristotle.* Chicago: University of Chicago Press, 1967.

Veatch, Henry B. *Aristotle: A Contemporary Appreciation.* Bloomington: Indiana University Press, 1974.

For an up-to-date, scholarly chronology of the life and works of St. Thomas, see:

Torrell, Jean-Pierre. *Saint Thomas Aquinas.* Vol. I: *The Person and His Work.* Translated by Robert Royal. Washington: The Catholic University of America Press, 1996.

Tugwell, O.P., Simon. Albert and Thomas: Selected Writings. New York: Paulist Press, 1988.

For an accurate and well-integrated condensed translation of the whole *Summa*, see:

Aquinas, St. Thomas. *Summa Theologiae: A Concise Translation.* Edited and translated by Timothy McDermott. Westminster, Maryland: Christian Classics, 1989.

For a guide to the context of St. Thomas's thought, see:

Pieper, Josef. *Guide to Thomas Aquinas.* Translated by Richard and Clara Winston. New York: Pantheon, 1962.

For expositions of St. Thomas's general philosophy, see:

Copleston, S.J., Frederick. *A History of Philosophy* 2:302–424. Westminster, Maryland: Newman, 1950. Also available in Image Books, Doubleday (vol. 2, part 2).

Davies, O.P., Brian. *The Thought of Thomas Aquinas.* Oxford, England: Oxford University Press, 1992.

Gilson, Etienne. *The Christian Philosophy of St. Thomas Aquinas.* New York: Random House, 1956.

McInerny, Ralph. *A First Glance at St. Thomas Aquinas: A Handbook for Peeping Thomists.* Notre Dame, Indiana: Notre Dame University Press, 1990.

For a study of the body-soul composition in Thomistic anthropology,
see:
Pegis, Anton C. *At the Origins of the Thomistic Notion of Man.* New
   York: Macmillan, 1963.

On Aristotle and St. Thomas on the nature and functions of the
intellect, see:
Adler, Mortimer. *Intellect: Mind over Matter.* New York:
   Collier-Macmillan, 1990.

For a systematic exposition of Thomistic anthropology, see:
Klubertanz, S.J., George P. *The Philosophy of Human Nature.* New
   York: Appleton-Century-Crofs, 1953.

For a personalist interpretation of Thomistic anthropology, see:
Clarke, S.J., W. Norris. *Person and Being.* Milwaukee: Marquette
   University Press, 1993.

For a transcendental interpretation of Thomistic anthropology, see:
Donceel, Joseph F. *Philosophical Psychology.* 2nd edition. New York:
   Sheed and Ward, 1961.

INDEX